Oracle Application Express 5 For Beginners

A practical guide to rapidly develop data-centric web applications accessible from desktop, laptops, tablets, and smartphones.

Riaz Ahmed

Oracle Application Express 5 For Beginners

Copyright © 2015 Riaz Ahmed

All rights reserved.

ISBN-13: 978-1-512-12354-8
ISBN-10: 1512123544

No part of this publication may be reproduced, stored in a retrieval system or transmitted in any form or by any means, electronic, mechanical, photocopying, recording, scanning or otherwise, except as permitted under Sections 107 or 108 of the 1976 United States Copyright Act, without the prior written permission of the Author.

Limit of Liability/Disclaimer of Warranty: The author make no representations or warranties with respect to the accuracy or completeness of the contents of this work and specifically disclaim all warranties, including without limitation warranties of fitness for a particular purpose. No warranty may be created or extended by sales or promotional materials. The advice and strategies contained herein may not be suitable for every situation. This work is sold with the understanding that the author is not engaged in rendering legal, accounting, or other professional services. If professional assistance is required, the services of a competent professional person should be sought. The author shall not be liable for damages arising here from. The fact that an organization or Web site is referred to in this work as a citation and/or a potential source of further information does not mean that the author endorses the information the organization or Web site may provide or recommendations it may make. Further, readers should be aware that Internet Web sites listed in this work may have changed or disappeared between when this work was written and when it is read.

Trademarks: Oracle is a registered trademark of Oracle Corporation. All other trademarks are the property of their respective owners. The author is not associated with any product or vendor mentioned in this book.

PREFACE

Oracle Application Express has taken another big leap towards becoming a true next generation RAD tool. It has entered into its fifth version to build robust web applications. One of the most significant features in this release is a new page designer that helps developers create and edit page elements within a single page design view, which maximizes developer productivity.

Without involving the audience too much into the boring bits, the book adopts an inspiring approach that helps beginners practically evaluate almost every feature of Oracle Application Express, including all features new to version 5.

The most convincing way to explore a technology is to apply it to a real world problem. In this book, you'll develop a sales application that demonstrates almost every feature to practically expose the anatomy of Oracle Application Express 5.

The short list below presents some main topics of Oracle APEX covered in this book:

- Rapid web application development for desktops, laptops, tablets, and latest smartphones
- Create comprehensive applications declaratively without writing tons of code
- Design application pages using new Page Designer
- Create applications with the help of wizards
- Create custom application pages by adding components manually
- Use same interface and code to develop applications for a wide array of devices
- Present data using a variety of eye-catching charts
- Produce highly formatted PDF reports, including invoices, grouped reports, and pivot tables
- Design and implement a comprehensive security module

If you are looking for a concise and concrete book on Oracle Application Express 5, then I must say that this is the book that will return more than what you have paid for it. The sticky inspirational approach adopted in this book not only exposes the technology, but also draws you in and keeps your interest up till the last exercise.

Download Book Code

Download book's code from: http://www.creating-website.com/apex5code.rar
Errata: http://oracleapex5.blogspot.com/2015/06/errata.html

- Riaz Ahmed
Author
oratech@cyber.net.pk

ABOUT THE AUTHOR

Riaz Ahmed is an IT professional with more than 23 years experience. He started his career in early 90's as a programmer, and has been employed in a wide variety of information technology positions, including analyst programmer, system analyst, project manager, data architect, database designer and senior database administrator. Currently he is working as head of IT for a group of companies. His core areas of interest include web-based development technologies, business intelligence, and databases. Riaz possesses extensive experience in database design and development. Besides all versions of Oracle, he has worked intensively in almost all the major RDBMS on the market today. During his career he designed and implemented numerous databases for a wide range of applications, including ERP. In addition to the best-selling title *Create Rapid Web Applications Using Oracle Application Express* (two editions), he has authored *Implement Oracle Business Intelligence*, *The Web Book – Build Static and Dynamic Websites*, and *SQL - The Shortest Route For Beginners*. You can reach him through: **oratech@cyber.net.pk**

Implement Oracle Business Intelligence
Analyze the Past
Streamline the Present
Control the Future
ISBN-10: 1475122012

The Web Book
Build Static and Dynamic Websites
The ultimate resource to building static and dynamic websites
http://www.creating-website.com
ISBN-10: 1483929272

Create Rapid Web Applications Using
Oracle Application Express – Second Edition
A practical guide to rapidly develop professional web & mobile applications
ISBN-10: 1492314188

SQL – The Shortest Route For Beginners
A hands-on book that covers all top DBMS and teaches SQL in record time
ISBN-10: 1505805600

CONTENTS

Chapter 1: Learn Rapid Web Application Development in Oracle Application Express 5	1
Chapter 2: Oracle Application Express Concepts	14
Chapter 3: Create Application Components	28
Chapter 4: Prepare Application Dashboard	38
Chapter 5: Customers Profiling	54
Chapter 6: Setup Products Catalog	66
Chapter 7: Taking Orders	78
Chapter 8: Present Data Graphically	128
Chapter 9: Produce Advance Reports	144
Chapter 10: Develop A Mobile Version for Smartphones	160
Chapter 11: Define Application Segments for Security	186
Chapter 12: Create Groups and Assign Application Privileges	192
Chapter 13: Create User and Assign Groups	202
Chapter 14: Implement Application Security	210
Chapter 15: Deploy APEX Applications	214

Chapter 1

Learn Rapid Web Application Development In Oracle Application Express 5

Chapter 1 - Learn Rapid Web Application Development In Oracle Application Express 5

1.1 What are you going to create?

Oracle Application Express (APEX) is a browser-based rapid application development (RAD) tool that helps you create rich interactive Oracle-based web applications very quickly and with relatively little programming effort. A web application is an application that is accessed by users over a network such as the Internet or an intranet. It is an application software that is coded in a browser-supported programming language (such as JavaScript, combined with a browser-rendered markup language like HTML) and dependent on a common web browser to render the application. The popularity of web applications is due to the ubiquity of web browsers, which is the only requirement to access such applications. Another major reason behind the popularity of web applications is the ability to update and maintain these applications without distributing and installing software on potentially thousands of client devices.

Developing Web applications can be a real challenge as it's a multidisciplinary process. You have to be proficient in all the core technologies involved such as HTML, CSS, JavaScript (on the client side) and PHP or any other scripting language to interact with the database on the server side. Also, you've to take into account the type-less nature of the Web environment and above all, the need to put it all together in a manner that will allow the end users to execute their jobs efficiently and in a simplified manner.

Oracle Application Express is a hosted declarative development environment for developing and deploying database-centric web applications. Oracle Application Express accelerates the application development process. Thanks to its built-in features such as user interface themes, navigational controls, form handlers, and flexible reports that off-loads the extra burden of proficiency acquisition in the core technologies.

The format of this book is to introduce you to the art of building desktop and mobile web applications by iteratively developing the sample sales application – provided with Oracle Application Express – from scratch. This application has been chosen as an example because you can learn most of the techniques from it for your own future work. The primary purpose of this book is to teach you how to use Oracle Application Express to realize your own development goals. Each chapter in this book explores a basic area of functionality and delivers the development techniques to achieve that functionality. By the time you reach the end of the examples in this book, you will have a clear understanding of Oracle Application Express and will be able to extend the application in almost any direction. There are a number of features that provide APEX a clear edge over other available RAD development tools. First of all, APEX uses SQL and PL/SQL as core languages for development. Due to this ability, people who have been working with Oracle database can easily tread the path. Following are some of the major benefits of developing web applications in Oracle APEX:

- **Declarative Development:** Declarative development is the most significant feature which makes Oracle APEX a good choice for rapid application development. Most of the tasks are performed with the help of built-in wizards that help you create different application pages. Each wizard walks you through the process of defining what you are expecting to achieve. After getting the input, the wizard data is stored as metadata in Oracle database tables. Later on, you can call page definition to modify or enhance the metadata to give your page the desired look. You can even add more functionality by putting your own custom SQL and PL/SQL code. Once you're comfortable with Oracle APEX, you can ignore the wizards and generate your application directly. The Application Express engine renders applications in real time using the metadata. When you create or extend an application, Oracle Application Express creates or modifies metadata stored in database tables. When the application is run, the Application Express engine reads the metadata and then displays the application.

- **Mobile Applications:** Another significant feature provided in Oracle APEX is the ability to create applications for mobile devices. Content to these devices are delivered through jQuery Mobile that is incorporated in APEX. jQuery Mobile supports mobile device-specific events, such as orientation change and touch events. You easily change the look and feel of jQuery Mobile-based applications by modifying the CSS using tools such as ThemeRoller. Being the future, mobile application development is the need of the hour. This platform will definitely aid the over burdened business professionals, facing increasing time constraints, to increase their productivity by enabling them to work from anywhere at any time. These applications will make the busy community more effective as the features they carry allow people of high cadre to stay informed and take correct in-time decisions even sitting away from their desks.

1.2 Understanding the Application

The application you will be creating in this book features an easy-to-use interface for adding, updating, deleting and viewing order and related products and customers' information. Users can navigate among the pages using a new desktop navigation menu. In addition to the desktop version, you'll be guided to create a mobile version of the same application so that it could be accessed from a variety of mobile devices including latest smartphones and tablets. Let's have a quick look at some of the major areas of our sample Sales Web Application to know what we're going to create.

1.2.1 Chapter 4 - Prepare Application Dashboard

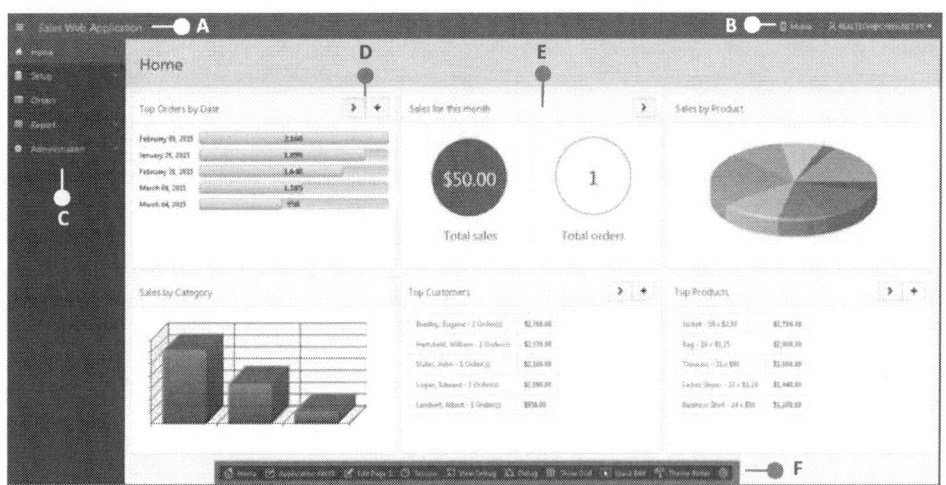

What You'll Learn

- 12 columns grid layout
- Multiple regions to hold different content
- Using APEX URL syntax in SQL statements
- Drill-down links
- Plug-ins
- CSS bar chart
- Badge list
- Pie chart
- Column chart
- Summarized text information
- Buttons to drill into details

In chapter 4, you'll create the home page of the application. It is a dashboard that users see when they successfully access the application after providing valid credentials. Let's first take a look at the tagged areas to acquaint ourselves with different sections of this page:

- A - Application name or logo
- B - Navigation Bar
- C - Main Navigation Menu
- D - Buttons
- E - Region
- F - Developers Toolbar

The page contains six regions to display different summarized information. It uses a 12 grid layout to place these regions accordingly. Besides application name or logo, the page displays a main navigation menu of the application, which is used to move to other application segments. The navigation bar, on the right side, allows you to switch to application's mobile version. It also displays the currently logged in user, along with a log out link. The data from different perspectives is displayed in multiple regions. Some regions have buttons on their top that allow you to drill into further details. In addition to buttons, the page also contains text links to dig details of the summarized information. Using the Developers Toolbar, you can switch to other pages instantly to perform various development tasks. A new feature (Theme Roller) is added to the toolbar in this version, using which you can change the whole complexion of your page.

1.2.2 Chapter 5 – Customers Profiling

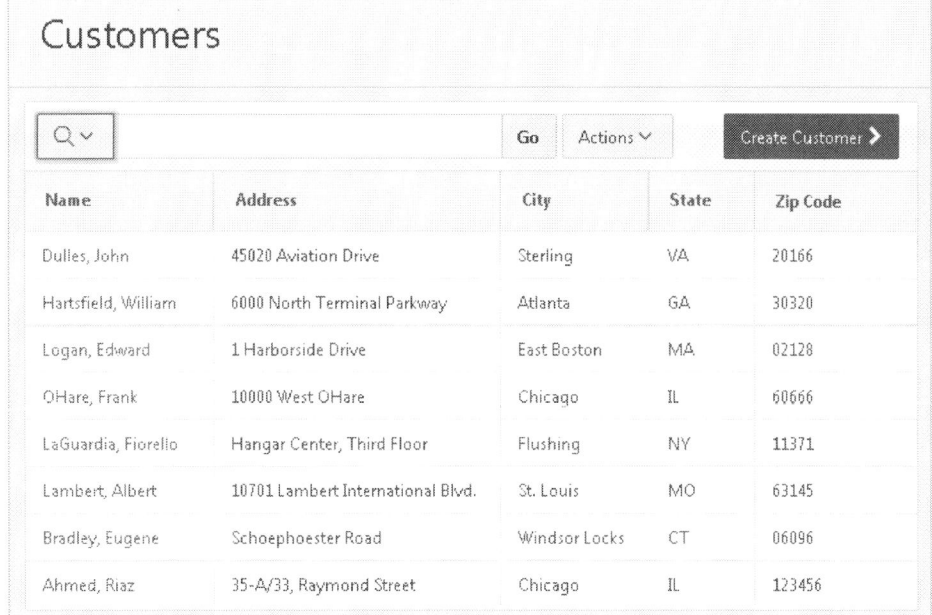

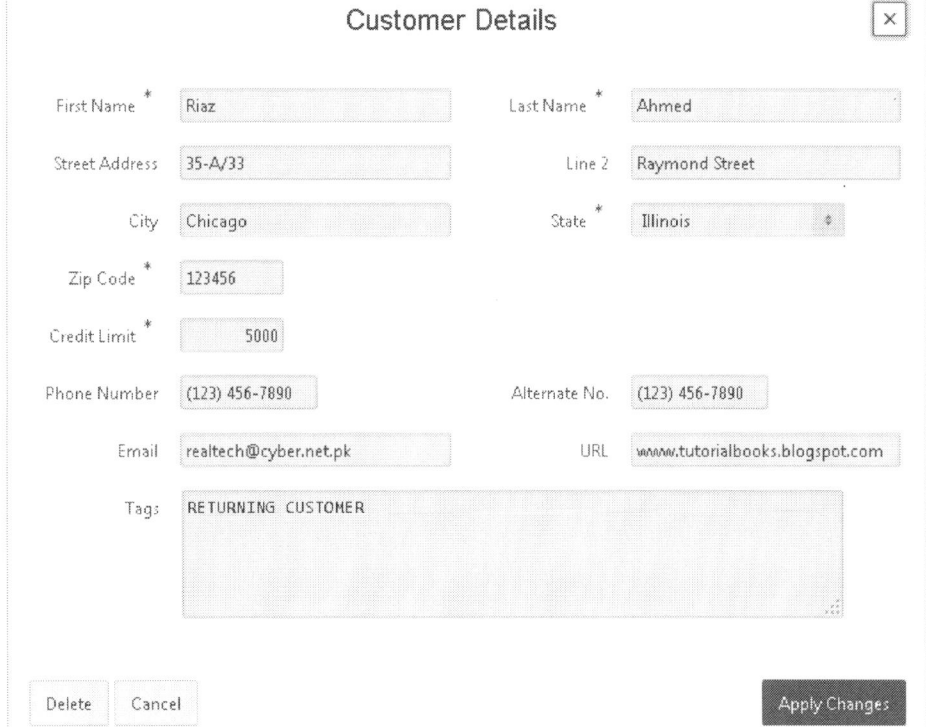

What You'll Learn

- Create application pages using wizards
- Add Interactive Reports
- Input form
- Using Modal Page (a new feature in APEX 5)
- Customizing wizard-generated pages to make them more professional
- Creating custom links to switch between the two module pages
- Positioning page elements using grid layout
- Marking mandatory fields
- Enforce data validation
- Learn how APEX transparently manages DML operations, without writing a single line of code

The sales application created in this book comprises several setups, including this one. Using this module, you will create customers profiles. Each customer will be provided a unique ID that will be generated automatically through a database object called a Sequence. After creating customers profiles, you will use this information in Chapter 6 – Taking Orders, where you will select these customers to process orders. The setup consists of two pages. The first page is an interactive report that lists all customers along with other information. The page carries links to the details page, which is a form where you can create, modify, or delete customers' records.

5

1.2.3 Chapter 6 – Setup Products Catalog

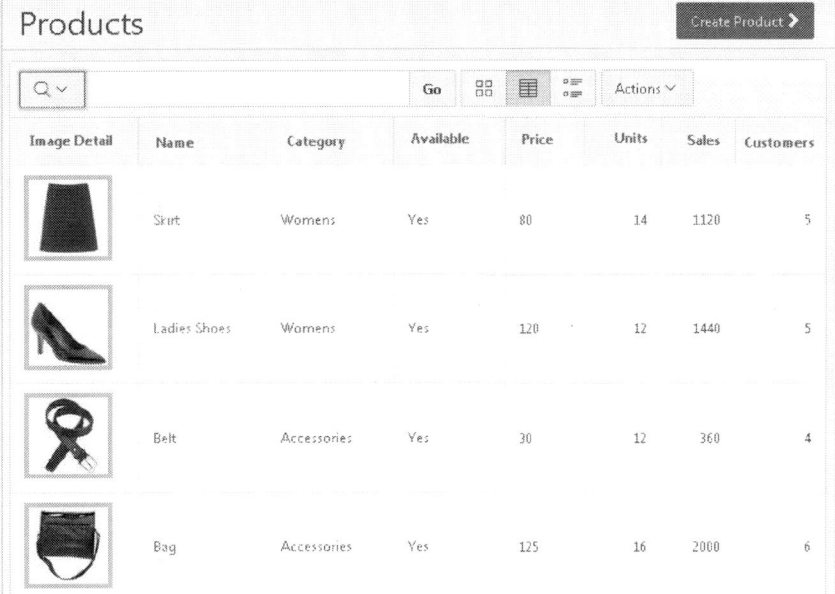

Since sales applications are developed to handle sales of products, therefore, a properly designed product setup is an integral part of this application. To fulfill this requirement, you will create a comprehensive product setup for the sales application to manage products information along with respective images. The products you incorporate here will be selected in customers' orders. Just like the Customers setup, this segment also comprises two pages. The initial page, comprising an interactive report, will be customized to create three different views to browse product information.

What You'll Learn

- Image handling through database
- Customize interactive report to have different views of data
- Using CSS to add custom styles
- Creating hidden items

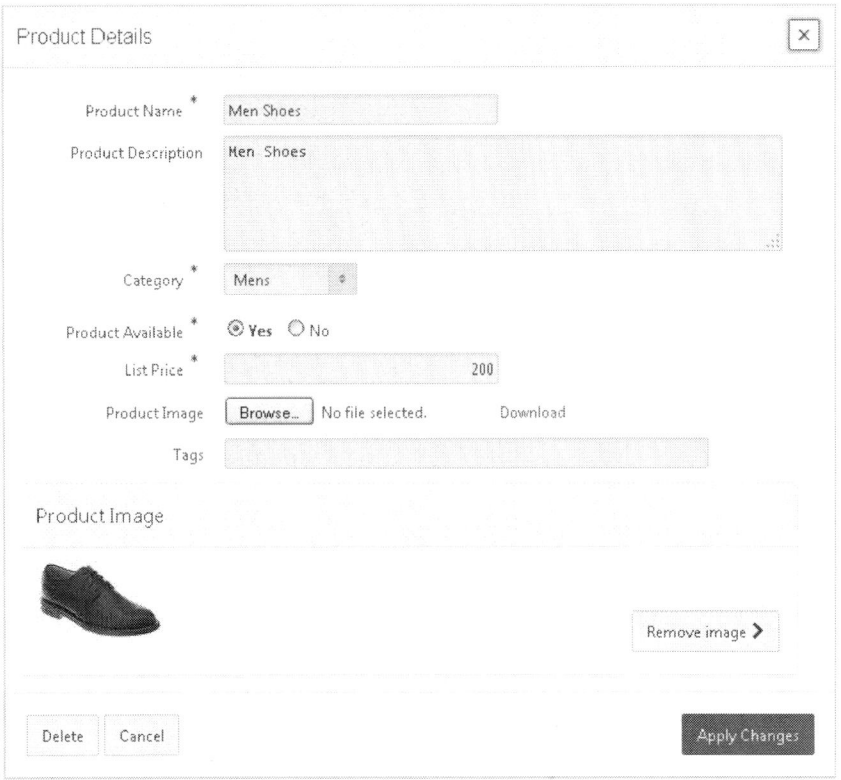

1.2.4 Chapter 7 – Taking Orders

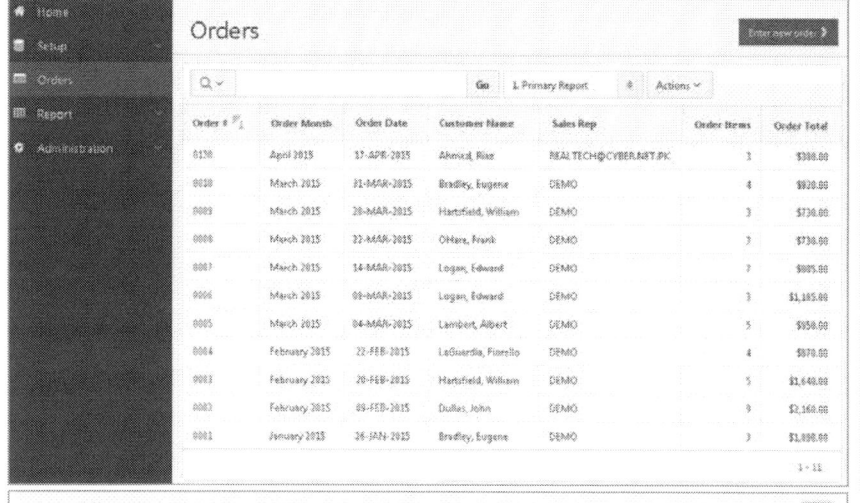

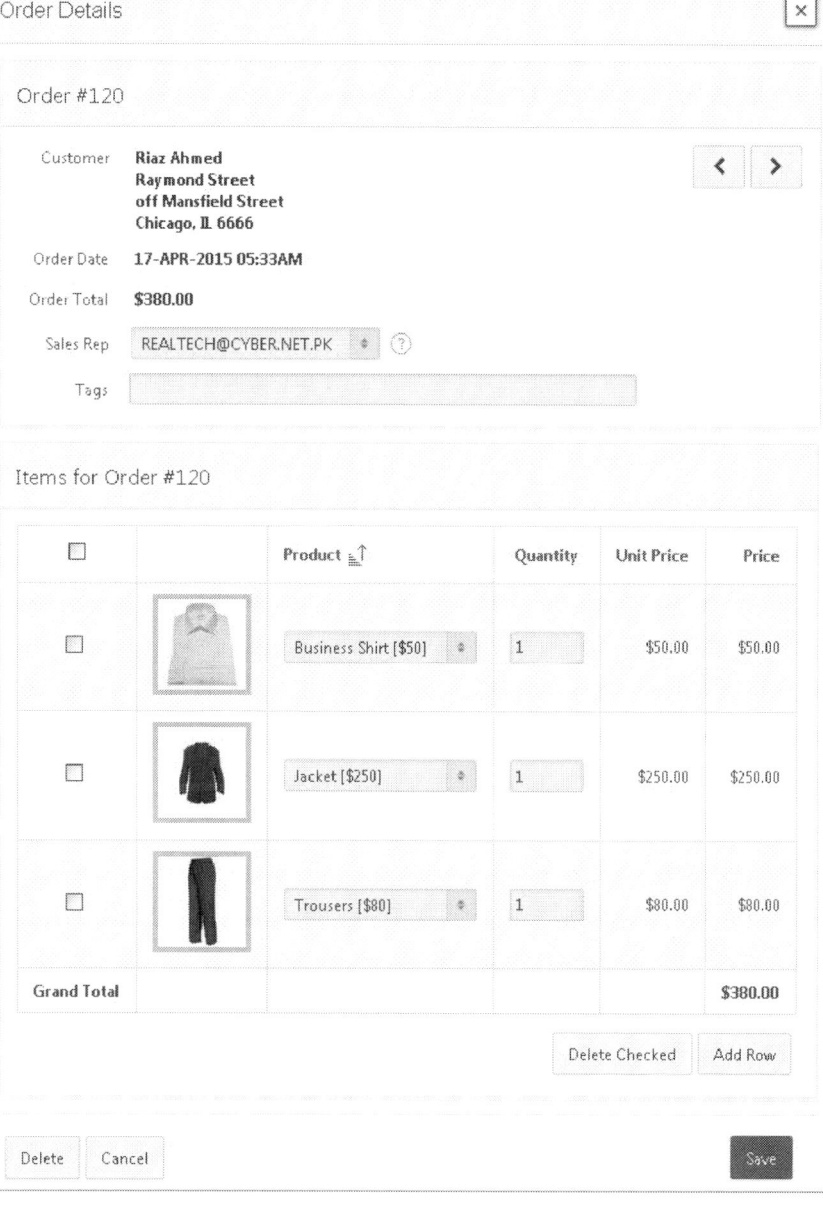

This is the most comprehensive chapter of the book. It will teach you lots of techniques. In this chapter, you will create a module to take orders from customers. Initially, you'll create this segment with the help of wizards, and later on, you will customize it to records orders through a sequence of wizard steps.

What You'll Learn

- Implement master/detail forms
- Sorting Interactive Report
- Add Control Breaks to interactive report to group related data
- Apply highlight rules to mark specific records
- Using Aggregate functions
- Using Chart and Group By views
- Creating Primary, Public, and Alternative versions of interactive report
- Utilizing Copy Page utility
- APEX Collections
- Adding custom processes and dynamic actions
- Using HTML in PL/SQL code

Chapter 1 - Learn Rapid Web Application Development In Oracle Application Express 5

1.2.5 Chapter 8 – Present Data Graphically

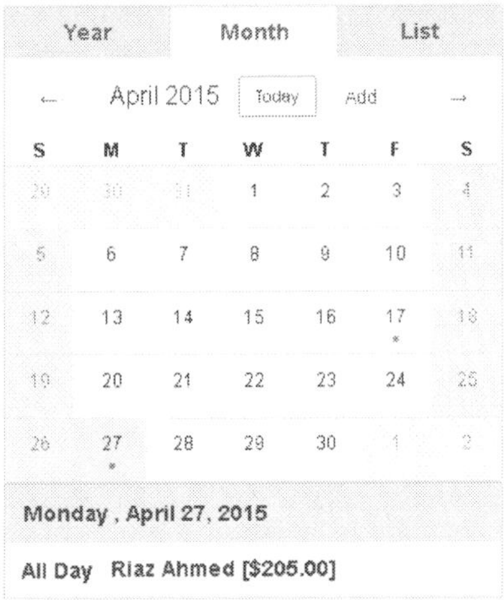

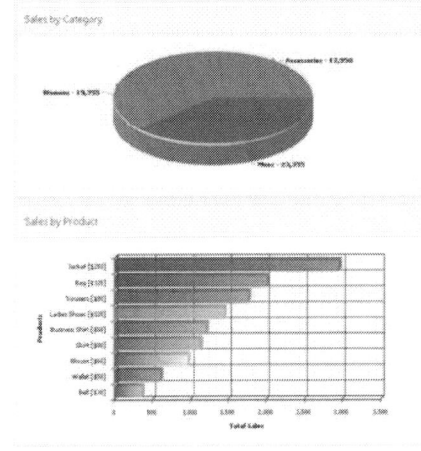

After getting thorough knowledge of data manipulation techniques, you move on to present output of the entered data graphically. In this chapter, you will be taught the use of different types of charts, maps, tree, and calendar to present data from different perspectives.

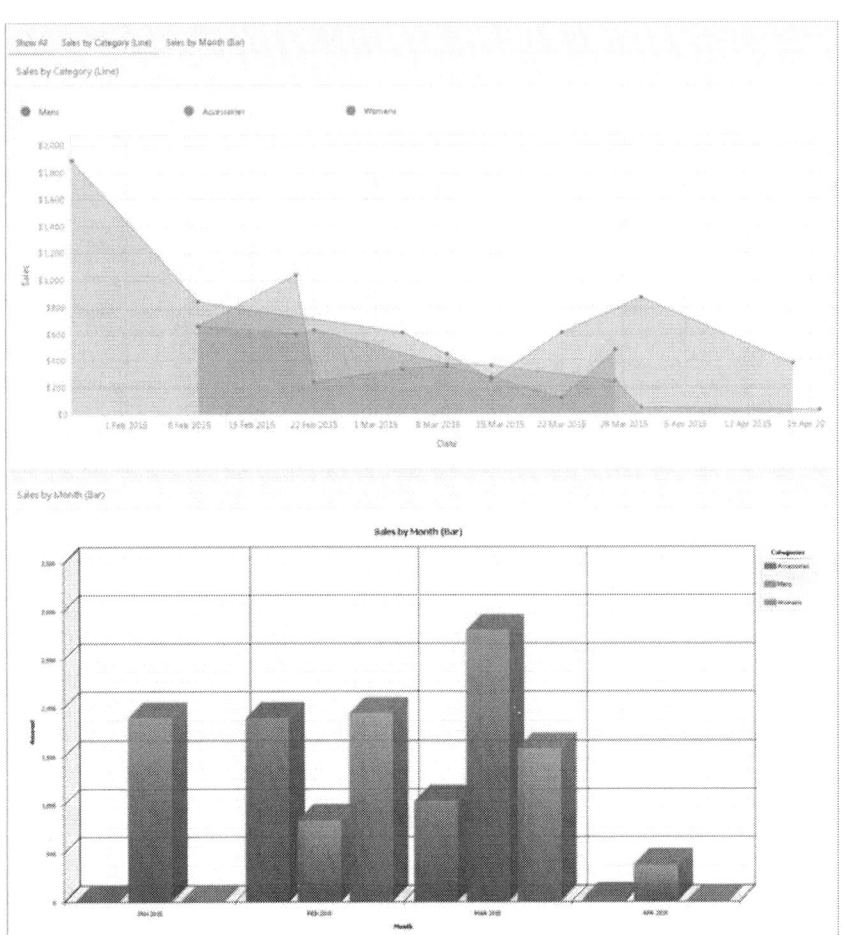

What You'll Learn

- Stacked Bar chart
- 3d Pie, Bar, and Column Charts
- Display customer orders in a calendar
- Show number of customers in different states using a map
- Hierarchical presentation of data using a tree component
- Drill down to details from charts

1.2.6 Chapter 9 – Produce Advance Reports

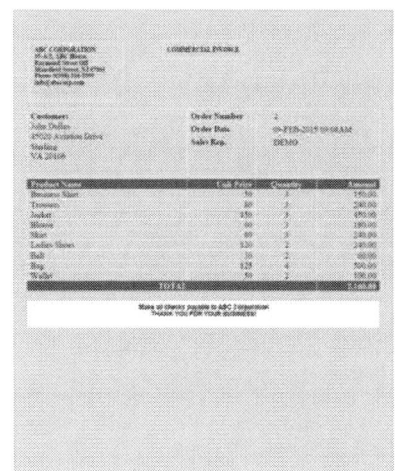

By default APEX has the ability to produce generic simple matrix reports, comprising rows and columns. This chapter will show you how to produce advance report in APEX. Here, you will be provided step by step instructions to generate:

- A highly formatted MIS report
- Commercial Invoice
- Pivot Table

What You'll Learn

- Create Report Query
- Design report layout in MS Word using XML data
- Data grouping and sorting
- Formatting reports using standard MS Word tools
- Add conditional formatting to display data differently in the same report
- Add calculations
- Create parameterized report
- Offline report testing
- Upload RTF layout to APEX
- Attach custom report layout to the default report query
- Add link in the application to run advance reports

1.2.7 Chapter 10 – Develop Mobile Version for Smartphones

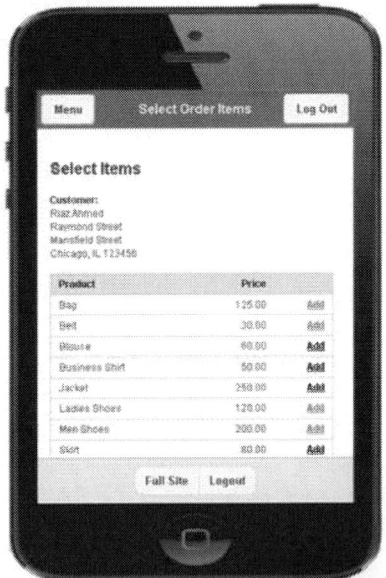

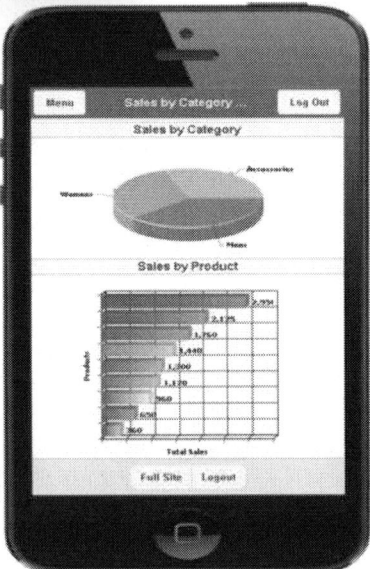

Due to an eruption in the market for smartphones and mobile devices, there is a huge demand of applications for this platform. Things that used to be done traditionally by people on their laptops are now being done increasingly on mobile devices. Feeling the heat, APEX incorporates a significant feature to build applications specifically for latest smartphones and tablets. In this chapter, you will completely explore mobile platform development by creating a mobile version of the desktop sales web application.

What You'll Learn

- Create mobile interface
- Add styles to mobile pages
- Mobile menus
- Present table data on mobile pages
- Mobile input forms
- Product catalog including images
- Taking orders
- Graphical reports

1.2.8 Application Security (Chapters 11-14)

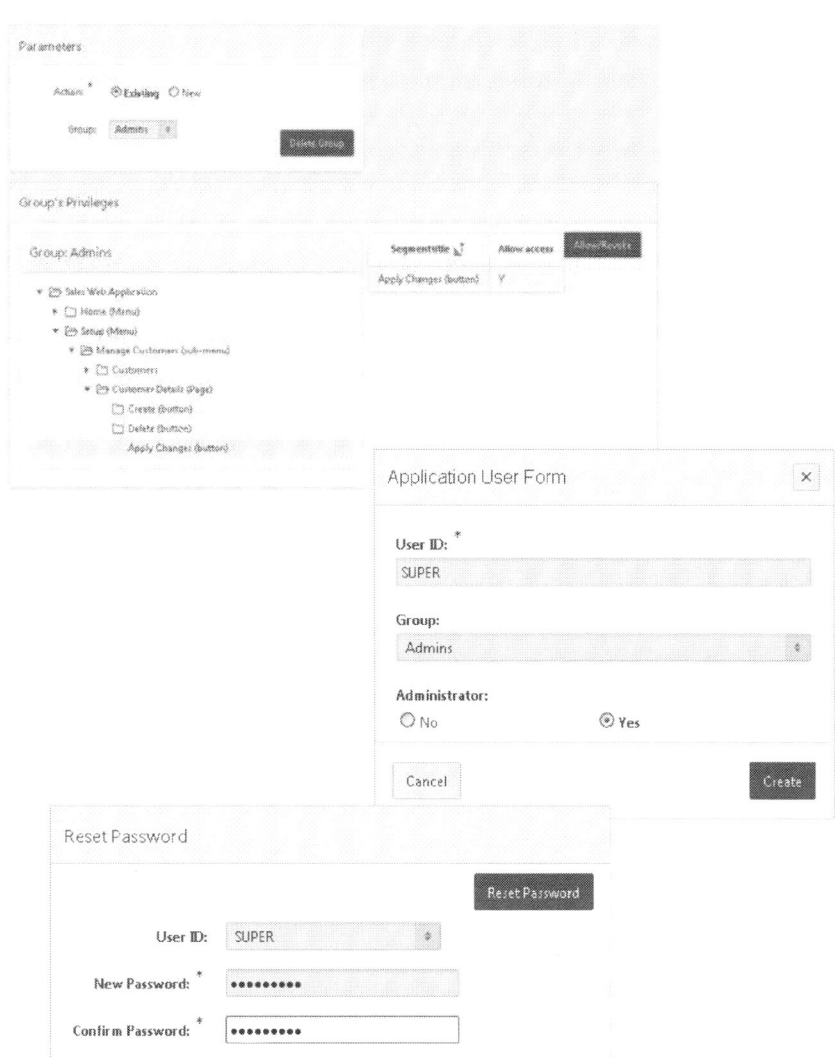

In this book you will create a comprehensive security module. The first step in developing this module is to define all application segments that you want to apply security on. These segments include: menus, pages, and page items. After defining all application segments in Chapter 11, you will create user groups in Chapter 12 where you will assign access privileges to each group on the default application segments. Next, you will create a setup in Chapter 13 to create application users. Each user is created and assigned a group. This way all the privileges granted to a group are automatically inherited to the users enrolled under it. In the same chapter, you will allow users to set/reset their passwords. Finally, in chapter 14, you will create authorization schemes and will modify all application segments to incorporate these schemes.

What You'll Learn

- Create a hierarchy of application segments
- Present application segments hierarchically in a tree view
- Create groups with different application privileges
- Allow/revoke access right on individual application segments
- Implement custom authentication scheme
- Add custom validations, processes and dynamic actions

1.2.9 Deploy APEX Application (Chapters 15)

In this chapter you will be guided to export an application from your development PC to a production environment. For this purpose, you will utilize APEX's Export and Import utilities. To keep things simple, you will deploy the application in the same workspace to understand the deployment concept. First, you will export the application to a script file, and then, using the Import utility, the same script file will be imported to create the application in the same workspace with a new id. The same technique is applicable to the production environment.

Summary

This chapter provided an overview about the essence of the book: a web-based data-centric application. You'll create this application in two flavors using the browser-based declarative development environment provided by Oracle APEX. The next chapter is aimed at providing some core concepts about Oracle APEX. Read the chapter thoroughly because the terms used in that chapter are referenced throughout the book.

Chapter 2

Oracle Application Express Concepts

Chapter 2 – Oracle Application Express Concepts

2.1 Introduction to Oracle Application Express

If you are interested in developing professional web applications, then you have chosen the right track. Oracle Application Express (Oracle APEX) is a rapid application development (RAD) tool that runs inside an Oracle database instance and comes as a free option with Oracle database. Using this unique tool you can develop and deploy fast and secure professional web application. The only requirements are a web browser and a little SQL and PL/SQL experience.

Free Offer: Please provide the purchase proof of this book at oratech@cyber.net.pk to get my free SQL ebook: SQL - The Shortest Route For Beginners.

Application Express provides a declarative programming environment, which means that no code is generated or compiled during development. You just interact through wizards and property editor to build web applications on existing database schemas. Reports and charts are defined with simple SQL queries, so some knowledge of SQL is very helpful. Besides, if procedural logic is needed, you can also write PL/SQL code. Oracle Application Express is a declarative tool and has a vast collection of pre-defined wizards, HTML objects, database handling utilities, page rendering and submission processes, navigation and branching options, and more. You can use all these options to build your database-centric web applications comprising web pages carrying forms, reports, charts, etc., with their layouts and business logic. The APEX engine translates it all into an HTML code for the client side, and SQL and PL/SQL code for the server side. If you do not get a solution from predefined options, you are allowed by APEX to create your own SQL and PL/SQL code for the server side, and HTML, CSS, and JavaScript code, for the client side.

2.2 Why Use Oracle APEX

Velocity in the demand for new applications and functionality rises as businesses grow. As a developer, you are expected to rapidly respond to these needs. Over the years, desktop database and spreadsheet tools have enormously contributed to data management due to the ease and user friendliness these applications extend to their audience. Besides benefits, these applications have scalability and functionality limitations that not only results in dozens of different applications and data sources but also adds extra overhead in their maintenance. Due to these issues, organizations are unable to continue their standard practices, leaving mission-critical data at risk. These fragmented systems may also cause loss of business opportunity. Finally, significant amount of time and resource is required to put these data blocks together to get the desired information. The following table lists some more drawbacks of desktop applications and presents advantages of using Oracle APEX:

Desktop Applications Drawbacks	APEX Advantages
▪ Installation of client software, such as Excel, on every machine ▪ Lack of data sharing with other applications ▪ Simultaneous data access inability in spreadsheets ▪ May not be the part of regular data backup ▪ Critical and confidential data can easily be moved via email or pocket storage devices	▪ Central management of data and applications ▪ No installation of software is required on client machines, the only requirement is a supported browser ▪ Shared development and application access ▪ Being central, data and applications become a part of regular backup procedure ▪ Data and application access control, empowered by audit trail

2.3 Oracle APEX Structure

I know you are keen to start the proceedings, but first you need to understand some basic concepts before you dive into APEX pool. This chapter introduces some basic structures of APEX that you must be aware of prior to executing the exercises.

Workspace

To access Oracle Application Express development environment, users sign in to a shared work area called a workspace. A workspace is a virtual private container allowing multiple users to work within the same Oracle Application Express installation while keeping their objects, data and applications private. You have to create a workspace before you create an application. It is necessary because you have to specify which workspace you want to connect to at the time of login. Without this piece of information, you are not allowed to enter Oracle Application Express.

In order to use the exercises presented in this book, you have to select one option from the following:
- Download and install Oracle APEX on your own PC or within your private cloud. Please visit my blog http://oracleapex5.blogspot.com for details.
- Get your own free workspace from Oracle to execute the exercise online on their servers. This is the most convenient way for beginners. So, go to https://apex.oracle.com/en/ and request a free workspace that will be provided to you in minutes. See page 17 for further details.

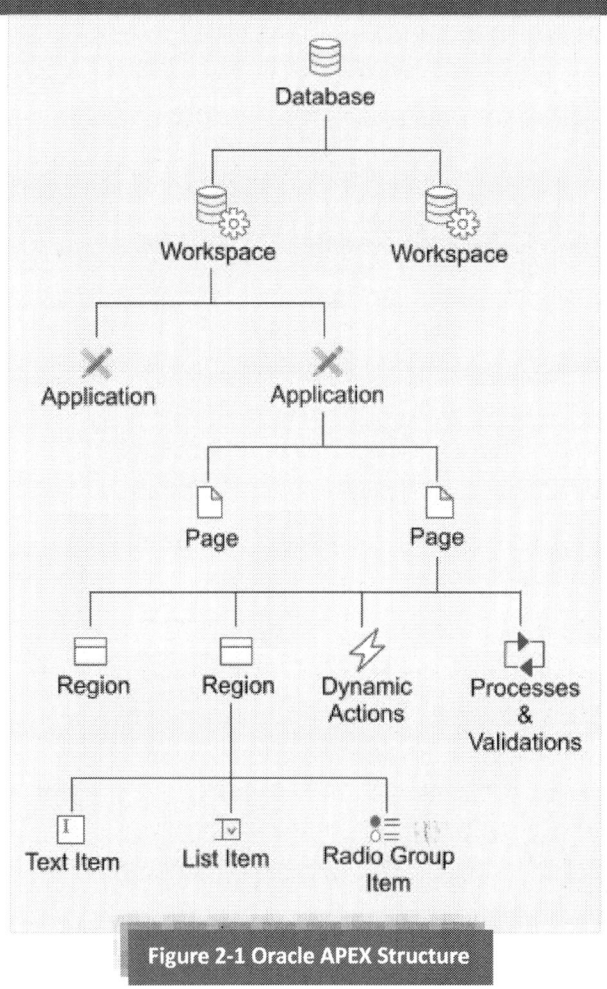

Figure 2-1 Oracle APEX Structure

Application

Applications in APEX are created through Application Builder and each application consists of one or more pages that are linked together using navigation menu, buttons, or hypertext links. Usually each page carries items, buttons, and application logic. You can show forms, reports, charts, and calendars on these pages and can perform different types of calculations and validations. You can also control movement within an application using conditional navigation. You do all this declaratively using built-in wizards or through custom PL/SQL code.

At this stage, it is necessary to introduce you to the two new features added to APEX 5: Universal Theme and Theme Roller. The Universal Theme is new application user interface that does away with excessive templates and supports effortless customizations with Theme Roller, Template Options, and Theme Styles. The Universal Theme empowers developers to build modern, responsive, sophisticated, accessible applications without requiring expert knowledge of HTML, CSS, or JavaScript.

Theme Roller displays in the Runtime Developer Toolbar. It is a live CSS editor that enables developers to quickly change the colors, rounded corners and other attributes of their applications without touching a line of code. To change all the colors of the theme style at once, drag the circles in the color wheel. Adjust a number of style attributes and see changes applied to your

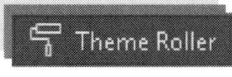

application in real time. Once you are satisfied with the result, you can save your changes as a Theme Style directly to your application.

There are three types of applications that you can create using the Application Builder: Desktop, Mobile, and Websheet. The *Create Application* wizard helps you to create these applications. While desktop and mobile applications are geared towards application developers, Websheet applications are designed for end users with no development experience.

Desktop Applications: These applications interact with a backend database to store and retrieve data. It is a collection of pages linked together using menus, buttons, or hypertext links. Pages are created declaratively through wizards. Each page can have multiple containers called regions. Each region can contain text, reports, charts, maps, web service content, calendars, or forms. Web forms hold items such as text fields, radio groups, check boxes, date pickers, list of values and more. In addition to these built-in types, you can create your own item types using plug-ins. When you build a database application, you can include different types of navigation controls, such as navigation menu, navigation bar entries, lists, breadcrumbs, and trees. Most of these navigation controls are shared components which mean that you create them at the application level and use them in any page within your database application. All pages in a database application share a common session state that is transparently managed by APEX.

Mobile Applications: Mobile database applications are designed to run specifically on smartphone devices.

Websheet Applications: Besides professional developers, APEX also cares for those who are not expert in the development field. It offers Websheet applications to such users to manage structured and unstructured data. Websheet applications are interactive web pages that combine text with data. These applications are highly dynamic and defined by their users. Websheet applications include navigation controls, search capabilities, and the ability to add annotations such as files, notes, and tags. Websheet applications can be secured using access control lists and several built-in authentication models. Pages can contain sections, reports, and data grids and everything can be linked together using navigation. All information is searchable and completely controlled by the end-user.

Page

A page is the basic unit of an application. When you build an application using Application Builder, you create pages that contain user interface elements, such as regions, items, navigation menu, lists, buttons and more. Each page is identified by a unique number. By default, page creation wizards automatically add controls to a page based on your selection. You can add more controls to a page later on by using the Page Designer interface. Usually the Create Page wizard is used to add components such as report, chart, form, calendar, or tree to a page. You also have the option to create a blank page and add components to it according to your own specific needs. In addition to different types of pages, you can add a Global Page to your application. A Global Page functions as a master page in your application. You can define separate Global Page, Login Page, and Home Page for desktop and mobile interfaces. This facilitates different pages being shown to end users when they access the application from a mobile device as opposed to a desktop system. The Application Express engine renders all components you add to a Global page on every page within your application. You can further control whether the Application Express engine renders a component or runs a computation, validation, or process by defining conditions.

Region

You can add one or more regions to a single page in an Oracle Application Express application. It is an area on a page that serves as a container for content. You control the appearance of a region through a specific region template. The region template controls the look of the region, the size, determines whether there is a border or a background color, and what type of fonts to display. A region template also determines the standard placement for any buttons placed in region positions. You can use regions to group page elements (such as items or buttons).

Item

After creating a region on a page, you add items to it. An item can be a text field, text area, password, select list, check box, and so on. Each item has its own specific attributes that affect the display of items on a page. For example, these attributes can impact where a label displays, how large an item is, and if the item displays next to or below the previous item.

Requesting a Free Workspace

Go to https://apex.oracle.com/en/ and click on the Free Workspace option. Follow the instructions mentioned below to get a free workspace:

1. On the Type page, select Application Development.
2. On the Identification page, enter your first and last names, email address, and the name of the workspace you intend to create (e.g. ORATECH).
3. On the next wizard page, enter a Schema Name (e.g. ORATECH69). Also select 25MB from the Space Allocation list and click Next. A schema is the set of metadata (data dictionary) used by the database, typically generated using DDL statement. You should consider a schema to be the user account and collection of all objects therein. APEX will create the schema you specify here with some default objects including data tables carrying some dummy data for evaluation.
4. Fill out the short survey questionnaire and move on.
5. Accept the terms and click Next.
6. On the final wizard page, enter case sensitive verification code and click the Submit Request button. Please note down your credentials from this page as you'll need this information to access APEX development environment. After submitting the request, you'll get a message "Your workspace (workspace name) has been successfully requested". Once this request is approved, your login credentials will be emailed to your email address.
7. Soon after submitting the request, you'll get an email from Oracle. Click on the provided link in this email to complete the approval process. The link will take you to APEX's website, and after a little while, your request will be approved with a message "Workspace Successfully Created".
8. Click on the button labeled Continue to Sign In Screen.
9. A screen would appear, requesting to change password. Enter and confirm your password and click the Apply Changes button.
10. Here you go. Your Workspace Home Page would appear, resembling the one illustrated below.

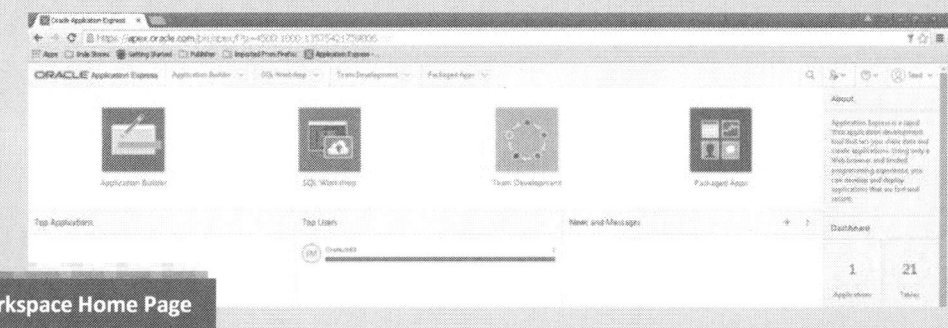

Figure 2-2 Workspace Home Page

Chapter 2 – Oracle Application Express Concepts

Oracle APEX has the web-based application development environment to build web applications. You are not required to install any client software to develop, deploy, or run APEX applications. Following are the primary tools provided by Oracle APEX:

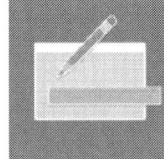

Application Builder – to create dynamic database driven web applications. This is the place where you create and modify your applications and pages. It comprises the following:
- **Create:** Using this option in the Application Builder you can create four types of applications: Desktop, Mobile, Websheet and Packaged applications.
- **Import:** Used to import an entire application and related files.
- **Dashboard:** Presents different metrics about applications in your workspace including: Developer Activity, Page Events, Page Count by Application, and Most Active Pages.
- **Workspace Utilities:** It contains various workspace utilities. The most significant one is Export. Using this utility, you can export application and component metadata to SQL script file format that you can import on the same or another compatible instance of Application Express.

SQL Workshop – to browse your database objects and to run ad-hoc SQL queries, SQL Workshop is designed to allow Application Developers to maintain database objects such as tables, packages, functions, views, etc. It is beneficial in hosted environments like apex.oracle.com where direct access to underlying schemas is not provided. It has five basic components:
- **Object Browser:** to review and maintain database objects.
- **SQL Commands:** to run SQL queries.
- **SQL Scripts:** to upload and execute script files.
- **Utilities:** includes Query Builder, Data Workshop, Generate DDL, Schema Comparison and more.
- **RESTful Services:** to define Web Services using SQL and PL/SQL against the database.

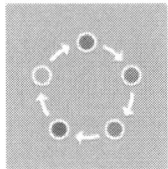

Team Development – Team Development allows development teams to better manage their APEX projects by defining milestones, features, to-dos and bugs. Features, to-dos and bugs can be associated with specific applications and pages as necessary. Developers can readily configure feedback to allow their end-users to provide comments on applications. The feedback also captures relevant session state details and can be readily converted to a feature, to-do or bug.

Packaged Apps – Packaged applications are a suite of business productivity applications, easily installed with only a few clicks. These solutions can be readily used as production applications to improve business processes and are fully supported by Oracle.

Oracle Application Express 5 For Beginners

2.4 Oracle Application Express Environments

The APEX environment has two broad categories:

Development Environment: Here you have complete control to build and test your applications as mentioned in this book.

Runtime Environment: After completing the development and testing phase, you implement your applications in a production environment where users can only run these applications and do not have the right to modify them. See Chapter 15 for further details.

2.5 About Browser Requirements

Because Oracle Application Express relies upon standards-compliant HTML5, CSS3, and JavaScript, Oracle recommends that you use the latest web browser software available for the best experience.

2.6 Page Designer

Page Designer is the main development interface where you manipulate page components. You use the Page Designer to view, create, and edit the controls and application logic that define a page. It is a new feature incorporated in APEX 5 to greatly improve developer's productivity and quickly enhance and maintain pages within Oracle Application Express. It allows you to undo and redo changes as necessary, before saving the page. In the Grid Layout, it visually presents how your regions and items appear on the page. Moreover, you can drag new components from Component Gallery, and move and copy existing components within a page. Similarly, you can drag to move multiple components at once in the Tree pane. It also has a new code editor with new functionalities, such as: SQL and PL/SQL validation with inline errors, auto completion, syntax highlighting, search and replace, and undo/redo support.

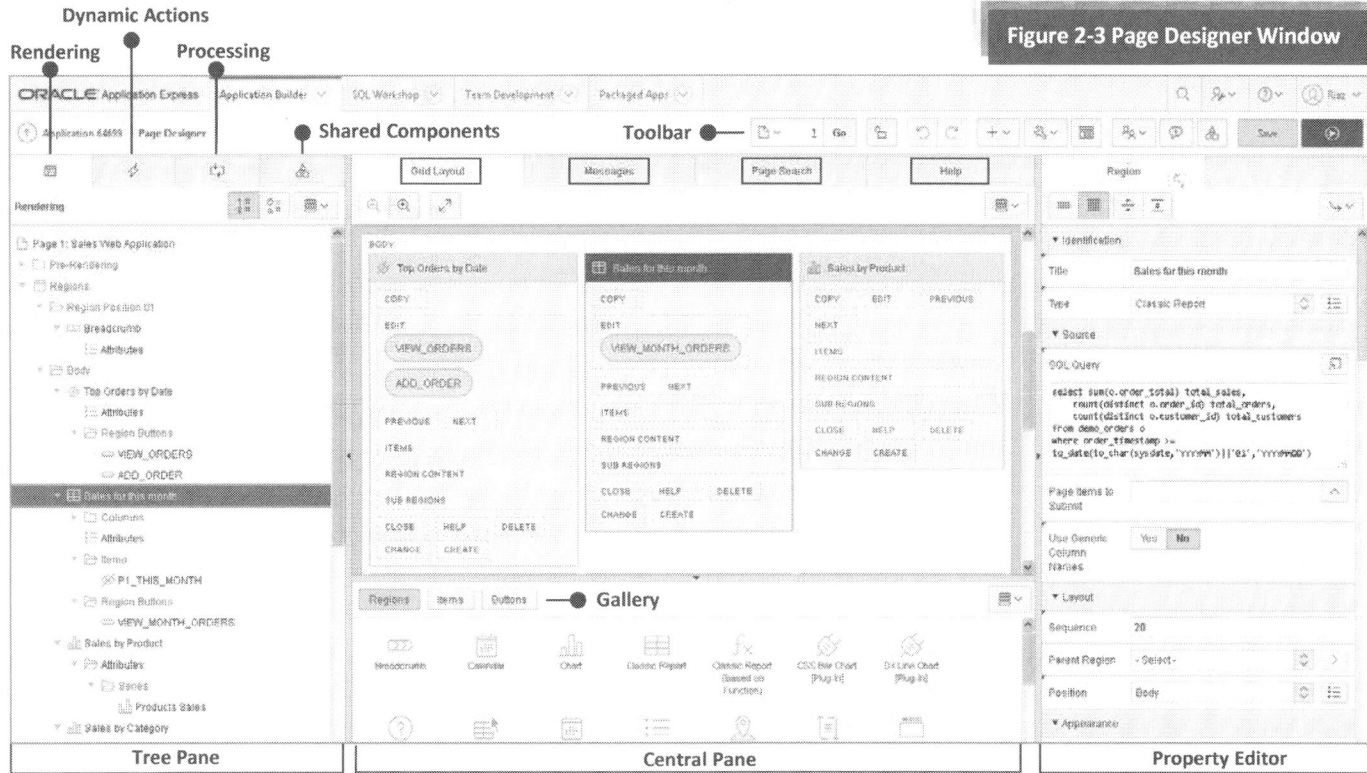

Figure 2-3 Page Designer Window

Toolbar

The Page Designer toolbar appears at the top of the page. It comprises various tools to: find a page, lock/unlock a page, undo/redo actions, save and run page, and so on. When you pass your cursor over an active button and menu, a tooltip displays that indicates what that particular toolbar option does.

Tree Pane

The Tree pane is displayed on the left side in Page Designer. It contains regions, page items, buttons, application logic (such as computations, processes, and validations), dynamic actions, branches, and shared components as nodes on a tree. It comprises four tabs:

- **Rendering** - Displays regions, page items, page buttons, and application logic as nodes in a tree.
- **Dynamic Actions** - Displays dynamic actions defined on this page. By creating a dynamic action, you can define complex client-side behavior declaratively without the need for JavaScript.
- **Processing** - Displays application logic defined on this page. Processes are logic controls used to execute Data Manipulation Language (DML) or PL/SQL. Processes are executed after the page is submitted. A page is typically submitted when a user clicks a button. Use this tab to specify application logic such as computations, validations, processes, and branches. Computations are APEX's declarative way of setting an item's values on the page. These are units of logic used to assign session state to items and are executed at the time the page is processed. Validation is a server-side mechanism designed to check and validate the quality, accuracy, and consistency of the page submitted data, prior to saving it into the database. Branches enable you to create logic controls that determine how the user navigates through the application.
- **Page Shared Components** - Displays shared components associated with this page.

Central Pane

The central pane in Page Designer has two sections. The upper section contains four tabs: Grid Layout, Messages, Page Search and Help. The lower pane is called Gallery and it is associated with Grid Layout.

- **Grid Layout:** Grid Layout is a visual representation of the regions, items, and buttons that define a page. You can add new regions, items and buttons to a page by selecting them from the Gallery at the bottom of the page.
- **Messages:** Displays to right of Grid Layout. When you create components or edit attributes in Page Designer, Messages notifies you of errors and warnings you need to address.
- **Page Search:** Displays to the right of Messages. Use Page Search to search all page metadata including regions, items buttons, dynamic actions, columns, and so on.
- **Help:** Help displays Help text for Property Editor attributes.

Property Editor

The Property Editor displays in the right pane and displays all attributes for the current component. As you select different components in either Tree View or Grid Layout, the Property Editor automatically updates to reflect the current selection. Attributes are organized into functional groups that describe their purpose. Required attributes display a red triangle in the upper left corner above the attribute label.

2.7 Understanding URL Syntax

Each application has its own unique ID and is referenced by this ID in URL. Similarly, you create pages in an application with respective numbers that uniquely identify each page. The Application Express engine assigns a session ID which is used as a key to the user's session state when an application is run. Here is the URL syntax example: http://apex.abc.com/pls/apex/f?p=101:1:440323506685863558

This example indicates:
- apex.abc.com is the URL of the server
- pls is the indicator to use the mod_plsql cartridge
- apex is the database access descriptor (DAD) name. The DAD describes how HTTP Server connects to the database server so that it can fulfill an HTTP request. The default value is apex.
- f?p= is a prefix used by Oracle Application Express
- 101 is the application being called
- 1 is the page within the application to be displayed
- 440323506685863558 is the session number

It is important to understand how f?p syntax works. Application Builder includes many wizards that automatically create these references for you. However, you may have to create the syntax yourself in some situations. In section 4.3.1 (chapter 4), we will create a manual link using this syntax, and in section 4.3.2, a link will be created on a couple of columns using the Target property of those columns.

Using f?p Syntax to Link Pages

You can create links between pages in your application using the following syntax:
f?p=App:Page:Session:Request:Debug:ClearCache:itemNames:itemValues:PrinterFriendly

The following are the arguments you can pass when using f?p syntax:
App: Indicates an application ID or alphanumeric alias.

Page: Indicates a page number or alphanumeric alias.

Session: Identifies a session ID. Web applications use HTTP by which browsers talk to Web servers. Since HTTP doesn't maintain state, it is known as a stateless protocol. Here, your Web server reacts independently to each individual request it receives and has no way to link requests together even if it is logging requests. For example, a client browser requests a page from a web server. After rendering the page, the server closes the connection. When a subsequent request is forwarded from the same client, the web server doesn't know how to associate the current request with the previous one. To access values entered on one page on a subsequent page, the values must be stored as session state. It is very crucial to access and manage session state while designing an interactive, data-driven web application. Fortunately, Oracle Application Express transparently manages session state behind the scenes for every page and provides developers with the ability to get and set session state values from any page in the application. When a user requests a page, the Application Express engine uses session ID to get session state information from the database. You can reference the session ID either using &SESSION. substitution string or by using :APP_SESSION bind variable.

Request: Here you place an HTML request. Each application button sets the value of REQUEST to the name of the button which enables the called process to reference the name of the button when a user clicks it. You can assess requests using the :REQUEST bind variable. See pages 81, 115 and 195.

Debug: Displays application processing details. Valid values for the DEBUG flag include: Yes or No. Setting this flag to YES you get details about application processing. You can reference the Debug flag using &DEBUG. substitution string. See page 39.

ClearCache: You use Clear Cache to make item values null. To do so, you provide a page number to clear items on that page. You can also clear cached items on multiple pages by adding a list of page numbers separated by comma. See page 43.

itemNames: Comma-delimited list of item names used to set session state with a URL.

itemValues: List of item values used to set session state within a URL. See Chapter 4 Section 4.3.1 for the utilization of these two syntax parameters.

PrinterFriendly: Determines if the page is being rendered in printer friendly mode. If PrinterFriendly is set to Yes, then the page is rendered in printer friendly mode. The value of PrinterFriendly can be used in rendering conditions to remove elements such as regions from the page to optimize printed output.

2.8 Start Building the Application

1. If you have logged out, then sign in to APEX development environment using the URL https://apex.oracle.com/pls/apex in your browser's address bar.
2. Enter the credential comprising your Workspace, Username, and Password in the Sign In form:

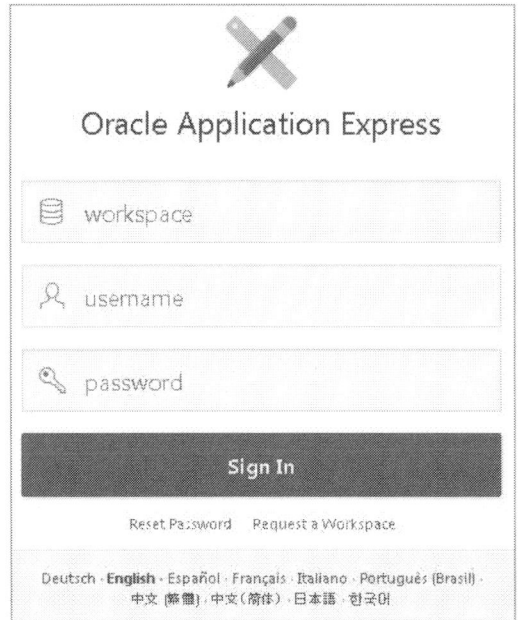

3. Click on the **Application Builder** icon.

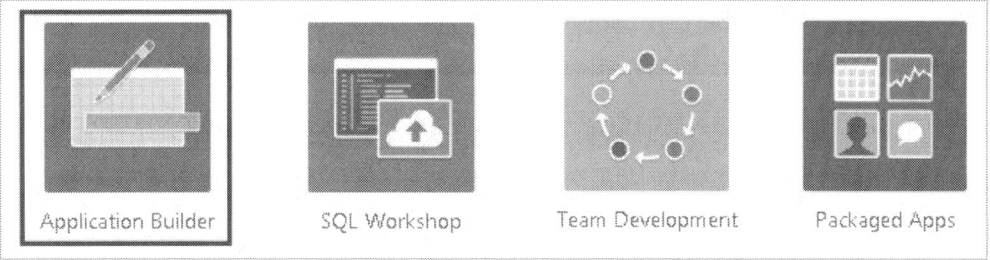

4. In the Application Builder page, click the **Create** icon or button to create a new application.

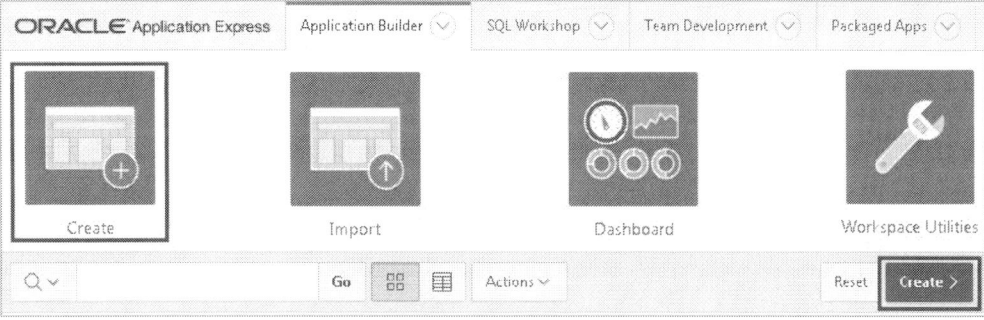

Chapter 2 – Oracle Application Express Concepts

5. Select the first **Desktop** option for the Type of application. You will create a mobile application in Chapter 10.

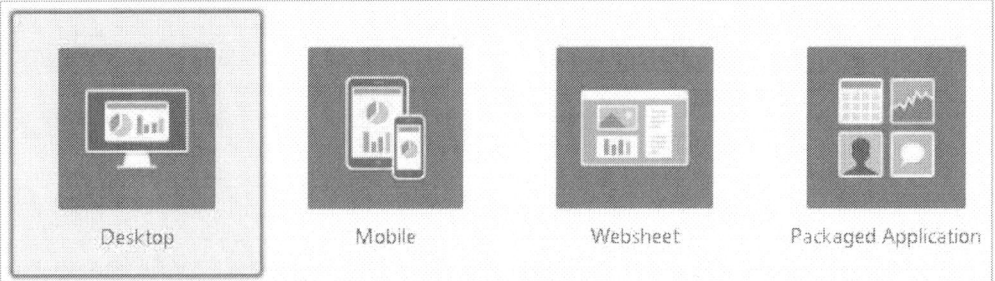

6. Enter **Sales Web Application** in the Name box and match other attribute values with those set in the following figure, except schema and Application number that would be different in your scenario. Accept the default values appearing for these two attributes and click **Next**.

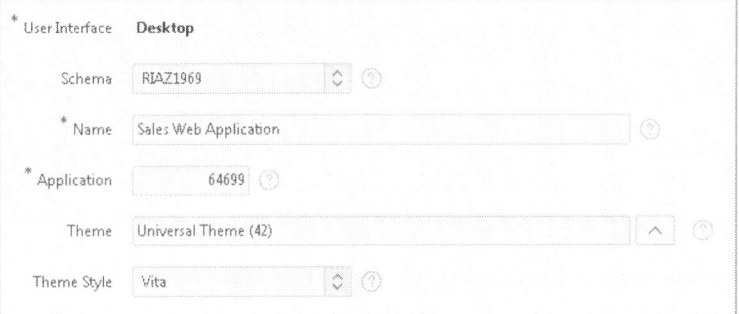

7. Accepting default values on the "Pages" page, and click **Next** to move on. By default, the application builder wizard creates a blank Home page along with a login page. This step shows the Home page information.

8. In Shared Components Page, select **No** for *Copy Shared Components from Another Application* and click **Next**.

9. In the Attributes page, set Date and Time formats using the adjacent LOV buttons. Accept default values for Authentication Scheme and other attributes as shown in the figure below. Oracle APEX provides a number of predefined authentication mechanisms, including a built-in authentication framework and an extensible custom framework. In the selected default scheme (Application Express Accounts) users are managed and maintained in the APEX workspace. Note that in Chapter 13 we will replace the default Application Express Authentication Scheme with custom authentication for this application. For the time being, click **Next** to proceed.

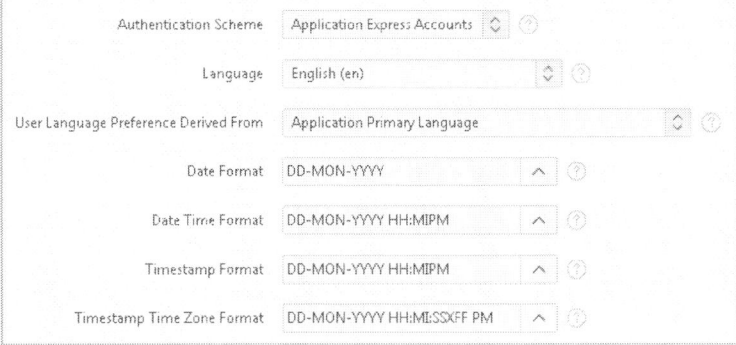

10. Click the **Create Application** button in the confirm page. Your screen should resemble the one presented hereunder. Note that APEX created the application with two pages: Page 1 (Home) and Page 101 (Login). This main application interface can be viewed differently using the two buttons: icon and report. The screen shot presented below presents the icon view.

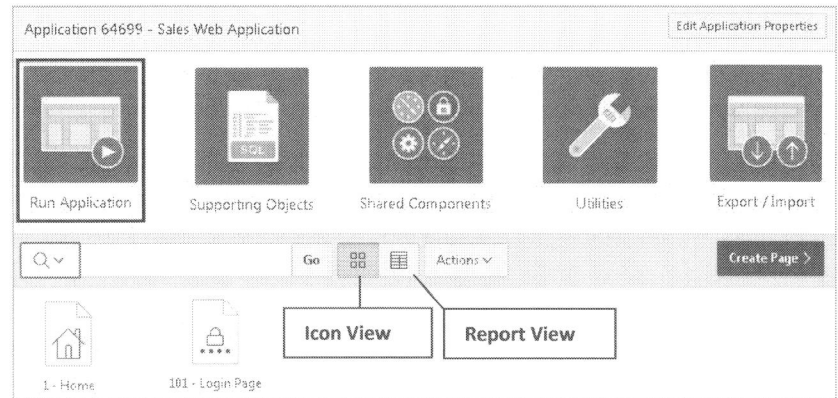

11. Click on **Run Application**. The application login form, created by the application builder, will come up. Type the same username (your email id) and password you entered earlier to access the development environment. Click the **Login** button. A new browser window will open, and you'll see the Home page of your application, also created by the application builder. Click the **Logout** link to exist the application.

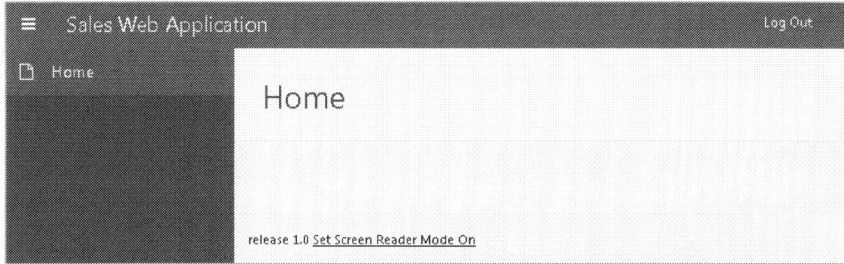

2.9 The Underlying Database Objects

While creating the workspace, you provided a schema name to hold database objects for your application. The following table lists some default objects created by APEX. These are the objects that you'll use in this book to build the sales application. You can view these objects using the Object Browser utility under SQL Workshop. In addition to the following, you will create some more tables in the final chapters of this book to set up a security module.

Tables	Sequences
DEMO_CUSTOMERS	DEMO_CUST_SEQ
DEMO_ORDERS	DEMO_ORDER_ITEMS_SEQ
DEMO_ORDER_ITEMS	DEMO_ORD_SEQ
DEMO_PRODUCT_INFO	DEMO_PROD_SEQ
DEMO_STATES	-
DEMO_TAGS	-

Summary

This chapter introduced you to some of the important basic concepts of Oracle Application Express. Besides the theoretical stuff, you were guided to request a free workspace. You also created the basic structure of your application with two default pages (you will work in detail on these pages in subsequent chapters to add useful content) and went through the underlying database objects that APEX created for you.

In the next chapter, you will create the building blocks (shared components) for your application. The Shared Components wizards allow us to define a variety of components that we can use, and re-use, throughout our application. In the coming chapters, our main focus will be on the practical aspect of this robust technology. Once you get familiar with Oracle Application Express, you can explore other areas on your own to become a master. The rest of the book will guide you to build professional looking web-based data-centric desktop and mobile applications, which will provide you the techniques in building your own.

Chapter 3
Create Application Components

Chapter 3 – Create Application Components

3.1 The Shared Components

Shared components are application structures that are used in application pages. These structures are called shared components because you create them once and utilize them across all the pages in the application. For example, in this chapter you will create a list comprising application menu options that will appear on every application page. The Page Shared Components tab in the Page Designer contains a list of common elements that are applied to a particular page. Note that Shared Components are only displayed under this tab after you add them. The following are some of the Shared Components that you will create for the Sales Web Application:

- Lists
- List of Values (LOV)
- Plug-ins
- Application Logo

If you are logged off, log back in to the application development environment.

1. Click on the **Application Builder** icon.
2. Click on the Edit button for Sales Web Application.
3. Click on the **Shared Components** icon, as illustrated below.

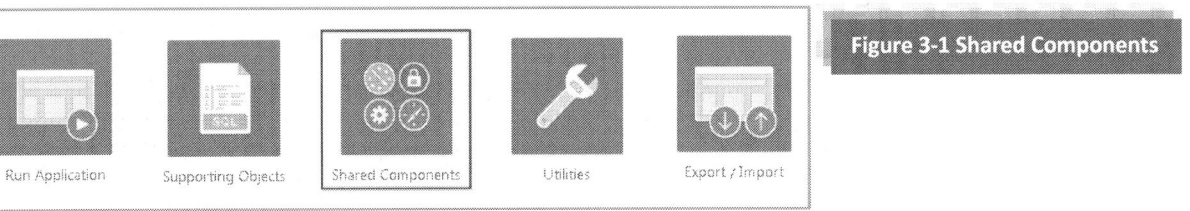

Figure 3-1 Shared Components

3.2 Lists

A list is a collection of links that is rendered using a template. For each list entry, you specify display text, a target URL, and other attributes that control when and how the list entry displays. You control the display of the list and the appearance of all list entries by linking the list to a template.

3.2.1 Modify Desktop Navigation Menu List

APEX used Tabs that acted as application's main menu till version 4.2. Now in version 5, a default navigation list named Desktop Navigation Menu is created with each new application in Shared Components. It is a hierarchical list of navigation which incorporates additional features like pull-down menus and sub-menus. It is displayed as a responsive side bar. Based on the available space, the navigation bar displays a full menu or collapses to a narrow icon bar. The default list carries just one item (Home). In this exercise, you'll modify this list to add more application menu entries.

1. In Shared Components, click the **Lists** option in the Navigation section.
2. Select **Desktop Navigation Menu** option, which carries one entry (Home) created by the application builder wizard. Modify this entry by clicking its name. In the attributes page of this menu item, click the popup LOV icon representing Image/Class attribute. From the Show list, select **Font Awesome Icons**, and from Category, select **Web Application**. Click the **Go** button to refresh the view. Select **fa-home** icon from the icons list. This image will be displayed for the Home menu at run time. Hit the **Apply Changes** button to save your work.
3. Click the button labeled **Create List Entry** to create a new menu item. Enter the following values against the specified attributes. You won't select anything in the first attribute (Parent List Entry), because initially

you will create level 1 entries that do not have parent entries. The target is either a page in the current application, or any valid URL. Since the Setup menu entry itself is not associated to any application page, its Target Type is set to No Target.

Attribute	Value	Attribute	Value
Parent List Entry	No Parent List Item	List Entry Label	Setup
Image/Class	fa-database	Target Type	No Target

4. Using the button **Create and Create Another**, create three more level-1 entries as follows. Combined together, the Target Type and Page attributes inform APEX where to land when a menu item is clicked.

Parent List Entry	List Entry Label	Image/Class	Target Type	Page
No Parent List Item	Orders	fa-list-alt	Page in this Application	4
No Parent List Item	Reports	fa-table	Page in this Application	26
No Parent List Item	Administration	fa-gear	No Target	-

The above four entries will form main menu of our application and due to this reason we set *No Parent List Item* for all four entries. Note that Setup and Administration entries have no target, because these two entries are not directly linked to application pages. In the next step, you will create sub-menus under these two main entries to call respective pages.

5. Create level-2 menu entries like this:

Parent List Entry	List Entry Label	Image/Class	Target Type	Page
Setup	Manage Customers	fa-users	Page in this Application	2
Setup	Manage Products	fa-shopping-cart	Page in this Application	3
Setup	Reset Password	fa-ellipsis-h	Page in this Application	65
Reports	Graphical Reports	fa-bar-chart	Page in this Application	26
Reports	Advance Reports	fa-file-pdf-o	Page in this Application	26
Administration	Application Segments	fa-sitemap	Page in this Application	60
Administration	User Groups	fa-group	Page in this Application	62
Administration	Users	fa-male	Page in this Application	63

The first three entries will come under the main Setup menu item. The Reports menu will contain two child entries, while Administration will have 3 entries.

6. Now create level 3 entries. The Page attribute for Monthly Review Report entry is set to zero, because it will be invoked through a print request - to be configured in chapter 9.

Parent List Entry	List Entry Label	Target Type	Page
Graphical Reports	Customer Orders	Page in this Application	17
Graphical Reports	Sales By Category/Products	Page in this Application	16
Graphical Reports	Sales by Category/Month	Page in this Application	5
Graphical Reports	Order Calendar	Page in this Application	10
Graphical Reports	Customer Map	Page in this Application	15
Graphical Reports	Product Order Tree	Page in this Application	19
Advance Reports	Monthly Review Report	Page in this Application	0
Advance Reports	Customer Invoice	Page in this Application	50

Chapter 3 – Create Application Components

The first six entries will appear as sub-menu under Graphical Reports menu. Similarly, Monthly Review Report and Customer Invoice will be placed under Advance Reports. All the above settings will setup a hierarchical navigation for your application as shown in Figure 3-2.

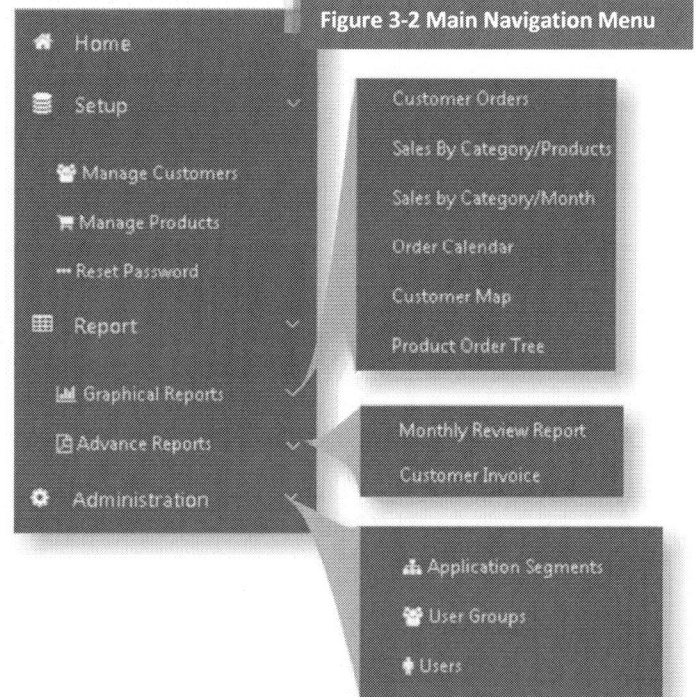

3.2.2 Reports List

This list contains six links that lead to different graphical reports in our desktop application. It will be utilized in Chapter 8 section 8.2

1. Go to Shared Components | Navigation Section | Lists. Click the **Create** button.
2. Select **From Scratch**. Enter **Reports List** for Name, select **Static** as the list Type, and click **Next**.
3. Enter the following values in *Query or Static Values* page. Initially, the wizard allows you to create five entries. The remaining entries are created after saving the first five.

Figure 3-2 Main Navigation Menu

List Entry Label	Target Page ID	Image/Class
Customer Orders	17	fa-money
Sales by Category and Product	16	fa-sort-amount-desc
Sales by Category / Month	5	fa-cogs
Order Calendar	10	fa-calendar
Customer Map	15	fa-map-marker
Product Order Tree	19	fa-sitemap
Monthly Review Report	0	fa-bar-chart-o
Customer Invoice	50	fa-print

4. Click **Next**, accept the default values in the next screen and click the **Create List** button.
5. Modify the list by clicking the **Reports List** name. Click the **Create List Entry** button to add the sixth entry.
6. Enter **Product Order Tree** in List Entry Label.
7. Set Target Type to Page in this Application and enter **19** in the Page attribute. Click the **Create List Entry** button. Using the same process, create the final two entries.
8. Modify each entry by clicking its name in the Lists interface and add image references as shown in the above table.

3.2.3 Order Wizard List

This is another utilization of lists. Rather than associating list items to pages in the application, you'll use it for visual representation. This list is used while creating orders in Chapter 7. In our application, we will create an order using a set of wizard steps in the following sequence:

a) Identify Customer
b) Select Items
c) Order Summary

Oracle Application Express 5 For Beginners

1. Go to Shared Components | Navigation Section | Lists and click the **Create** button.
2. Select the first option **From Scratch** and click **Next**.
3. Type **Order Wizard** in the Name box, set Type to **Static** and click **Next**.
4. On the next page, enter the following values and click Next.

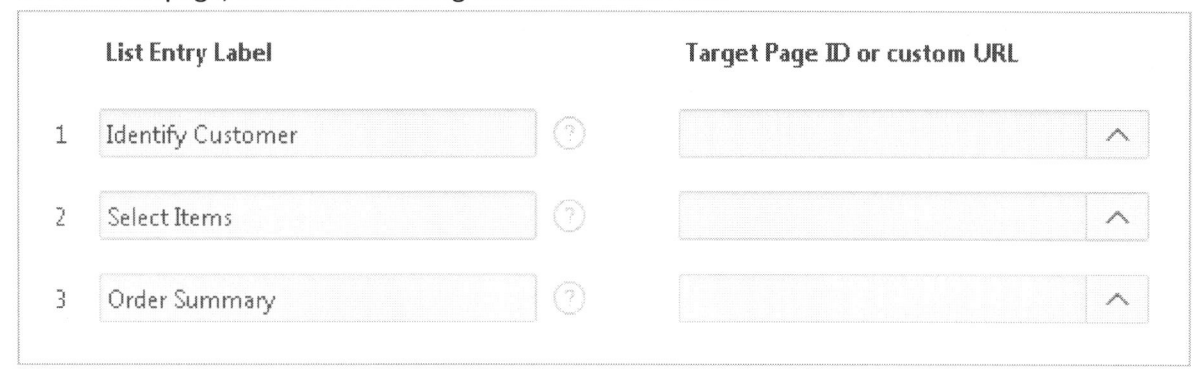

	List Entry Label	Target Page ID or custom URL
1	Identify Customer	
2	Select Items	
3	Order Summary	

5. Click **Create List** button on the confirmation page.
6. Click on the newly created Order Wizard list.
7. Edit each list item, set *Target Type* attribute to **No Target** for all three list items. The No Target is being set because this list is intended to display the current order wizard step the user is on, and not to call a page in the application. In the Current List Entry section, set List Entry Current for Pages Type to **Comma Delimited Page List** for the three list items mentioned below, and set the List Entry Current for Condition attribute individually as shown in the following table.

Attribute	Identify Customer	Select Items	Order Summary
List Entry Current for Condition	11	12	14

The attribute - List Entry Current for Pages Type - specifies when this list entry should be current. Based on the value of this attribute, you define a condition to evaluate. When this condition is true then the list item becomes current. The template associated with list item gives users a visual indication that the current list item is selected. The following figure illustrates the use of a list in our application. Being the first step in the order wizard, the *Identify Customer* list item is marked as current, while the remaining two are displayed as non-current.

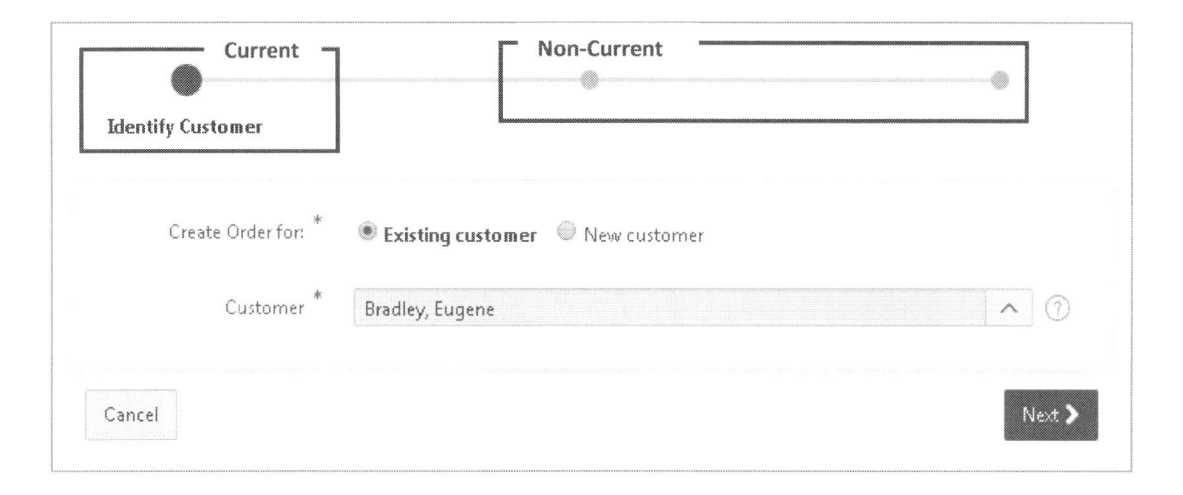

31

Chapter 3 – Create Application Components

3.3 Desktop Navigation Bar

A navigation bar is used to link users to various pages within an application. Typically a navigation bar is used to access Help pages and also carries a Sign Out link. The location of a navigation bar depends upon the associated page template. When you create a navigation bar you can specify an image name, label, display sequence, and target location (a URL or page).

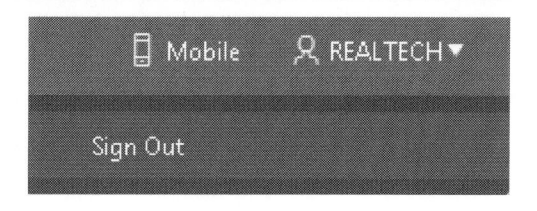

The navigation bar used in our application will have Mobile and Sign Out links. Besides, it will show the currently logged in user associated to the Sign Out link, as illustrated in the above figure. In this exercise we are going to create just the mobile link, because the Sign Out entry was created automatically when we initially created the application in the previous chapter.

3.3.1 Mobile Entry

This navigational bar entry will take users to the home page of the mobile application.

Go to Shared Components. Once again select the **Lists** option and click on **Desktop Navigation Bar**. This will bring up the default navigation bar carrying the sole Logout entry. Click the **Create List Entry** button to add some more entries, using the following table. The page id (30) defined for the mobile entry will be generated by application builder wizard in Chapter 10, where you will create mobile interface. After creating the mobile interface in that chapter, replace this id with that of yours. By defining a parent entry, the Sign Out entry appears as a sub-menu item. APP_USER and LOGOUT_URL are built-in substitution strings. APP_USER is the current user running the application, while LOGOUT_URL is an application-level attribute used to identify the logout URL. This is a URL that navigates the user to a logout page or optionally directly logs out a user. In order to use these substitution variables in your application attributes, you have to prefix them with an & and postfix with a period.

Attribute	New Entry	New Entry	Modify Log Out Entry
Parent List Entry	No	No	&APP_USER.
Image/Class	fa-mobile	fa-user	-
List Entry Label	Mobile	&APP_USER.	Sign Out
Target Type	Page in this Application	No Target	URL
Page	30 *(in my scenario)*	-	-
URL Target	-	-	&LOGOUT_URL.

3.4 List of Values (LOV)

List of values is used to control the values displayed and limits the user's selection. You can define two types of lists: Static and Dynamic. A static list of values is based on predefined display and return values. A dynamic list of values is based on a SQL query, executed at runtime. In the following exercise we are going to create both types of LOVs.

3.4.1 CATEGORIES LOV

In our application we have two integrated setups: Categories and Products. The application uses three categories. Each product in the application falls under one of these categories. This LOV is created with the intention to provide three static values to the user (while creating a product record) to choose a category the product belongs to. This LOV is utilized in Chapter 6 section 6.4.2, and Chapter 10 section 10.8.1.

1. In Shared Components, click **Lists of Values** under the Other Components section.
2. Click the **Create** button.
3. Select the **From Scratch** option and click **Next**.
4. Enter **Categories** in the Name box, select the default **Static** type, and click **Next**.
5. Fill in the values as shown in the following figure and click **Create List of Values** button.

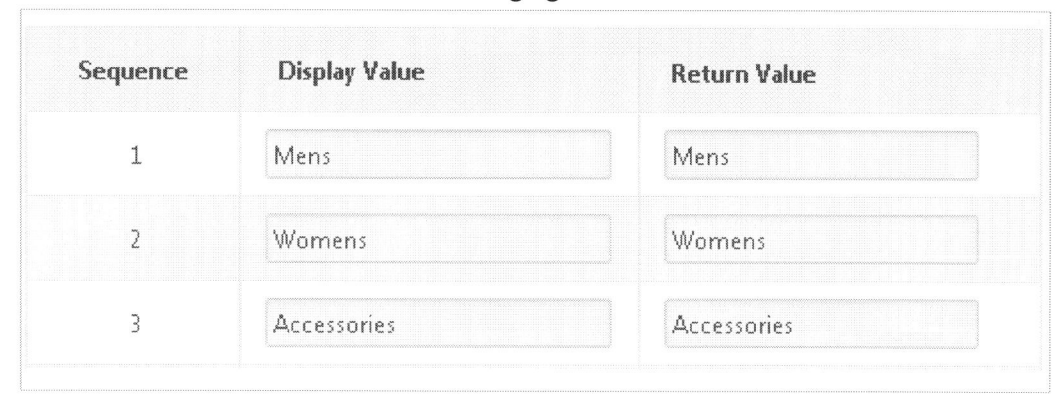

Sequence	Display Value	Return Value
1	Mens	Mens
2	Womens	Womens
3	Accessories	Accessories

In the last step, you entered a pair of static Display and Return values. These entries will display in the order entered. Return Value does not display, but is the value that is returned as a user selection to the Application Express engine.

3.4.2 PRODUCTS WITH PRICE LOV

Similar to the categories list of value, this one also limits user's selection by displaying product names with prices during order creation. Here you'll generate the list dynamically with the help of a SQL statement. It will be utilized in Chapter 7 section 7.4.2.

1. Once again click the **Create** button in Lists of Values.
2. Select **From Scratch** and click **Next**.
3. Enter **Products with Price** in the Name box. This time select the **Dynamic** Type and click **Next**.
4. In the Query box type:
   **select apex_escape.html(product_name) || ' [$' || list_price || ']' d, product_id r
   from demo_product_info
   where product_avail = 'Y'
   order by 1**

APEX_ESCAPE.HTML
The function APEX_ESCAPE.HTML is used to protect against XSS (Cross Site Scripting) attacks. It replaces characters that have special meaning in HTML with their escape sequence. 　It converts occurrence of & to &amp 　It converts occurrence of " to &quot 　It converts occurrence of < to &lt 　It converts occurrence of > to &gt

5. Click **Create List of Values** button to finish the wizard.

Chapter 3 – Create Application Components

3.4.3 STATES LOV

This is a dynamic LOV and is based on a SQL SELECT query to fetch State names from DEMO_STATES table. The query fetches both columns from the table. This LOV is used in Chapter 5 section 5.4.2 and Chapter 10 section 10.6.1, where it is attached to an item in the customer form.

1. In Lists of Values, click the **Create** button.
2. Select the **From Scratch** option and click **Next**.
3. Enter **States** in the Name box, select **Dynamic** as Type, and click **Next**.
4. In the Query box type:
   select initcap(state_name) display_value, st return_value from demo_states order by 1
5. Click **Create List of Values** button.

3.4.4 Y or N LOV

This LOV will be used in Product setup module (Chapter 6 section 6.4.3) to specify whether the product is available or not.

1. In Lists of Values, click **Create**.
2. Select **From Scratch** and click **Next**.
3. Enter **Y or N** in the Name box, select **Static** as Type, and click **Next**.
4. Fill in the values as shown in the following figure and click **Create List of Values**.

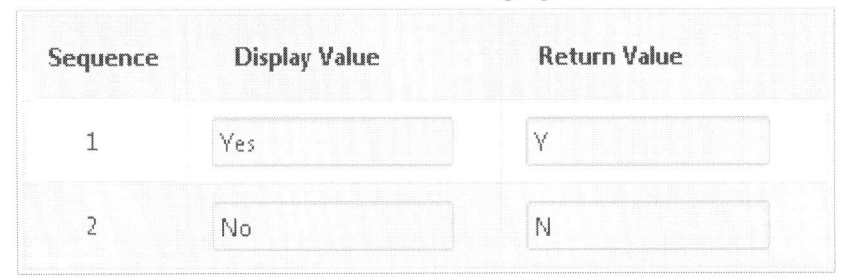

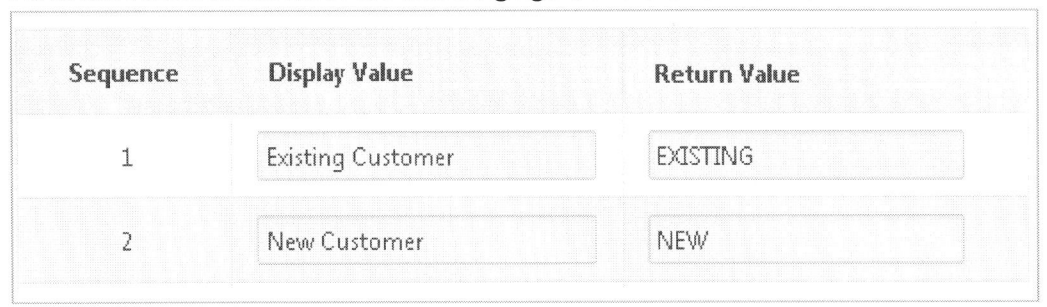

Sequence	Display Value	Return Value
1	Yes	Y
2	No	N

3.4.5 NEW OR EXISTING CUSTOMER LOV

This static list will be incorporated in the initial Order Wizard step (Chapter 7 Section 7.5.4) to select either an existing customer or to create a new one.

1. In Lists of Values, click **Create**.
2. Select **From Scratch** and click **Next**.
3. Enter **NEW OR EXISTING CUSTOMER** in the Name box, select **Static** as Type, and click **Next**.
4. Fill in the values as shown in the following figure and click **Create List of Values** button.

Sequence	Display Value	Return Value
1	Existing Customer	EXISTING
2	New Customer	NEW

3.5 Plug-Ins

Plug-ins enable developers to declaratively extend, share, and reuse the built-in types available with Oracle Application Express. Oracle Application Express supports a set group of authentication scheme, authorization scheme, item, region, dynamic action, and process types. Plug-ins offer a means of augmenting these built-in types by declaratively creating and using new types in your application. Because plug-ins are designed for reuse, developers can export and import them to other workspaces and also share them with others. The process of implementing a plug-in involves the following steps:

1. Create a plug-in or import a plug-in in to your application workspace.
2. Edit or create an authorization scheme, item, region, process, or dynamic action type to use the plug-in.
3. Run your application to test the plug-in.

3.5.1 Import CSS Bar Chart and D3 Line Chart Plug-Ins

You'll import a couple of charts in your application. The first one (CSS Bar Chart) will be created in the Home page (Chapter 4 section 4.3.1), while the second one (D3 Line Chart) will be utilized in a graphical report in Chapter 8 section 8.5. These charts are provided as plug-ins by APEX community and are included in the source code of this book. You just need to import these plug-ins to use them in your application pages. To do so, execute the following set of steps.

1. In Shared Components, click **Plug-ins** under Other Components section.
2. Click the **Import** button.
3. Click the **Browse** button, select **css_bar_chart.sql** file from Chapter3 folder in the downloaded book source, and click the **Open** button. Make sure that the option **Plug-in** is selected as File Type.
4. Click **Next** to move on.
5. A message saying *The export file has been imported successfully* would appear. Click **Next** to install the file.
6. Select your application (Sales Web Application) from the *Install Into Application* list and click the **Install Plug-in** button. The plug-in (CSS Bar Chart) will be installed.
7. Repeat the same process to import the **D3 Line Chart** plug-in by selecting D3_Line.SQL file from the same folder.

3.6 Images

You can reference images within your application by uploading them to the Images Repository. When you upload an image, you can specify whether it is available to all applications or a specific application. Images uploaded as shared components can be referenced throughout an application. They may include images for application menus or buttons or may represent icons that, when clicked, allow users to modify or delete data. One important point to remember here is that the images uploaded to the images repository should not be directly related to the application's data such as images of products and employees. Such images must be stored in the application's schema alongside the data to which the image is related. You'll follow this approach in chapter 6 (Setup Product Catalog) to save each product's image along with other information, in a database table.

Application Express images are divided into two categories:

- **Workspace images** are available to all applications for a given workspace
- **Application images** are available for only one application

In the following set of steps, you'll add your application's logo to the images repository. The logo appears at the top of every page in the application.

1. In Shared Components, click **Static Application Files** under Files section.
2. Click on the **Upload File** button.
3. Click the **Browse** button and select logo.png (available in book's code).

   ![Sales Web Application logo]

4. Click the **upload** button. After uploading the image, you need to tell APEX to use this file as your application logo. To pass this information, execute the following steps.
5. In Shared Components click **User Interface Attributes** under User Interface section.
6. For Logo Type, select **Image**.
7. Enter **#APP_IMAGES#logo.png** in the Logo box (Use the correct case for the image file name and extension else the logo will not be displayed) and click the **Apply Changes** button. The substitution string (APP_IMAGES) is used to reference uploaded images, JavaScript, and cascading style sheets that are specific to a given application and are not shared over many applications. If you upload a file and make it specific to an application, then you must use this substitution string, or bind variable.

Summary

In this chapter you created all the components required by the application with relevant references. These shared components were created declaratively with the help of APEX wizards to demonstrate yet another great feature of this technology to tackle redundancy. From the next chapter you will be creating all the pages of your web application (starting with the Home page), and will see all these shared components in action. After creating an application page, you can see a list of all Shared Components utilized on that page by accessing its Shared Components tab in the Page Designer.

Chapter 4
Prepare Application Dashboard

Chapter 4 - Prepare Application Dashboard

4.1 About the Home Page

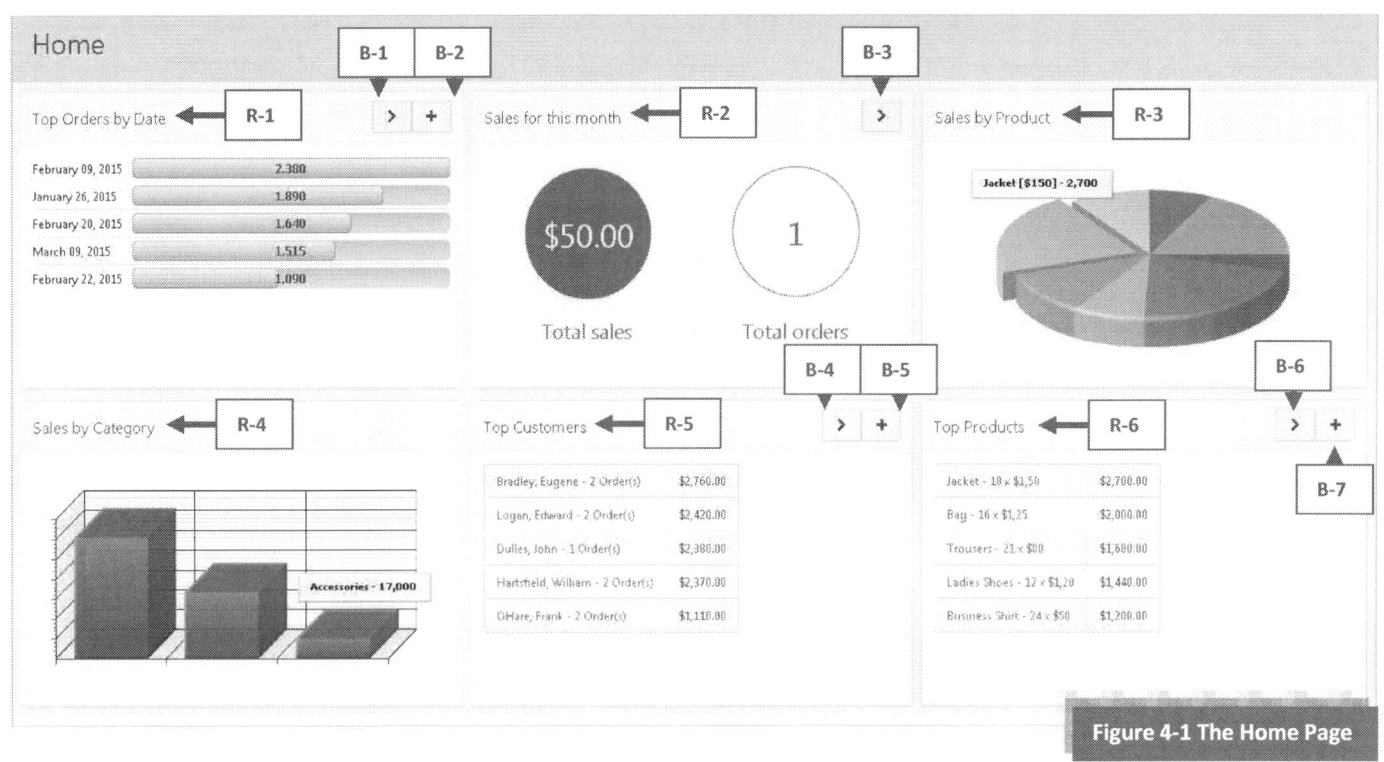

Figure 4-1 The Home Page

Every website on the internet has a home page. Technically referred to as the default page, it is the page that comes up when you call a website without mentioning a specific page. For example, if you call Oracle's official website using the URL www.oracle.com, the first page you see is the default or home page of the website. It is the page that represents the objective of a website. Similar to a website, a web application also carries this page. By default, Oracle APEX creates this page along with a login page, for both desktop and mobile applications. The desktop login page, that you used to access the application in a previous chapter, usually doesn't require any modification or enhancement. It comes with out-of-the-box functionalities and utilizes current authentication scheme to process the login request. The Home page, on the other hand, is created as a blank slate that you need to populate with content relevant to your application's theme. For instance, the Home page of your Sales Web Application will have stuff related to sales.

Let's experience the APEX declarative development environment by completing this page of our web application, which is a dashboard and holds six regions to present different views of sales data.

4.2 Modify the Home Page

Before starting the proceedings, I would recommend you to first have a look at Chapter 2 section 2.6 to acquaint yourself with the Page Designer interface. Once you're comfortable with it, then execute the following steps to modify attributes of the Home page.

1. Sign in to your workspace. Click on **Application Builder** and then click the **Edit** icon under Sales Web Application.
2. Click on the **Home** icon (if you're browsing the page in Icon view). This will bring up the Page Designer.

4.2.1 Modify Page Attributes

Modify Name and Title attributes of the Home page with meaningful labels. The Name attribute gives the page a meaningful name for recognition. The Application Express engine uses the title you specify here in place of the #TITLE# substitution string used in the page template. This title is inserted between the HTML tags <TITLE> and </TITLE>.

Under the Rendering tab to your left, click on the root node Page 1: Home to refresh the Property Editor (on the right side) with the main page attributes. Set the following attributes and click the **Save** button. These are the attributes that are enough to set for the main page. However, there are many others that you must be curious to know about. Click each attribute in the Property Editor, and click on the Help tab (in the Central pane) to see what that attribute does.

Attribute	Value
Name	Sales Web Application
Title	Sales Web Application
Page Template	Standard

> **NOTE**
> To remove a component (e.g. a region) from a page, right click the desired component in the Rendering section, and select Delete from the context menu.

4.3 Create Regions

You put items on a page under a specific region. A region is an area on a page that serves as a container for content. You can create multiple regions to visually segregate different sections on a page and to group page elements. A region may carry a SQL report, static HTML content, items, and buttons. Each region can have its own template applied which controls its respective appearance. The following sub-sections demonstrate how you can create multiple regions to present different information on a single page.

4.3.1 Top Orders by Date ➔ (R-1)

This region will display top five orders by date from the database using a CSS Bar Chart plug-in that we imported in Chapter 3 section 3.5.1. The chart is populated using a SQL SELECT statement, which fetches summarized sales figures for each date from the Orders table. Under Rendering section, right-click **Regions** and select **Create Region** from the context menu. This will create a new node named Body ☐ Body and will place a new region </> New under it. Click on the </> New entry and set the following attributes (in the Property Editor) for it:

Attribute	Value
Title	Top Orders by Date
Type	CSS Bar Chart (Plug-in)

SQL Query	select to_char(o.order_timestamp,'Month DD, YYYY') order_day,
	    SUM(o.order_total) sales,
	    'f?p=&APP_ID.:4:'||:app_session||
	    '::&DEBUG.:RIR,4:IREQ_ORDER_DATE:'||
	    to_char(trunc(order_timestamp),'MM/DD/YYYY') the_link
	from demo_orders o
	group by to_char(o.order_timestamp,'Month DD, YYYY'), order_timestamp
	order by 2 desc nulls last

Click on the link beside the Template Options attribute to set Body Height as follows	
Body Height	240px
Grid	Start New Row=Yes, Column=Automatic, Column Span=4

Chapter 4 - Prepare Application Dashboard

In the above SQL query, we created a link on the ORDER_TIMESTAMP column, using APEX's f?p URL syntax. The following table elaborates the arguments used in the link:

Argument	Explanation
&APP_ID.	The first argument in the URL is reserved for application ID. The expression used here is called a substitution string that holds application ID. Instead of hard-coding application ID, we used this substitution variable. Note that substitution variables are always preceded with an & and end with a period.
:	The colon special character is used in the URL as an argument separator. Since the URL contains no REQUEST argument, the position of this argument is left empty. See an additional colon before the &DEBUG. Argument.
4	This is the target page (Page 4 – Orders) that we are calling in this URL.
||	The concatenation operator is used to join the preceding text arguments (enclosed in single quotes) first with the numeric application session, and then with a date value.
:app_session	It is the session ID of our application and is used to create links between application pages by maintaining the same session state among them. Again, instead of using a hard-coded session number, which is rendered by the APEX engine, we used this bind variable. Bind variables always start with a colon.
&DEBUG.	References the debug flag to display application processing details.
RIR,4	Placed in the URL's ClearCache position, this argument resets interactive report on Page 4.
IREQ_ORDER_DATE	This argument is used in the itemNames position. The IR (Interactive Report) string is used along with the equal operator (EQ), followed by an item name (ORDER_DATE - an item on Page 4). This argument actually acts as a filter that is used in conjunction with the itemValue (mentioned underneath) to only display the clicked order.
to_char(trunc(order_timestamp),'MM/DD/YYYY')	Used in the itemValue position, the expression forwards the clicked ORDER_TIMESTAMP value to the target page. The TRUNC (date) function returns date with the time portion of the day truncated. To create a filter on an interactive report in a link, use the string *IR<operator>_<target column alias>* in the ItemNames section of the URL, and pass the filter value in the corresponding location in the ItemValues section of the URL. See section 2.7 in chapter 2 on APEX f?p syntax. Other operators that you can use to filter an interactive report include: - EQ = Equals (the default operator) - LT = Less than - GT = Greater than - LTE = Less than or equal to - GTE = Greater than or equal to - LIKE = SQL LIKE operator - N = Null In order to apply the filter, you must use correct date format mask for order_timestamp column. For example, if the Order Date column on Page 4 appears as 09-FEB-2015, then you must use 'DD/MON/YYYY' format mask in the above SQL query.

If you execute the above SQL statement in SQL Command, the output would resemble something like this:

ORDER_DAY	SALES	THE_LINK
February 09, 2015	2380	f?p=4500:4:108274172486899::NO:RIR,4:IREQ_ORDER_DATE:02/09/2015
January 26, 2015	1890	f?p=4500:4:108274172486899::NO:RIR,4:IREQ_ORDER_DATE:01/26/2015
February 20, 2015	1640	f?p=4500:4:108274172486899::NO:RIR,4:IREQ_ORDER_DATE:02/20/2015
March 09, 2015	1515	f?p=4500:4:108274172486899::NO:RIR,4:IREQ_ORDER_DATE:03/09/2015
February 22, 2015	1090	f?p=4500:4:108274172486899::NO:RIR,4:IREQ_ORDER_DATE:02/22/2015
March 22, 2015	1060	f?p=4500:4:108274172486899::NO:RIR,4:IREQ_ORDER_DATE:03/22/2015
March 04, 2015	950	f?p=4500:4:108274172486899::NO:RIR,4:IREQ_ORDER_DATE:03/04/2015
March 14, 2015	905	f?p=4500:4:108274172486899::NO:RIR,4:IREQ_ORDER_DATE:03/14/2015
March 31, 2015	870	f?p=4500:4:108274172486899::NO:RIR,4:IREQ_ORDER_DATE:03/31/2015
March 28, 2015	730	f?p=4500:4:108274172486899::NO:RIR,4:IREQ_ORDER_DATE:03/28/2015

The database applications created in APEX use a grid layout (comprising 12 columns) to position page elements. The first Grid attribute (Start New Row) used in this region is set to Yes to put the region on a new row. Compare this value with the next region (Sales for This Month), where it is set to No to place that region adjacent to this one. The value Automatic in the Column attribute automatically finds a column position for the region. Since there exists no elements on the current row, column number 1 will be used as the starting place to position this region. As you can see in the following figure, we have placed three regions on a single row. Equally divided in a 12 columns grid layout, each region spans 4 columns and this is the value we set for all the six regions on the Home page. The first region will span from column number 1 to 4, the second one from 5 to 8, and the third one from 9 to 12, as illustrated below.

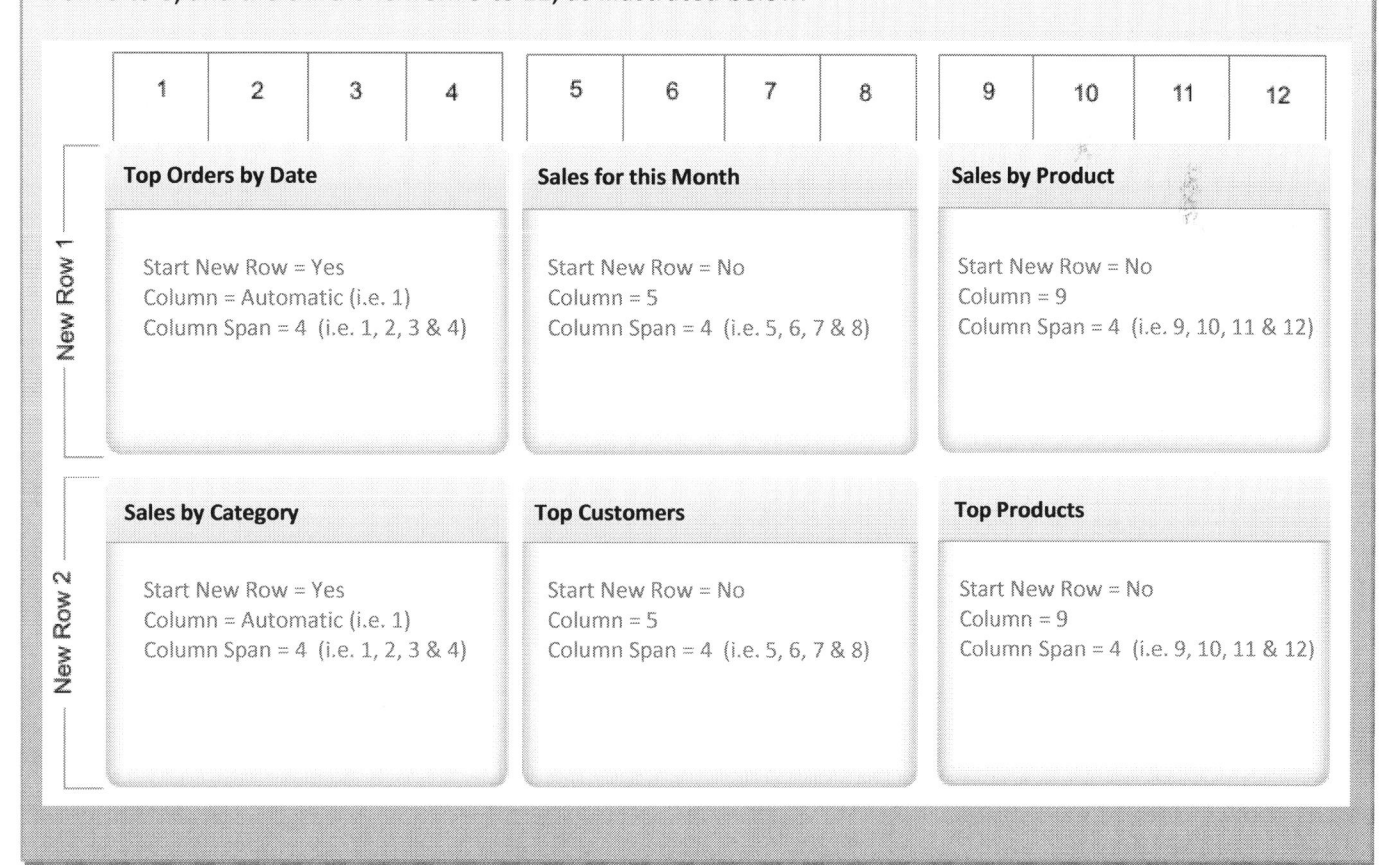

Figure 4-2 Grid Layout

New Row 1

Top Orders by Date
Start New Row = Yes
Column = Automatic (i.e. 1)
Column Span = 4 (i.e. 1, 2, 3 & 4)

Sales for this Month
Start New Row = No
Column = 5
Column Span = 4 (i.e. 5, 6, 7 & 8)

Sales by Product
Start New Row = No
Column = 9
Column Span = 4 (i.e. 9, 10, 11 & 12)

New Row 2

Sales by Category
Start New Row = Yes
Column = Automatic (i.e. 1)
Column Span = 4 (i.e. 1, 2, 3 & 4)

Top Customers
Start New Row = No
Column = 5
Column Span = 4 (i.e. 5, 6, 7 & 8)

Top Products
Start New Row = No
Column = 9
Column Span = 4 (i.e. 9, 10, 11 & 12)

Chapter 4 - Prepare Application Dashboard

APEX enables you to test your work from time to time. For example, after completing this region you can save and run the page (by clicking the Save and Run Page button) to check how the region appears on it. At this stage your Home page will be carrying just one region (Top Orders by Date), containing a bar chart. If you click any bar in the chart or any of the provided date links, the application tries to open Page 4 and throws an error, because the page doesn't exist. After completing Page 4 (Orders) in chapter 7, when you run the Home page and click any of these links, the interactive report defined on the target page would appear with a filter applied (as shown below) to display the selected order.

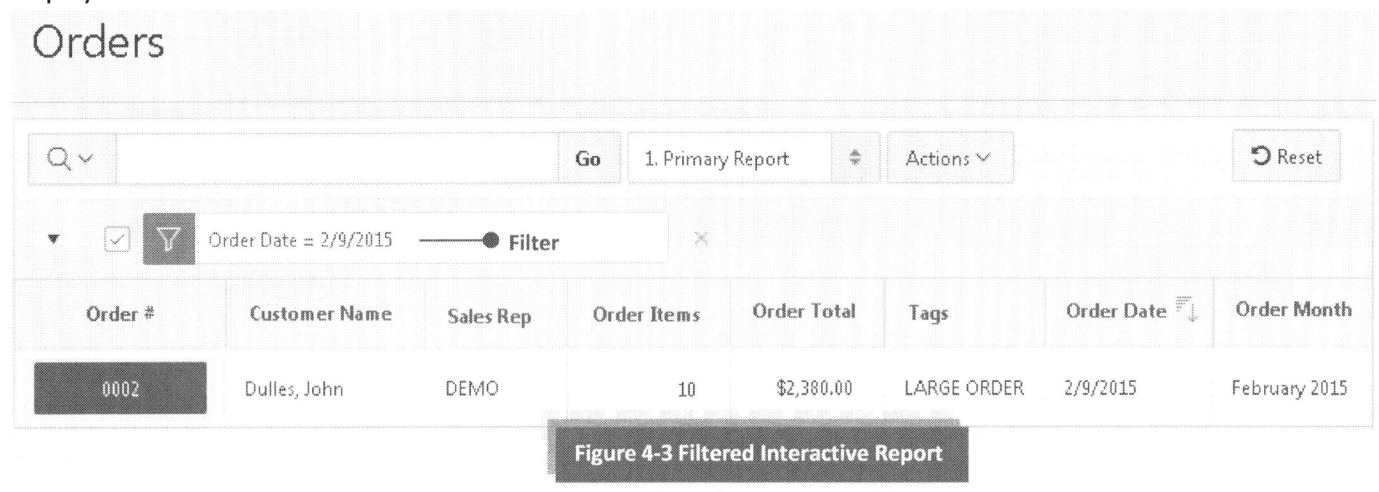

Figure 4-3 Filtered Interactive Report

4.3.2 Sales For This Month ➔ (R-2)

As the name implies, this region will present sales figures in graphical format (using a Badge List) along with number of orders placed, for the current month. The list is dynamically rendered based on a SQL Statement each time the page is viewed.

Under Rendering section, right-click **Regions** and select **Create Region** from the context menu. Again, a new region will be created under the previous one. In the Property Editor, set the following attributes for this region:

Attribute	Value
Title	Sales for this month
Type	Classic Report

SQL Statement	select sum(o.order_total) total_sales,
	      count(distinct o.order_id) total_orders,
	      count(distinct o.customer_id) total_customers
	from demo_orders o
	where order_timestamp >=
	      to_date(to_char(sysdate,'YYYYMM')||'01','YYYYMMDD')

Click on the link beside the **Template Options** attribute to set **Body Height** as follows	
Body Height	240px
Grid	Start New Row=No, Column=5, Column Span=4

In the Rendering section, expand **Columns** node and click on **TOTAL_SALES** column. This will refresh the Properties pane to show attributes of the currently selected column. Set the following attributes for TOTAL_SALES to transform it into a link. In the first attribute (Type), you specify that the column is to be displayed as a link. The Format Mask attribute displays sales value, preceded with a $ sign, and including a thousand separator. The remaining attributes actually define the link. First, you specify that the link should call a page in the current application followed by the target page number (4). It is suffice to transform a column into a link by setting these three attributes (Link, Type, and Page). The Name and Value attributes form a filter to display current month's order on the target page (Page 4 – Orders, to be created in Chapter 7). In the previous region you formed a similar kind of link in the SELECT statement. At run-time this link would be formed like this:

f?p=&APP_ID.:Page:Sessionid::NO:RP,RIR,4:IRGTE_(itemname):itemvalue (held in &P1_THIS_MONTH item)
https://apex.oracle.com/pls/apex/f?p=64699:4:10935015015866::NO:RP,RIR,4:IRGTE_ORDER_DATE:04012015

The page item &P1_THIS_MONTH is a hidden item, created on the next page to store first day of the current month. Whenever you refer to a page item in links, you present it as a substitution string. The last attribute is set to #TOTAL_SALES#, which specifies the column name that will be displayed as a link. Note that column names are enclosed in # symbol when you specify them in Link Text attribute.

Attribute	Value
Type	Link
Format Mask	$5,234.10
Click on **No Link Defined** beside **Target** and set the following attributes in the **Link Builder** dialog:	
Type	Page in this application
Page	4
Name	IRGTE_ORDER_DATE
Value	&P1_THIS_MONTH. *(do not forget to add the trailing dot)*
Clear Cache	RIR,4
Reset Pagination	Yes(default)
Click **OK** to close the **Link Builder - Target** dialog box	
Link Text	#TOTAL_SALES#

Click on **TOTAL_ORDERS** column and set the following attributes. Here, you are transforming TOTAL_ORDERS column into a link, using the same attributes, values, and filter to call the same Orders page.

Attribute	Value
Type	Link
Format Mask	5,234
Click on **No Link Defined** beside **Target** and set the following attributes in the **Link Builder** dialog:	
Type	Page in this application
Page	4
Name	IRGTE_ORDER_DATE
Value	&P1_THIS_MONTH.
Clear Cache	RIR,4
Reset Pagination	Yes(default)
Click **OK** to close the **Link Builder - Target** dialog box	
Link Text	#TOTAL_ORDERS#

Select **TOTAL_CUSTOMERS** column and set Type to **Hidden Column**. By setting an item's Type attribute to Hidden, you make it invisible at run-time. Click on Attributes node under Sales for this Month region. Switch Template from Standard to **Badge List**, click on Template Options and set Badge Size to **128px**, Layout to **Span Horizontally** and click **OK**. By setting these region attributes, the derived one row summarized report will be presented as a badge list, spanned horizontally. Also set Pagination Type to **No Pagination (Show All Rows)**.

Right click on Sales for this Month region and select **Create Page Item**. A new node named Items Items will be created with a new item P1_NEW. Select the new item and set the following attributes. This is the hidden page item you referenced in the above tables. By using the system date, it evaluates current month. This evaluation is performed every time you access the Home page. A hidden item is used in APEX applications to hold crucial values for behind-the-scene processing.

Chapter 4 - Prepare Application Dashboard

Attribute	Value
Name	P1_THIS_MONTH
Type	Hidden
Value Protected	Yes (default)
Type	PL/SQL Expression
PL/SQL Expression	to_char(sysdate ,'MM')||'01'||to_char(sysdate ,'YYYY')

Again, if the Order Date column on Page 4 is rendered as 09-FEB-2015, then you have to change the above PL/SQL Expression like this: '01-'||to_char(sysdate ,'MON')||'-'||to_char(sysdate ,'YYYY')

Click **Save and Run Page** button to see this region having two badges on it displaying current month's sales and number of orders placed. Both these badges act as links and lead you to Page 4 to display details of this summarized data. Since Page 4 will be created in Chapter 7, once again you will get Page Not Found message if you click any of these badges.

4.3.3 Sales by Product → (R-3)

This region is intended to show individual product sale figures using a pie chart. If you move the mouse pointer over the pie slices, you'll see those figures. Create another region as mentioned in the previous exercises, and set the following attributes.

Attribute	Value
Title	Sales by Product
Type	Chart
Click on the link beside the Template Options attribute and set Body Height	
Body Height	240px
Grid	Start New Row=No, Column=9, Column Span=4

Click on the New node ✕ New and set the following attributes:

Attribute	Value
Name	Products Sales
Type (under Source)	SQL Query
SQL Query	SELECT null, p.product_name||' [$'||p.list_price||']' product, SUM(oi.quantity * oi.unit_price) sales FROM demo_order_items oi, demo_product_info p WHERE oi.product_id = p.product_id GROUP BY p.product_id, p.product_name, p.list_price ORDER BY p.product_name desc

> **NOTE**
>
> *In APEX you create a chart using a SQL query which has the following syntax:*
>   *SELECT link, label, value*
>   *FROM ...*
> *The link column helps you drill-down to further details. You'll use the link column in chapter 8 – Present Data Graphically. Right now the drill-down functionality is not being used, therefore, a null is put in the link position to follow the syntax rule.*

Click on the corresponding Attributes node 📂 Attributes and set the following chart attributes. You are free to change these values to test other settings.

Attribute	Value	Attribute	Value
Type	Pie	Height (Layout)	200
Title	*Clear Title*	Scheme	Look 6 (default)
Rendering	Flash Chart	Label Show	No
Marker	None	Value Show	No
Width (Layout)	400	-	-

NOTE

You can define custom color scheme by adding your own colors to the chart with the help of color picker palette or by adding hex color values. Custom color scheme is used by setting the following two attributes:
Series Color Scheme: **Custom**
Custom Colors: **05FA05,#FF0000,#00ABFA,#87FA03,#FF8400,#DBF705,#0857F7,#7700FF,#112E01,#781200**

4.3.4 Sales by Category ➔ (R-4)

This region demonstrates the use of a Column Chart and presents sale figures of each category through this chart type. Note that there are three categories in the products table, and these are: Men, Women, and Accessories. Each product in the DEMO_PRODUCT_INFO table belongs to one of these categories. This time we will add a region using the new drag and drop feature provided in APEX 5. Following the figure illustrated below, drag the **Chart** icon and drop it just under the Top Orders by Date region. After placing the region at its proper location, set the attributes presented in the table provided after the illustration.

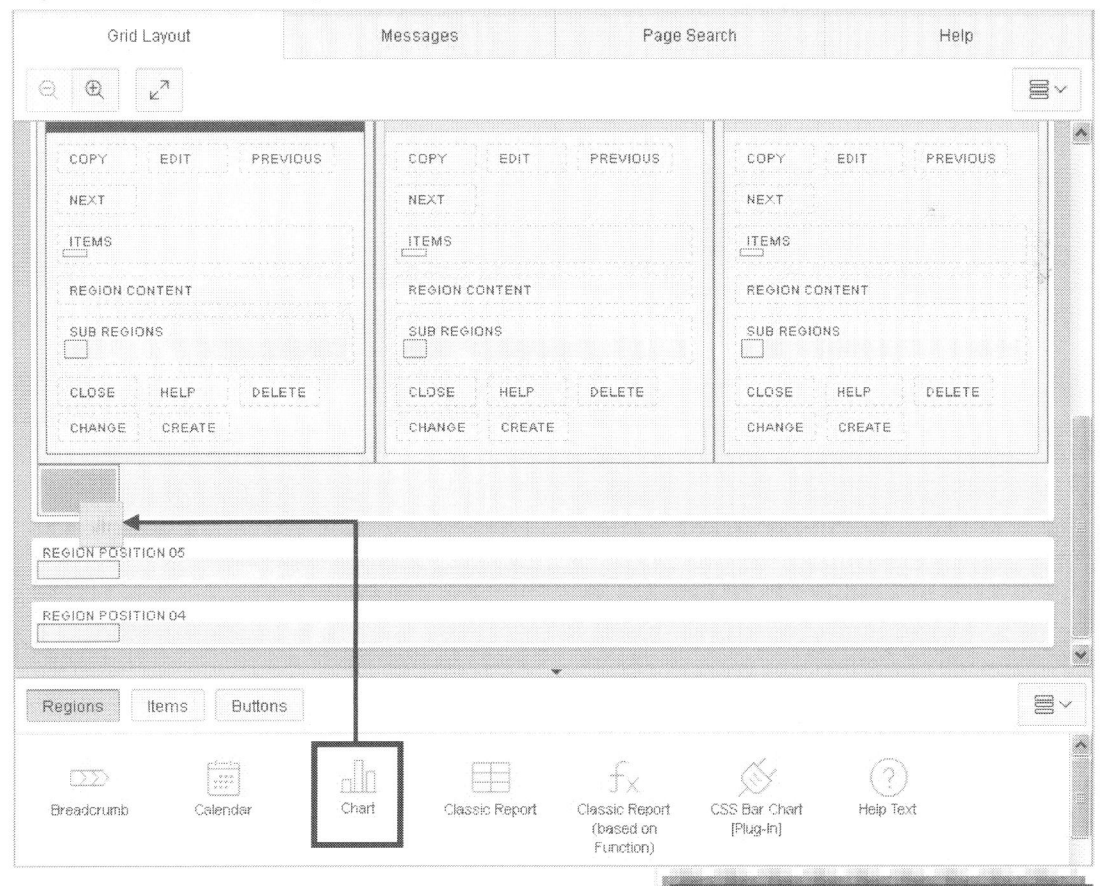

Figure 4-4 Drag Item in Page Designer

Here are the modified region attributes:

Attribute	Value
Title	Sales by Category
Type	Chart *(this time it will be set by default)*
Click on the link beside the Template Options attribute and set Body Height:	
Body Height	240px
Grid	Start New Row=Yes, Column=1, Column Span=4

Click on the **New** node and set the following attributes:

Attribute	Value
Name	Category Sales
Type (under Source)	SQL Query
SQL Query	SELECT null, p.category label, sum(o.order_total) FROM demo_orders o, demo_order_items oi, demo_product_info p WHERE o.order_id = oi.order_id AND oi.product_id = p.product_id GROUP BY category order by 3 desc

Click on region's Attributes node ▸ Attributes and set the following chart attributes:

Attribute	Value	Attribute	Value
Type	Column	Width (Layout)	400
Title	*Clear Title*	Height (Layout)	200
Rendering	Flash Chart	Scheme	Look 6 (default)
Show Grid	Both	Label Show	No
Show Scrollbars	None	Value Show	No
Marker	None	-	-

4.3.5 Top Customers Region ➔ (R-5)

This region will display top five customers with highest orders and will present the information in text format.
Create a new region by dragging the **Classic Report** icon and dropping it under the Sales by Category region.

Attribute	Value
Title	Top Customers
Type	Classic Report (should be already set)

SQL Statement	SELECT b.cust_last_name || ', ' || b.cust_first_name
	    || ' - '|| count(a.order_id) ||' Order(s)' customer_name,
	    SUM(a.ORDER_TOTAL) order_total, b.customer_id **id**
	FROM demo_orders a, DEMO_CUSTOMERS b
	WHERE a.customer_id = b.customer_id
	GROUP BY b.customer_id, b.cust_last_name || ', ' || b.cust_first_name
	ORDER BY NVL(SUM(a.ORDER_TOTAL),0) DESC

Click on the link beside the Template Options attribute and set Body Height:	
Body Height	240px
Grid	Start New Row=No, Column=5, Column Span=4

Expand Columns node and click on **CUSTOMER_NAME** column. Set the following attributes to transform this column into a link. The #ID# value references the third column in the above SELECT query. Just like you use substitution strings to reference a page item, the standard procedure in APEX to refer to a column value is to enclose it between the # symbols.

Attribute	Value
Type	Link
Click on **No Link Defined** beside **Target** and set the following attributes in the **Link Builder** dialog:	
Type	Page in this application
Page	7
Name	P7_CUSTOMER_ID
Value	#ID#
Clear Cache	7
Click OK to close the **Link Builder - Target** dialog box	
Link Text	#CUSTOMER_NAME#

In the above table, we specified attributes about a link we wish to create. The purpose of setting the above attributes is to place hyperlinks on customer name column to provide drill-down capability. We specified CUSTOMER_NAME column in the Link Text attribute. When you run this page, each customer's name would appear as a hyperlink and would call customer's profile page (Page 7), when you click any of these links. After specifying the Link Text, we set Page attribute to 7 which is the page we wish to navigate to. We also forwarded the customer's id (#ID#) to Page 7. The value P7_CUSTOMER_ID refers to an item on Page 7 that will be populated with the value held in #ID#. It is forwarded to Page 7 from the Home page to display profile of the selected customer.

Click on **ORDER_TOTAL** column and set Format Mask to **$5,234.10**.

Select **ID** column and set Type to **Hidden Column**, to hide this column at run-time. Click on **Attributes** node under this region to set the following attributes:

Attribute	Value	Attribute	Value
Number of Rows	5	Maximum Row Count	5
Template	Standard (default)	Heading Type	None
Pagination Type	No Pagination	-	-

We set Heading Type to None to suppress column headings. Similarly, pagination is suppressed since we want to see only five records in the region. Often only a certain number of rows of a report display on a page. In order to include additional rows, the application user needs to navigate to the next page of the report. Pagination provides the user with information about the number of rows and the current position within the result set. Pagination also defines the style of links or buttons that are used to navigate to the next or previous page.

Click **Save and Run Page** button to test the progress.

Chapter 4 - Prepare Application Dashboard

4.3.6 Top Products Region ➔ (R-6)

Add another classic report region as you just created above. This region is similar to Top Customers and displays five top selling products.

Attribute	Value
Title	Top Products
Type	Classic Report

SQL Statement	SELECT p.product_name||' - '||SUM(oi.quantity)||' x'
	           ||to_char(p.list_price,'L999G99')||'' product,
	           SUM(oi.quantity * oi.unit_price) sales, p.product_id
	FROM demo_order_items oi, demo_product_info p
	WHERE oi.product_id = p.product_id
	GROUP BY p.Product_id, p.product_name, p.list_price
	ORDER BY 2 desc

Click on the link beside the **Template Options** attribute and set **Body Height:**	
Body Height	240px
Grid	Start New Row=No, Column=9, Column Span=4

Expand Columns node and click on **PRODUCT** column to set the following attributes:

Attribute	Value
Type	Link
Click on **No Link Defined** beside **Target** and set the following attributes in the **Link Builder** dialog:	
Type	Page in this application
Page	6
Name	P6_PRODUCT_ID
Value	#PRODUCT_ID#
Clear Cache	6
Click OK to close the **Link Builder - Target** dialog box	
Link Text	#PRODUCT#

Click on **SALES** column and set Format Mask to **$5,234.10**.

Select **PRODUCT_ID** column and set Type to **Hidden Column** to hide this column at run-time. Click on Attributes node for this region to set the following attributes:

Attribute	Value	Attribute	Value
Number of Rows	5	Maximum Row Count	5
Template	Standard (default)	Heading Type	None
Pagination Type	No Pagination	-	-

Click **Save and Run Page** button to see how all the six regions appear on the page.

4.4 Create Buttons

After creating all the regions, your next task is to create buttons on top of each region. These buttons provide drill-down functionality and take user to relevant pages to dig further details for the provided summarized information. Some of these regions will have a pair of buttons (add and view), to create a new record and to browse further details of the provided information. For instance, if you click the Add Order button in the Top Order by Date region, you will be redirected to Page 11 to add a new order.

4.4.1 View Orders Button ➔ (B-1)

This button is used to view a list carrying all orders. To create this button, right-click **Top Orders by Date** region and select **Create Button** option from the context menu. A new node Region Buttons will be added with a ⌐ New button. Set the following attributes for the new button:

Attribute	Value
Button Name	VIEW_ORDERS
Label	View Orders *(appears as a tooltip when you move over the button)*
Region	Top Orders by Date (default)
Button Position	Edit *(try other options as well to observe different positions)*
Button Template	Icon *(the button will be displayed as an icon)*
Icon CSS Classes	fa-chevron-right *(the name of an icon residing in APEX's repository)*
Action	Redirect to Page in this Application
Target	Type=Page in this application, Page=4

4.4.2 Add Order Button ➔ (B-2)

This one calls Order Wizard (to be created in chapter 7), to place a new order. Right-click **Region Buttons** under Top Orders by Date region and select **Create Button** to add another button under this region. Set the following attributes for this new button:

Attribute	Value
Button Name	ADD_ORDER
Label	Enter New Order
Region	Top Orders by Date (default)
Button Position	Edit
Button Template	Icon
Icon CSS Classes	fa-plus
Action	Redirect to Page in this Application
Target	Type = Page in this application Page = 11 Clear Cache=11

Chapter 4 - Prepare Application Dashboard

4.4.3 View Orders For This Month Button → (B-3)

This button will drill down into current month's order details. As illustrated in the following figure, drag an icon button from the Buttons gallery and drop it in the EDIT position, under Sales for this Month region. A new button will be added to this region. Select it and set the attributes mentioned just after the illustration.

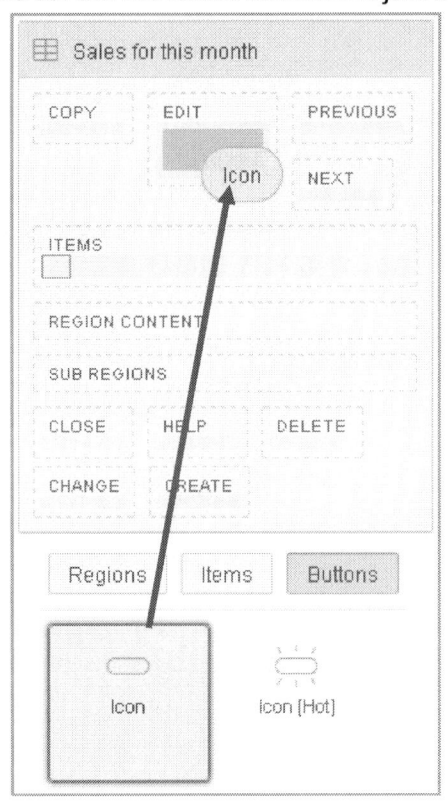

Attribute	Value	Attribute	Value
Button Name	VIEW_MONTH_ORDERS	Action	Redirect to Page in this Application
Label	View Orders for this Month	Target Type	Page in this Application
Region	Sales for this Month (default)	Page	4
Button Position	Edit (already set)	Name	IRGTE_ORDER_DATE
Button Template	Icon (already set)	Value	&P1_THIS_MONTH.
Icon CSS Classes	fa-chevron-right	Clear Cache	RIR,4

4.4.4 View Customers Button → (B-4)

You'll place two buttons in the Top Customers region. Create these buttons using either of the two methods applied above and set respective attributes as mentioned below. The first button will be used to view a list of customers on Page 2.

Attribute	Value	Attribute	Value
Button Name	VIEW_CUSTOMERS	Icon CSS Classes	fa-chevron-right
Label	View Customers	Action	Redirect to Page in this Application
Region	Top Customers	Target Type	Page in this Application
Button Position	Edit	Page	2
Button Template	Icon	-	-

4.4.5 Add Customer Button ➔ (B-5)

This button is used to add a new customer record. When clicked, this button will call Page 7 (Customers – to be created in the next chapter). This target page will appear on top of the Home page (as a modal dialog) carrying a blank form to enter new customer's credentials.

Attribute	Value	Attribute	Value
Button Name	ADD_CUSTOMER	Icon CSS Classes	fa-plus
Label	Add Customer	Action	Redirect to Page in this Application
Region	Top Customers (default)	Target Type	Page in this application
Button Position	Edit	Page	7
Button Template	Icon	Clear Cache	7

4.4.6 View Products Button ➔ (B-6)

Create the following two buttons in the Top Products region. The first one leads you to the main products page to view a list of all products.

Attribute	Value	Attribute	Value
Button Name	VIEW_PRODUCTS	Icon CSS Classes	fa-chevron-right
Label	View Products	Action	Redirect to Page in this Application
Region	Top Products	Target Type	Page in this Application
Button Position	Edit	Page	3
Button Template	Icon	-	-

4.4.7 Add Product Button ➔ (B-7)

This one calls Page 6 to add a new product.

Attribute	Value	Attribute	Value
Button Name	ADD_PRODUCT	Icon CSS Classes	fa-plus
Label	Add Product	Action	Redirect to Page in this Application
Region	Top Products	Target Type	Page in this Application
Button Position	Edit	Page	6
Button Template	Icon	Clear Cache	6

At this stage, all the seven buttons are placed at their proper locations with the expected functionalities and are ready for partial test. To remind you again, these buttons will be productive only after creating all relevant pages indicated in the Target attributes.

Chapter 4 - Prepare Application Dashboard

Test Your Work

Click **Save and Run Page** button to see the Home page, which should now look similar to the one illustrated at the beginning of this chapter.

Summary

Congratulations! You've created your first professional looking page in APEX. This chapter provided you with the flavor of declarative development where you added contents to a blank page, using simple procedures. You also learned how to modify attributes to customize the look and feel of this page. This is the uniqueness and beauty of Oracle Application Express that allows you to create pages rapidly without writing tons of code.

Chapter 5

Customers Profiling

Chapter 5 – Customers Profiling

5.1 About Customer Management

Whenever you create a sales application, you add a mandatory customer management module to it. In this setup, you maintain profiles of customers, including their names and addresses. This information appears on several reports, including customer invoices. Every new customer is provided with a unique ID, either manually or automatically by a built-in process. In this book these IDs will be generated automatically through a database object called a Sequence. Using the information from this module you can analyze a business from the perspective of customers. For example, you can evaluate how much business you have done with your customers either by location or by product. In this chapter, you will create a setup to manage customers' profiles. It will allow you to:

- Browse and search customer records
- Modify customers profile
- Add record of a new customer to the database
- Remove a customer from the database

> When creating a database application, you can include two types of reports: an interactive report or a classic report. The main difference between these two report types is the extent to which end users can customize the appearance of the data through searching, filtering, sorting, column selection, highlighting, and other data manipulations.

This module is based on a table named DEMO_CUSTOMERS. The table was created by the Application Builder when the application was created. It contains some seed data for testing purpose. In this chapter, you'll create two pages with the help of APEX wizard to view and edit customer information. The first one (Page 2 Figure 5-1) is an interactive report that displays a list of all customers from the aforementioned database table using a SQL SELECT query, while the second one (Page 7 Figure 5-2) is an input form to enter details of a new customer, modify the record of an existing customer, or delete one from the database. In order to keep data integrity, those customers who have some existing orders cannot be removed from the database. Each customer's name would act as a link in the interactive report. When you click the name of a customer, the form page appears with the complete profile of the selected customer. Let's get our hands dirty with some practical work to learn some more about the exciting declarative development environment offered by Oracle Application Express.

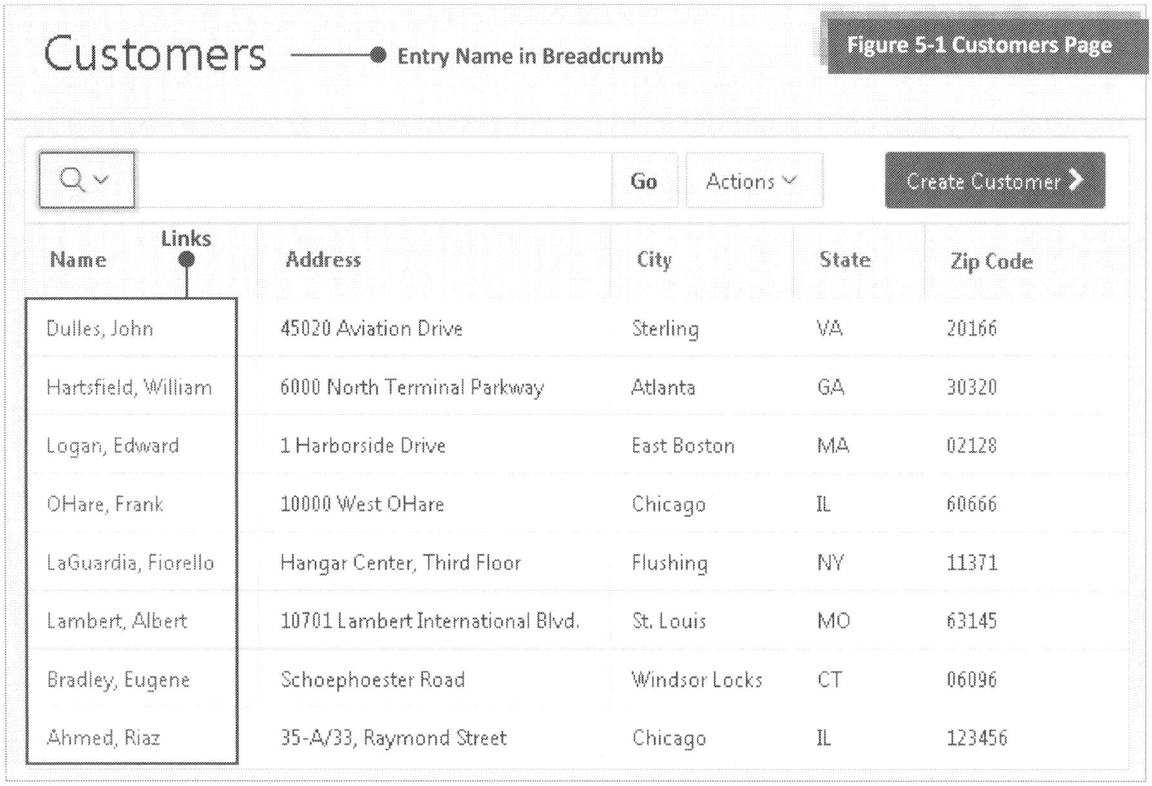

Customers — Entry Name in Breadcrumb

Figure 5-1 Customers Page

Name (Links)	Address	City	State	Zip Code
Dulles, John	45020 Aviation Drive	Sterling	VA	20166
Hartsfield, William	6000 North Terminal Parkway	Atlanta	GA	30320
Logan, Edward	1 Harborside Drive	East Boston	MA	02128
OHare, Frank	10000 West OHare	Chicago	IL	60666
LaGuardia, Fiorello	Hangar Center, Third Floor	Flushing	NY	11371
Lambert, Albert	10701 Lambert International Blvd.	St. Louis	MO	63145
Bradley, Eugene	Schoephoester Road	Windsor Locks	CT	06096
Ahmed, Riaz	35-A/33, Raymond Street	Chicago	IL	123456

5.2 Create Pages to Manage Customers

The Home page of our application was created by APEX, initially at the time when the application was created. The rest of the pages in this application will be created manually with the help of wizards and copy utility.

1. Click the **Create Page** button. You'll use this button throughout this book to create new application pages.
2. Click on the **Form** option. The initial wizard screen allows you to select a single option from a collection of multiple choices. Since you're creating a form to enter customer details, you'll select the Form option.
3. Select **Form on a Table with Report** option. This screen presents sub-categories of forms and requires a single selection the form will be based on. The option you selected here means that a form will be created along with an interactive report. Coupled together, these two steps inform APEX to generate two pages. The first page (Page 2 - Customers) will show an interactive report as shown in Figure 5-1, while the second page (Page 7 - Customer Details, Figure 5-2) will present a form to add, modify or delete a customer record. Subsequent inputs are received by the wizard based on these initial selections.
4. In the next wizard step, set the following attributes for the interactive report page, and click **Next**.

Attribute	Value	Attribute	Value
Implementation	Interactive	Region Template	Interactive Report
Page Number	2	Breadcrumb	Breadcrumb
Page Name	Customers	Parent Entry	No Parent Entry
Page Mode	Normal	Entry Name	Customers
Region Title	Manage Customers	-	-

For the report implementation type, you can either choose Classic to create SQL Report, or Interactive to create Interactive Report. In Application Express each page is identified with a unique number. The main page of this module (showing an interactive report) will be recognized by number 2, whereas the form page will have number 7. Just like numbers, a page is provided a unique name for visual recognition. The title of the sole region on this page is also set to uniquely identify it on the page. Recall that we created six regions in chapter 4, each with a unique title. A breadcrumb shared component was created initially by the Application Builder when you created this application earlier. In this step you selected the same breadcrumb component and added an entry name (Customers) to it. Have a look at Figure 5-1 to see where the provided entry name appears in the breadcrumb region.

5. On Data Source page, accept the default schema in Table/View Owner, select **DEMO_CUSTOMERS** for Table/View Name and click **Next**. After defining the main criteria for the page, you're asked to specify the schema to connect to for data manipulation. Once you select a schema, all tables within that schema are populated in the adjacent drop-down list. Note that in the current scenario you can select only one table from the provided list.
6. On the Navigation Menu page, set Navigation Preference to **Identify an existing navigation menu entry for this page**, set Existing Navigation Menu Entry to **Setup** and click **Next**. This step will highlight the Setup entry in the main navigation menu when this page is accessed.
7. In the next step, you select the desired columns from the DEMO_CUSTOMERS table to display on the main interactive report. By default, the Report Columns page selects all the columns from the selected table. Leave the following columns in the right pane, to include them in the report, and exclude others by

moving them to the left pane using ctrl+click and the left arrow ‹ icon. These are the columns that we want to show on the interactive report.

Cust_First_Name, Cust_Last_Name, Cust_Street_Address1, Cust_Street_Address2, Cust_City, Cust_State, and **Cust_Postal_Code**

8. Click **Next**.
9. You'll be presented with a list of Edit Link Images. Select any edit link image and click **Next**. The icon you select here will appear in the first column of the interactive report (for each record) as an edit link. When clicked, the link will call Page 7 where you can either modify or delete a customer's record. This is a conventional method to call a record from an interactive report. However, later on in this chapter, we will use another method by transforming customer names into links to serve the same purpose.
10. In the **Form Page**, set the following attributes and click **Next**. The wizard will create a child page (Page 7) named Customer Details that will be linked to the main Customers page (Page 2). This page will be called to create a new customer or to edit/delete record of an existing customer. The remaining steps in the wizard receive input for Page 7. A modal dialog page is a stand-alone page replaced for old-style popup window. An APEX page can be created as a dialog which supports for all the functionality of a normal page, including computations, validations, processes, and branches. You can also specify your own dimensions for such pages, as you'll see later in this chapter.

Attribute	Value	Attribute	Value
Page Number	7	Region Title	Customer Details
Page Mode	Modal Dialog	Region Template	Standard
Page Name	Customer Details	-	-

11. For *Primary Key Type*, select the second option **Select Primary Key Column(s)**. Set *Primary Key Column 1* attribute to **CUSTOMER_ID** and click **Next**.
12. Select the option *Existing sequence*, set *Sequence* to **DEMO_CUST_SEQ**, and click **Next**. The above two steps specify the primary key and the database sequence object the primary key will generate from. In the previous step, you set CUSTOMER_ID as the primary key. A primary key is a column or set of columns that uniquely identify a record in a table. In step 12, you selected the option *Existing sequence* and defined DEMO_CUST_SEQ as the existing sequence. A sequence is a database object that automatically generates primary key values for every new customer record. See section 2.9 – Underlying Database Objects.
13. Include all columns from the DEMO_CUSTOMERS table to Page 7 by clicking the double right arrow icon » and click **Next**. In this step, you selected all columns from the customers table, because these columns will appear in the entry form on Page 7 to receive corresponding values.
14. Select **Yes** for *Insert, Update,* and *Delete* and click **Next**. With the Yes values selected for the three options, you inform APEX to declaratively create respective processes to handle these DML operations. To avoid any of these processes, select the No option. For example, to prevent users from deleting data from this form, select No for the Delete option. This will prevent the Delete button from appearing on the form.
15. On the final confirmation page, click the **Create** button.
16. Click the **Application 64699** breadcrumb and see the two new pages, Customers and Customer Details, with their respective page numbers.

> **NOTE:** I will use **Application 64699** throughout this book to reference the ID of my application.

5.3 Modify Customers Page - Page 2

The main page of this module (Page 2) holds an interactive report which is generated by the wizard with some default values such as SQL SELECT statement and corresponding column names. In the following steps you will change these values to generate some meaningful output.

5.3.1 Modify Region Attributes

1. In the main Application 64699 interface, click the **Customers** page to call it in the Page Designer.
2. Click **Manage Customers** under Regions | Body node. The standard method to modify attributes of a page component is to click the corresponding node. This action refreshes the Properties section (located to your right) with the attributes of the selected page component for alteration.
3. Enter the following SQL statement in *Region Source*, replacing the existing one. The auto generated SELECT SQL statement is replaced with a custom statement that uses the concatenation operator '||' to join columns. The new statement joins last and first name of customers into a single column. The new concatenated column is recognized by a new name: customer_name. Similarly, the two address columns are combined together to form a single address.

```
select customer_id,
cust_last_name || ',' || cust_first_name customer_name, CUST_STREET_ADDRESS1 ||
decode(CUST_STREET_ADDRESS2, null, null, ',' || CUST_STREET_ADDRESS2) customer_address,
cust_city, cust_state, cust_postal_code
from demo_customers
```

DECODE FUNCTION

In the above SELECT statement, we used a DECODE function. The DECODE function has the functionality of an IF-THEN-ELSE statement. It compares expression to each search value one by one. If expression is equal to a search, then Oracle Database returns the corresponding result. If no match is found, then Oracle returns default. If default is omitted, then Oracle returns null. In the above statement, the Decode function assesses if the returned value of second street address is null, store null to the result; otherwise, concatenate it to the first address. The following syntax and example of the Decode function elaborates it further.

Decode Syntax:
decode(expression , search , result [, search , result]... [, default])

Example of Decode Function:
Select customer_name, decode(customer_id, 1, 'A', 2, 'B', 3, 'C', 'D') result
From customers;

The equivalent IF-THEN-ELSE statement for the above Decode function would be:

```
IF customer_id = 1 THEN
  result := 'A';
ELSIF customer_id = 2 THEN
  result := 'B';
ELSIF customer_id = 3 THEN
  result := 'C';
ELSE
  result := 'D';
END IF;
```

4. Save you work.

5. Run the page and click on the **Actions** menu [Actions]. Select the option **Select Columns**. Make sure that all columns appear in *Display in Report* section. If not, move all columns to it. Using the arrow icons (to your right), arrange columns in the following order:
   Customer Name, Address, City, State, and Postal Code

6. Click the **Apply** button to save the above alternations.

7. Click the Actions menu again and select the **Save Report** option. Select **As Default Report Settings** and set Default Report Type to **Primary**. Click the **Apply** button. After modifying an interactive report you must save it using this procedure, otherwise you'll lose the applied settings when you subsequently view this report. Developers can save two types of default interactive report: primary and alternative. Both reports display on the Report list on the Search bar. The primary default report (you just saved) cannot be renamed or deleted.

8. Click **Edit Page2** in the Developer Toolbar at the bottom of your screen to call the Page Designer.

9. Expand Manage Customers region and then expand the Columns node. Change column headings as follows:
   Name, **Address**, **City**, **State**, and **Zip Code**

10. Make sure that the value of Type attribute for CUSTOMER_ID column is set to Hidden to hide the column at runtime. Primary Key columns are added to database tables to enforce data integrity and are not displayed in applications. This is why such columns' Type attribute is set to hidden to make them invisible at runtime.

11. Click on the Attribute node under Manage Customers. Switch Link Column from Link to Custom Target to **Exclude Link Column**. This will exclude the default link column, carrying edit icons for each record. The default link column is excluded, because in the next step you will convert the customer name column into a link.

12. Select Manage Customers region and click on CUSTOMER_NAME column to set the following attributes. In these attributes you specify that the customer name column is to be displayed as a link that leads to Page 7. You created similar kind of link in Chapter 4 for a region named Sales for this Month.

Attribute	Value	Attribute	Value
Type	Link	Name (first row)	P7_CUSTOMER_ID
Target Type	Page in this application	Value (first row)	#CUSTOMER_ID#
Page	7	Link Text	#CUSTOMER_NAME#

5.3.2 Modify Button Attributes

The following modifications are applied to Create button. This is a default button created by the wizard to add a new customer record.

1. In Region Buttons node (under Manage Customers region), click on the **Create** button and set the following attributes.

Attribute	Value	Attribute	Value
Label	Create Customer	Hot	Yes
Button Template	Text with Icon	Icon CSS Classes	fa-chevron-right

2. Save and run Page 2, which should look similar to Figure 5-1.
3. Click the **Create Customer** button. This will call Customer Details page (Page 7) on top of the calling page as a modal dialog.

5.4 Modify Customer Details Page - Page 7

With Page 7 being displayed in your browser, click the link **Edit Page 7** in Developer Toolbar at the bottom of your screen to call this page in the Page Designer for modifications.

1. Right click Breadcrumb and select Delete to remove this region from the details page.
2. Click on the Page node Page 7: Customer Details. Set the following attributes in the Properties pane to set title and dimensions of this modal page.

Attribute	Value	Attribute	Value
Title	Customer Details	Height	480
Width	660	Maximum Width	1000

5.4.1 Modify Item Attributes

Click each item under ITEMS node and apply the following attributes. Just like region placement in a 12 columns grid layout that you performed for the Home page regions, the page items too, could be placed accordingly using APEX's gird layout, as follows. In the following table, some values for the Value Required attribute are set to Yes. If Value Required is set to Yes and the page item is visible, Oracle Application Express automatically performs a NOT NULL validation when the page is submitted. If you set it to No, no validation is performed and a NULL value is accepted.

Item	Label	Grid	Width	Value Required
P7_CUST_FIRST_NAME	First Name	Start New Row=Yes Column=Automatic Column Span=Automatic Label Column Span=2	40	Yes
P7_CUST_LAST_NAME	Last Name	Start New Row=No Column=Automatic New Column=Yes Column Span=Automatic Label Column Span=2	40	Yes
P7_CUST_STREET_ADDRESS1	Street Address	Start New Row=Yes Column=Automatic Column Span=Automatic Label Column Span=2	48	No

Item	Label	Grid	Width	Value Required
P7_CUST_STREET_ADDRESS2	Line 2	Start New Row=No Column=Automatic New Column=Yes Column Span=Automatic Label Column Span=2	48	No
P7_CUST_CITY	City	Start New Row=Yes Column=Automatic Column Span=6 Label Column Span=2	40	No
P7_CUST_STATE	State	Start New Row=No Column=Automatic New Column=Yes Column Span=Automatic Label Column Span=2	-	Yes
P7_CUST_POSTAL_CODE	Zip Code	Start New Row=Yes Column=Automatic Column Span=6 Label Column Span=2	8	Yes
P7_CREDIT_LIMIT	Credit Limit	Start New Row=Yes Column=Automatic Column Span=6 Label Column Span=2	8	Yes
P7_PHONE_NUMBER1	Phone Number	Start New Row=Yes Column=Automatic Column Span=Automatic Label Column Span=2	12	No
P7_PHONE_NUMBER2	Alternate No.	Start New Row=No Column=Automatic New Column=Yes Column Span=Automatic Label Column Span=2	12	No
P7_CUST_EMAIL	Email	Start New Row=Yes Column=Automatic Column Span=Automatic Label Column Span=2	30	No
P7_URL	URL	Start New Row=No Column=Automatic New Column=Yes Column Span=Automatic Label Column Span=2	64	No
P7_TAGS	Tags	Start New Row=Yes Column=Automatic Column Span=Automatic Label Column Span=2	64	No

Save and Run the page to observe the above modifications.

5.4.2 Change Item Type and Attach LOV

In the following set of steps you'll work on the State column, first by altering its type from Text to a Select List, and then attaching an LOV to it. APEX allows you to change an item's type from its default state to another desirable type. For example, the P7_CUST_STATE item was generated as a text type by the wizard. Now, we wish to change this item to a Select List to hold a predefined list of States. To display this list, you'll attach the STATES LOV to this item that was created in Chapter 3 section 3.4.3. That list will be screwed up with this field so that the user could save a valid State value to the database.

1. Click on **P7_CUST_STATE** item.
2. Change Type from Text to **Select List**.
3. Set Template to **Required**. This attribute will show an asterisk (*) with the label to mark the column as a mandatory field. Note that this attribute was set by the wizard for first and last name columns. Set this attribute for postal code and credit limit as well, to display them as mandatory fields.
4. Set *Value Required* to **Yes**. If set to Yes and the page item is visible, Application Express will automatically perform a NOT NULL validation when the page is submitted and will ask you to input a value in the field. This attribute usually works in conjunction with the previous one – Template = Required.
5. Set Type (under List of Values) to **Shared Components**, and List of Values to **STATES**.
6. Set *Display Extra Values* to **No**. An item may have a session state value which does not occur in its list of values definition. Select whether this list of values should display this extra session state value. If you choose not to display this extra session state value and there is no matching value in the list of values definition, the first value will be the selected value.
7. Set *Display Null Value* to **Yes**. (default)
8. Enter **-Choose State-** in *Null Display Value*. This step along with the previous one generates a manual entry that appears on top of the LOV whenever you call this page to create a new customer record.
9. Save your work.

5.4.3 Apply Input Mask to Items

Modify the two phone number items and set their Value Placeholder attribute to 999-999-9999. When a new customer record is added, this placeholder is shown in the two phone number items to receive input in the specified format. As you type in values, the placeholders will be replaced by the numbers entered.

5.4.4 Create Validation - Check Customer Credit Limit

Validations enable you to create logic controls to verify whether user input is valid. In this part, you'll create a validation to check customer's credit limit. The customer form contains a field named Credit Limit which is used to assign a cap to each customer with a figure of $5,000. If you enter a value more than the assigned cap, you'll be prevented by presenting an appropriate message.

Click on the Processing tab, right click the Validating node Validating, and select the Create Validation option. This action will add a new validation. Set the following attributes for the new validation:

Attribute	Value
Name	Check Credit Limit
Type	PL/SQL Expression
PL/SQL Expression	:P7_CREDIT_LIMIT <= 5000
Error Message	Customer's Credit Limit must be less than or equal to $5,000

5.4.5 Create Validation - Can't Delete Customer with Orders

This is the second validation to prevent deletion of those customers who have placed orders. This check is performed to retain application's integrity from the front-end. The validation is performed using a custom PL/SQL function which returns either a true or a false value. The return value is based on a SELECT query which returns false if records exist for the selected customer. If the returned value is false, the error message is displayed and the record deletion process is prevented. The validation is associated to the DELETE button in the last attribute, which means that the validation will be performed only when the Delete button is pressed.

Once again right click the Validating node, and select the **Create Validation** option to add a new validation under the previous one. Set the following attributes for this new validation.

Attribute	Value
Name	Can't Delete Customer with Orders
Type	PL/SQL Function Body (Returning Boolean)

PL/SQL Function Body (Returning Boolean)	begin
	  for c1 in (select 'x' from demo_orders
	      where customer_id = :P7_CUSTOMER_ID) loop
	    RETURN FALSE;
	  end loop;
	    RETURN TRUE;
	end;

Error Message	Can't delete customer with existing orders
When Button Pressed	DELETE

Test Your Work

Before running the customer module, let's have a look at the definitions of the two pages. Call Page 2 - Customers and closely look at the Shared Components tab. The entries contained in this tab were automatically generated by APEX based on your selections in the wizard steps. Similarly, the Create Customer button (in the Rendering Tab) was generated by the wizard with a default action to redirect users to the appropriate page (Page 7), when this button is clicked. If you see definition of Page 7, you'll see some more auto-generated buttons with default functionalities. Just like buttons, APEX performs many other tasks transparently without us having to write a single line of code. For instance, click on the root node (Page 7: Customer Details) under Rendering tab in Page 7 and scroll down to Function and Global Variable Declaration section. Here you'll see a global variable defined as var htmldb_delete_message. This variable was generated automatically along with a corresponding shortcut named DELETE CONFIRM MSG (in Shared Components) to control record deletion process by presenting a confirmation dialog box, before deleting a customer's record. Moreover, the wizard created a Dynamic Action under the Processing tab to close this form when the Cancel button is clicked. These are some of the beauties of declarative development that not only generates basic functionalities of an application, but on the same time doesn't limit our abilities to manually enter specific and tailored code, both on the client and server sides to answer our specific needs.

Save and run the application. Access this module by clicking Manage Customers menu item (under Setup). You'll see Page 2 – Customers, as shown in Figure 5-1, carrying an interactive report. The report has a search bar comprising a magnifying glass, a text area, and a button labeled Go. The bar allows you to search a string in the report appearing underneath. The magnifying glass is a drop down list. You can use this list to limit your search to a specific column. Type **albert** in the text area and click the Go button. You'll see a row displaying record of Albert

Lambert. Click the remove filter icon ⊠ to reinstate the report to its previous state. The Actions menu has several other options that we'll apply in chapter 7. The Create Customer button calls the second page of this module (Page 7) to enter profile of a new customer. As you can also see that the Customer Name column is appearing as a link. If you want to modify a specific record, click the corresponding link. Again, the same form page comes up where all fields are populated with relevant information from the database. Click the name of any customer to see the information, as presented in the following figure.

You are free to test your work. Try by adding, modifying, and deleting a new customer. Try to delete Eugene Bradley; you won't be able to do that because there are some orders placed by this customer and the validation that you created in section 5.4.5 will prevent the deletion process. Also check the credit limit validation by entering a value more than 5000 in the Credit Limit box.

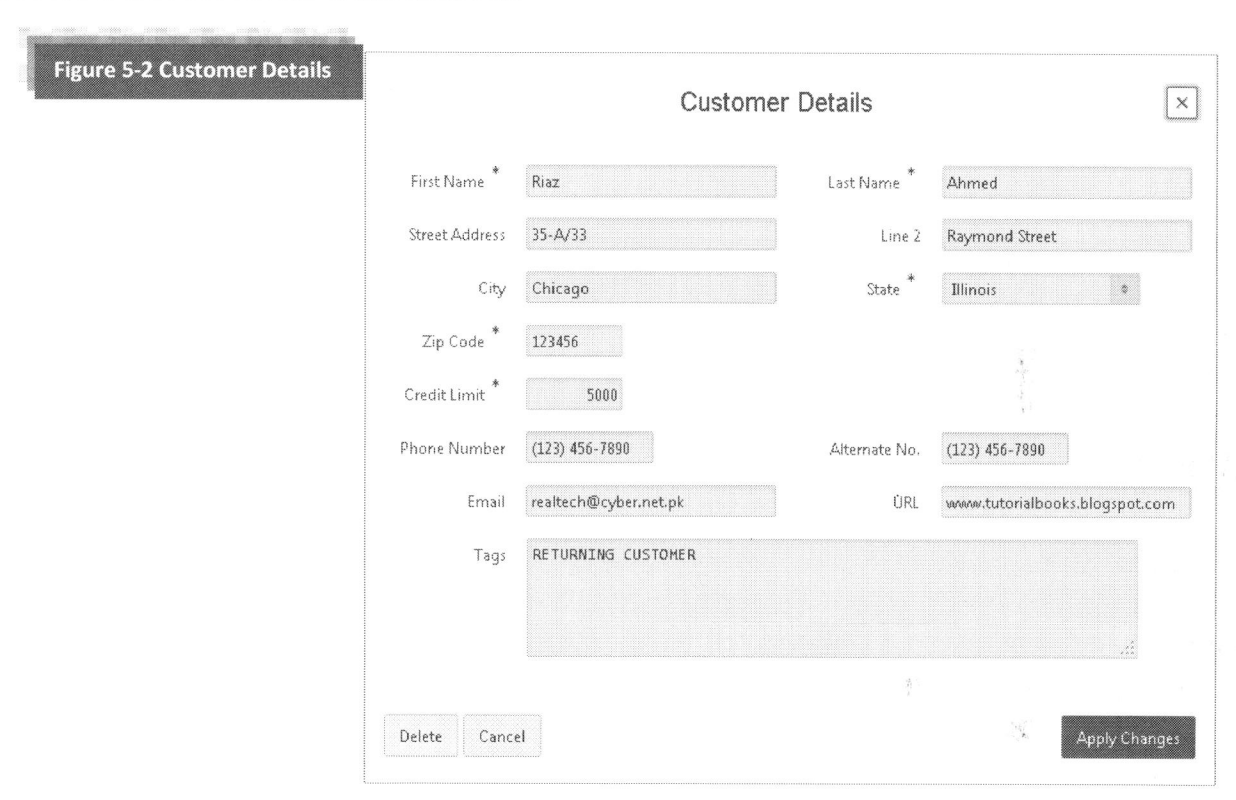

Figure 5-2 Customer Details

First Name *	Riaz	Last Name *	Ahmed
Street Address	35-A/33	Line 2	Raymond Street
City	Chicago	State *	Illinois
Zip Code *	123456		
Credit Limit *	5000		
Phone Number	(123) 456-7890	Alternate No.	(123) 456-7890
Email	realtech@cyber.net.pk	URL	www.tutorialbooks.blogspot.com
Tags	RETURNING CUSTOMER		

Delete Cancel   Apply Changes

Summary

Let's go through the summary of this chapter to see what we grasped in it. We learned the following techniques while performing various exercises in this chapter:

- Declaratively created report and form pages and linked them together.
- Used an interactive report.
- Changed type of an item and attached a list of value (LOV) to it.
- Created validations to prevent customer record deletion having existing orders and to check customers' credit limits.

The next chapter discusses how to manage products in a database application with some more useful techniques to explore APEX.

Chapter 6
Setup Products Catalog

Chapter 6 – Setup Products Catalog

6.1 About Products Setup

Just like the Customers module, you'll create a Products setup that will allow you to manage products information. This module will also have two pages: Products and Product Details. The main products page (Page 3 – Figure 6-1) will have three different views: Icon, Report, and Details. Initially, the wizard will create the Report View version that you'll modify with a custom SQL statement. The remaining two views (Detail and Icon) are placed on the page by enabling respective attributes found under the main Products region. Once you enable these views, their respective icons appear on the main Search bar. Using these icons you can switch among different views to browse products information.

Figure 6-1 Products Page

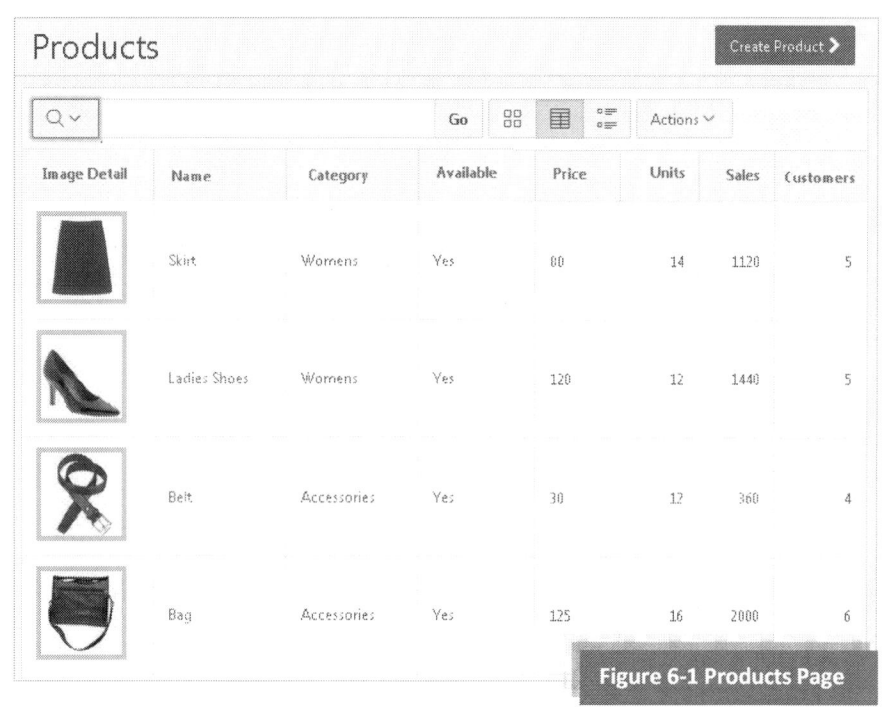

The Product Details page (Page 6) will be created to add, modify, and delete a product. To create these two pages you'll follow the same approach as you did in the previous chapter. Since most of the steps are similar to those already briefed in the Customers setup chapter, we'll elaborate the features new to this module.

The new stuff added to this module includes: image handling and styling. This module is based on DEMO_PRODUCT_INFO table in the database. Among conventional columns exists the following four special columns to handle images in the database. A question arises here: why do we need extra columns? BLOBs fall outside the range of normal data, and in a normal scenario, require specialized processing to handle their use. The APEX environment has eliminated the need to perform all that specialized processing with these additional columns. Your APEX application will use these columns to properly process images in the BLOB column.

> **PRODUCT_IMAGE:** This column uses BLOB data type. A BLOB (Binary Large Object) is an Oracle data type that can hold up to 4 GB of data. BLOBs are handy for storing digitized information (e.g., images, audio, and video).

> **MIMETYPE:** A Multipurpose Internet Mail Extension (MIME) type identifies the format of a file. The MIME type enables applications to read the file. Applications such as Internet browsers and email applications use the MIME type to handle files of different types. For example, an email application can use the MIME type to detect what type of file is in a file attached to an email. Many systems use MIME types to identify the format of arbitrary files on the file system. MIME types are composed of a top-level media type followed by a subtype identifier, separated by a forward slash character (/). An example of a MIME type is image/jpeg. The media type in this example is image and the subtype identifier is jpeg. The top-level media type is a general categorization about the content of the file, while the subtype identifier specifically identifies the format of the file.

FILENAME: A case sensitive column name used to store the filename of the BLOB (e.g. bag.jpg).

IMAGE_LAST_UPDATE: A case sensitive column name used to store the last update date of the BLOB.

Besides image handling, you'll also learn the technique to incorporate style sheet in an APEX page. Web browsers refer to Cascading Style Sheets (CSS) to define the appearance and layout of text and other material.

6.2 Create Pages for Products Setup

The following set of steps use the same approach you followed in the previous chapter to create an interactive report with a form.

1. Click the **Create Page** button in Application Builder.
2. Click on the **Form** option, followed by **Form on a Table with Report**.
3. On the next wizard page (Report), set the following attributes and click **Next**. These are the same attributes that you set in the previous chapter.

Attribute	Value	Attribute	Value
Implementation	Interactive	Region Template	Interactive Report Region
Page Number	3	Breadcrumb	Breadcrumb
Page Name	Products	Parent Entry	No Parent Entry
Page Mode	Normal	Entry Name	Products
Region Title	Products	-	-

4. On Data Source page, accept the default schema in Table/View Owner, select **DEMO_PRODUCT_INFO** for Table/View Name and click **Next**.
5. On the Navigation Menu page, set Navigation Preference to **Identify an existing navigation menu entry for this page**, and set Existing Navigation Menu Entry to **Setup**. Click **Next**.
6. For the time being, select all columns from the products table and click **Next**. In the next section, you will add a custom SQL query for this page.
7. Select an edit link image and click **Next**.
8. On the **Form Page**, set the following attributes and click **Next**. The wizard will create a child page (Page 6) named Product Details that will be linked to the main Products page (Page 3). This page will be called to create and manipulate product information.

Attribute	Value	Attribute	Value
Page Number	6	Region Title	Product Details
Page Mode	Modal Dialog	Region Template	Standard
Page Name	Product Details	-	-

9. For Primary Key Type, select the second option **Select Primary Key Column(s)** and set Primary Key Column 1 attribute to **PRODUCT_ID**. Click **Next**. PRODUCT_ID is the primary key column which uniquely identifies a product and is populated using a database sequence object (DEMO_PROD_SEQ).
10. Select **Existing sequence** option, set Sequence to **DEMO_PROD_SEQ**, and click **Next**.
11. Add all columns from DEMO_PRODUCT_INFO table to Page 6, except MIMETYPE, FILENAME, and IMAGE_LAST_UPDATE. Click **Next**. These three columns are used in the background to handle images.
12. Select **Yes** for *Insert, Update,* and *Delete* options and click **Next**.
13. On the final confirmation page, click the **Create** button.

Chapter 6 – Setup Products Catalog

14. Once again the wizard creates two pages to handle the module. We used the same procedure to create the initial structure for this module as we did for the Customers module. In the upcoming exercises you will undergo some new techniques to transform these pages and provide them a professional look.

6.3 Modify Products Page - Page 3

Execute the instructions provided in the following sub sections to first modify the Products (interactive report) page.

6.3.1 Modify Region Attributes

1. Call **Products** page (Page 3) for few modifications.
2. Click on the Products node Products.
3. Replace the existing SELECT statement with the following in SQL Query attribute:

   select p.product_id, p.product_name, p.product_description, p.category,
   decode(p.product_avail, 'Y','Yes','N','No') product_avail, p.list_price,
   (select sum(quantity) from demo_order_items where product_id = p.product_id) units,
   (select sum(quantity * p.list_price) from demo_order_items where product_id = p.product_id) sales,
   (select count(o.customer_id) from demo_orders o, demo_order_items t
   where o.order_id = t.order_id and t.product_id = p.product_id group by p.product_id) customers,
   (select max(o.order_timestamp) od from demo_orders o, demo_order_items i where o.order_id = i.order_id and i.product_id = p.product_id) last_date_sold, p.product_id img,
   apex_util.prepare_url(p_url=>'f?p='||:app_id||':6:'||:app_session||
   '::::P6_PRODUCT_ID:'||p.product_id) **icon_link**,
   decode(nvl(dbms_lob.getlength(p.product_image),0),0,null,
   '<img alt="'||p.product_name||'" title="'||p.product_name||'" style="border: 4px solid #CCC;
   -moz-border-radius: 4px; -webkit-border-radius: 4px;" '||
   'src="'||apex_util.get_blob_file_src('P6_PRODUCT_IMAGE',p.product_id)||'" height="75" width="75" />') detail_img,
   decode(nvl(dbms_lob.getlength(p.product_image),0),0,null,
   apex_util.get_blob_file_src('P6_PRODUCT_IMAGE',p.product_id)) detail_img_no_style,
   tags
   from demo_product_info p

   The icon link column is formed using the same APEX syntax you went through in the previous chapter to create a link. This link is used to call Product Details (Page 6). The detail_img column holds images of products. We used HTML <img> tag to form this column in conjunction with a built-in function. APEX_UTIL.GET_BLOB_FILE_SRC is an APEX function which provides the ability to more specifically format the display of the image (with height and width attributes). The image is styled using CSS inline styling method. The getlength function of the dbms_lob package (dbms_lob.getlength) is used to estimate the size of a BLOB column in the table. The selection of the BLOB size is made to facilitate the inclusion of a download link in a report. If the length is 0, the BLOB is NULL and no download link is displayed.

4. Expand Columns node and set meaningful **headings** for all columns as follows:
   Name, Description, Category, Available, Price, Units, Sales, Customers, Last Sold, Image, Icon Link, Image Detail, Detail Image No style, and **Tags**

5. Modify the following columns using the specified attributes. These columns are marked as hidden to make them invisible at runtime. However, they will be visible to your application for handling images. These columns were also derived through the SQL SELECT statement in step 3.

Column	Attribute	Value
IMG	Type	Hidden Column
ICON_LINK	Type	Hidden Column
DETAIL_IMG	Escape special characters	No *(otherwise image will not appear)*
DETAIL_IMG_NO_STYLE	Type	Hidden Column

6. Click on PRODUCT_NAME column to transform it into a link, as you did with customer name in the previous chapter.

Attribute	Value	Attribute	Value
Type	Link	Name	P6_PRODUCT_ID
Target	Page In this application	Value	#PRODUCT_ID#
Page	6	Link Text	#PRODUCT_NAME#

7. Under Products region, click on its Attributes node and set Link Column to **Exclude Link Column** to eliminate first column. You performed the same action in the Customers module to remove the first column carrying edit links.

8. In the same Attributes node, scroll down to **Icon View** section and set the following attributes. By default, most interactive reports display as a report. You can optionally display columns as icons. When configured, an icon labeled View Icons displays on the Search bar. To use this view, you must identify the columns to identify the icon, the label, and the target (that is, the link). As a best practice, the Type attribute of these columns is set to hidden (as you did in step 5), because they are typically not useful for end users.

Attribute	Value
Icon View Enabled	Yes
Columns Per Row	5 *(to display 5 images on a single row in View Icons interface)*
Link Column	ICON_LINK
Image Source Column	DETAIL_IMG_NO_STYLE
Label Column	PRODUCT_NAME
Image Attributes	width="75" height="75" *(styles height and width of images)*

9. In **Detail View** section set *Enabled* to **Yes**. When configured, a *View Details* icon displays on the Search bar.

10. In **Before Rows**, enter the following code. This attribute of the Detail View enables you to enter HTML code to be displayed before report rows. For example, you can use the <TABLE> element to put the database content in row/column format. Besides adding HTML code, styling information can also be incorporated using this attribute. The <style> tag is used to define style information for an HTML document. Inside the <style> element you specify how HTML elements should render in a browser. A cascading style sheet (CSS) provides a way to control the style of a web page without changing its structure. When used properly, a CSS separates visual attributes such as color, margins, and fonts from the structure of the HTML document. Oracle Application Express includes themes that contain templates that reference their own CSS. The style rules defined in each CSS for a particular theme also determine the way reports and regions display. The code below uses custom CSS rules to override the default APEX Interactive Report (apexir) styles.

```
<style>
  table.apexir_WORKSHEET_CUSTOM {
    border: none !important;
    box-shadow: none;
    -moz-box-shadow: none;
    -webkit-box-shadow: none;}

  .apexir_WORKSHEET_DATA td {
   border-bottom: none !important;}

  table.reportDetail td {
    padding: 2px 4px !important;
    border: none !important;
    font: 11px/16px Arial, sans-serif;}

  table.reportDetail td.separator {
    background: #F0F0F0 !important;
    padding: 0 !important;
    height: 1px !important;
    padding: 0;
    line-height: 2px !important;
    overflow: hidden;}

  table.reportDetail td h1 {margin: 0 !important}

  table.reportDetail td img {
    margin-top: 8px;
    border: 4px solid #CCC;
    -moz-border-radius: 4px;
    -webkit-border-radius: 4px;}
</style>
<table class="reportDetail">
```

> **NOTE:** Remember that all APEX pages are HTML pages controlled by HTML attributes and cascading style sheet (CSS) settings. When you create an interactive report, Oracle APEX renders it based on CSS classes associated with the current theme. Each APEX interactive report component has a CSS style definition that may be changed by applying standard CSS techniques to override the defaults. Such changes may be applied to a single interactive report, to a page template to effect changes across several interactive reports, or to all page templates of a theme to enforce a common look and feel for all reports in an application.
>
> In the current step, you are changing the appearance of the report by overriding built-in styles for the table and subordinate elements.

11. In **For Each Row**, enter the following code. The code is applied to each record. In every <td> element you are referencing interactive report columns and labels with the help of a special substitution string (#) and are styling each record using inline CSS method. You used the substitution string to reference table column names and labels of page items as #PRODUCT_NAME# and #CATEGORY_LABEL#, respectively.

```
<tr>
  <td rowspan="5" valign="top"><img width="75" height="75" src="#DETAIL_IMG_NO_STYLE#"></td>
  <td colspan="6"><h1><a href="#ICON_LINK#"><strong>#PRODUCT_NAME#</strong></a></h1></td>
</tr>
<tr>
  <td><strong>#CATEGORY_LABEL#:</strong></td><td>#CATEGORY#</td>
  <td><strong>#PRODUCT_AVAIL_LABEL#:</strong></td><td>#PRODUCT_AVAIL#</td>
  <td><strong>#LAST_DATE_SOLD_LABEL#:</strong></td><td>#LAST_DATE_SOLD#</td>
</tr>
<tr>
  <td align="left"><strong>#PRODUCT_DESCRIPTION_LABEL#:</strong></td>
  <td colspan="5">#PRODUCT_DESCRIPTION#</td>
```

```
      </tr>
      <tr>
        <td style="padding-bottom: 0px;"><strong>#LIST_PRICE_LABEL#</strong></td>
        <td style="padding-bottom: 0px;"><strong>#UNITS_LABEL#</strong></td>
        <td style="padding-bottom: 0px;"><strong>#SALES_LABEL#</strong></td>
        <td style="padding-bottom: 0px;"><strong>#CUSTOMERS_LABEL#</strong></td>
      </tr>
      <tr>
        <td style="padding-top: 0px;">#LIST_PRICE#</td>
        <td style="padding-top: 0px;">#UNITS#</td>
        <td style="padding-top: 0px;">#SALES#</td>
        <td style="padding-top: 0px;">#CUSTOMERS#</td>
      </tr>
      <tr>
        <td colspan="7" class="separator"></td>
      </tr>
```

12. In **After Rows**, enter **</table>**. In this attribute you enter the HTML to be displayed after report rows. Here, you used the closing table tag </TABLE> to end the table.
13. Click on the View Reports icon .
14. Click the **Actions** menu and click on **Select Columns**. Make sure all columns (except Description, Last Sold, and Tags) appear in *Display in Report section*. If not, move all columns to it. Using the arrow icons, arrange columns in a desired order and click the **Apply** button.
15. Click on the **Actions** menu again. Select **Save Report**. From the *Save* drop-down list, select **As Default Report Settings**. Set *Default Report Type* to **Primary** and click **Apply**.

6.3.2 Modify Button Attributes

Modify the following attribute of the Create button. Currently it is lying under the Products region and is being switched to Breadcrumb region to make it more visible. We are also creating a link to call Product Details page (Page 6).

Attribute	Value	Attribute	Value
Label	Create Product	Icon CSS Classes	fa-chevron-right
Region	**Breadcrumb**	Action	Redirect to Page in this Application
Button Position	Create	Target Type	Page in this application
Button Template	Text with Icon	Page	6
Hot	Yes	Clear Cache	6

Click **Save and Run Page** button to test Page 3. You will see three icons beside the Search Bar: View Icon, View Report, and View Detail. Click each icon to see the corresponding output.

Chapter 6 – Setup Products Catalog

6.4 Modify Product Details Page - Page 6

Call **Page 6** and click on the root node Page 6: Product Details. Set the following attributes for the Product Details page.

Attribute	Value	Attribute	Value
Title	Product Details	Height	530
Width	660	Maximum Width	1000

6.4.1 Making Page Item Mandatory

Make product name (**P6_PRODUCT_NAME**) item mandatory using the following attributes:

Attribute	Value	Attribute	Value
Template	Required	Value Required	Yes

The first attribute above marks mandatory items on a page with an asterisk (*), while the second one ensures that the marked fields are not null. Set these two attributes for P6_CATEGORY, P6_PRODUCT_AVAIL, and P6_LIST_PRICE as well.

6.4.2 Attach Categories LOV

We created a list of values (CATEGORIES) in Chapter 3 section 3.4.1. Here we're going to use that list to display pre-defined values of categories in a Select List. First, you will change the Category item from Text to a Select List, and then you'll define the list of values (LOV) the item will bound to. Recall that you used this process in the Manage Customers module to display STATES LOV. From the Items node under Product Details region, click on **P6_CATEGORY** item and amend the following attributes in the Property Editor:

Attribute	Value	Attribute	Value
Type	Select List	Display Extra Values	No
Type (under List of Values)	Shared Component	Display Null Value	No
List of Values	CATEGORIES	-	-

6.4.3 Attach LOV to Product Available Column

Next, you will change Product Available field to Radio Group having two options Yes and No. This LOV was also created in Chapter 3 section 3.4.4. Just like the previous steps, here as well, you're changing item type from text to a new one: Radio Group. At runtime, this item will show two options (as shown in the Figure 6-2) to specify whether the selected product is available or not. If you ignore this exercise and leave the item to its default type, users can enter whatever value they like, resulting in compromising application's integrity. This is a good example to restrict users to select valid values. Select **P6_PRODUCT_AVAIL** item and set the following attributes. Note that you are also setting a default value (Y) for this item.

Attribute	Value	Attribute	Value
Type	Radio Group	Display Extra Values	No
Label	Product Available	Display Null Value	No
Number of Columns	2	Default Type	Static Value
Type (under List of Values)	Shared Component	Static Value	Y
List of Values	Y or N	-	-

6.4.4 Handling Image (Handle Image Exercise A)

Modify the following attributes of P6_PRODUCT_IMAGE item to handle product image.

Attribute	Value	Attribute	Value
MIME Type Column	MIMETYPE	BLOB Last Update Column	IMAGE_LAST_UPDATE
Filename Column	FILENAME	-	-

In Settings section, the attribute Storage Type is set to **BLOB column specified in item source attribute**. The Storage Type attribute specifies where the uploaded file should be stored at. It has two values:
- BLOB column specified in item source attribute - Stores the uploaded file in the table used by the "Automatic Row Processing (DML)" process and the column specified in the item source attribute. The column has to be of data type BLOB.
- Table APEX_APPLICATION_TEMP_FILE - Stores the uploaded file in the table APEX_APPLICATION_TEMP_FILE.

6.4.5 Create Region – Product Image (Handle Image Exercise B)

To show images of selected products on Product Details page, we will create a Static Content sub region. Note that this section will only create a blank region to hold an image. The image will be added to it in a subsequent section. To create a sub region, right click Product Details region </> Product Details and select **Create Sub Region** from the context menu. A sub region is a region that resides in a parent region. Select the new sub region and modify the following attributes. The region will be displayed only when there exists an image, and this evaluation is made using a condition that is based on a PL/SQL function.

Attribute	Value
Title	Product Image
Type	Static Content
Parent Region	Product Details
Type (under Condition)	PL/SQL Function Body

PL/SQL Function Body	declare
	begin
	  if :P6_PRODUCT_ID is not null then
	    for c1 in (select nvl(dbms_lob.getlength(product_image),0) A
	              from demo_product_info
	              where product_id = :P6_PRODUCT_ID)
	    loop
	      if c1.A > 0 then
	        return true;
	      end if;
	    end loop;
	  end if;
	  return false;
	end;

NOTE: Page items are referenced in PL/SQL block using bind variables i.e. a colon(:) prefixed to the item name, for example :P6_PRODUCT_ID

Chapter 6 – Setup Products Catalog

Code Explained

In APEX you make use of conditions to control appearance of page items. In the current scenario, you set a condition based on a PL/SQL function which returns a single Boolean value: True or False. If the code returns True, the region is displayed carrying the image of the selected product. After selecting a condition type, you inform APEX to execute the defined PL/SQL code. The code first executes an IF condition (line 3) to check whether the product ID is not null by evaluating the value of the page item P6_PRODUCT_ID. If the value is null, the flow of the code is transferred to line 13, where a false value is returned and the function is terminated. If there exists a value for the product ID, then line 4 is executed which creates a FOR loop to loop through all records in the DEMO_PRODUCT_INFO table to find the record (and consequently the image) of the selected product (line 4-11). On line 8, another IF condition is used to assess whether the image is found. If so, a true value is returned on line 9 and the function is terminated.

6.4.6 Create Item – IMAGE (Handle Image Exercise C)

In this section you will create a new item named Image to display product image in the Product Image region created just above. Right click Product Image region </> *Product Image* and select Create Page Item from the context menu. Set the following attributes for the new item. The code defined in PL/SQL Function Body fetches image of the selected product using a function (apex_util.get_blob_file_src). By setting a condition, we ensured that an image exists in the table.

Attribute	Value
Name	P6_IMAGE
Type	Display Only
Region	Product Image
Label	*Clear Label*
Template	No template *(Set it to -Select- placeholder)*
Type (under Source)	PL/SQL Function Body
PL/SQL Function Body	return '<img src="'||apex_util.get_blob_file_src('P6_PRODUCT_IMAGE',:P6_PRODUCT_ID)||'" />';
Type (under Condition)	Rows Returned
SQL Query	SELECT mimetype from demo_product_info WHERE product_id = :P6_PRODUCT_ID AND mimetype like 'image%'
Escape Special Characters	No *(Otherwise the image won't appear)*

6.4.7 Create Button Remove Image (Handle Image Exercise D)

An image can be removed from the Product Details page and consequently from the underlying table by clicking this button. It is attached to a process (Delete Image) defined in the next section. Right-click Product Image region and select **Create Button**. Set the following attributes for the new button. The URL value set in the Action attribute calls a confirmation box. This call is made using an APEX function (apex.confirm) by passing a message and the name of the Delete button. In the confirmation box, if you click Yes, then the process associated with the Delete button removes image references from the products table.

Attribute	Value	Attribute	Value
Name	DELETE_IMAGE	CSS Classes	close iconLeft
Label	Remove Image	Icon CSS Classes	fa-chevron-right
Button Template	Text with Icon	Action	Redirect to URL
URL (under Target)	javascript:apex.confirm('Are you sure you want to delete this image? It will no longer be available for others to see if you continue.','DELETE_IMAGE');		

6.5 Create Process Delete Image Under Processing (Handle Image Exercise E)

This is the process we were talking about in the previous section. It will be associated with the Delete button. Click on the **Processing** tab and then right click on the **Processing** node. From the context menu select **Create Process**. Set the following attributes for the new process:

Attribute	Value
Name	Delete Image Process
Type	PL/SQL Code
PL/SQL Code	update demo_product_info set product_image = null, mimetype = null, filename=null, image_last_update=null where product_id = :P6_PRODUCT_ID;
Success Message	Product image deleted.
When Button Pressed	DELETE_IMAGE

NOTE: To remove images stored in database table, you are required to replace the content of the relevant columns with a null.

Test Your Work

Save your work and run the application. From the main navigation menu, select Manage Products entry. On the main interactive report page, click the three report icons individually to see different views of products information. Clicking **View Icons** will present small icons of products. Each product is presented as a linked icon. If you click any icon, you'll be taken to another page (Page 6) where you'll see details of the selected product. Click the Report View icon. The Report View presents data in a tabular form. Here you can access the details page by clicking products' names. Click the Detail View icon. This View presents products information from a different perspective. You can access details of a product by clicking its name. This is the view that was styled in section 6.3.1 steps 9-12.

Click any product's name to call its details page (as illustrated in Figure 6-2). The main region (Product Details) was created by the wizard incorporating all relevant fields. The Product Image sub region appears within the parent region. This region was created in section 6.4.5. Also note that the Remove Image button (you created in section 6.4.7) appears within the child region.

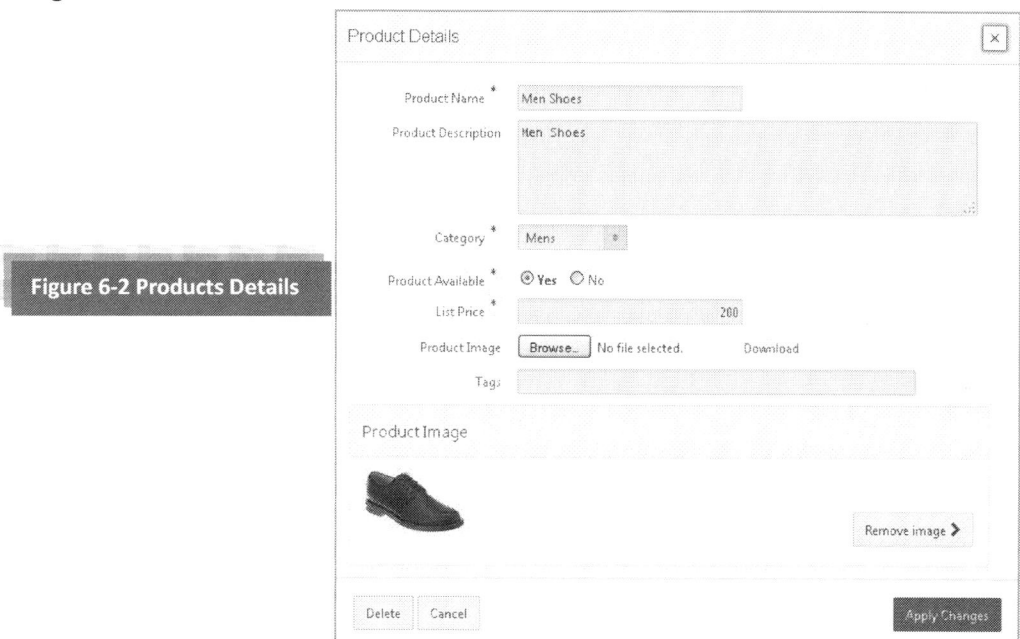

Figure 6-2 Products Details

Create a new product record using the Create Product button on the main Products page. Click the browse button and select any small image file to test image upload. Fill in all the fields except List Price. Try to save this record by clicking the Create button. A message will appear at the top of your screen to inform you that some value for the List Price must be provided. Now, provide some alpha-numeric value like abc123 in the List Price. Again, an appropriate message will come up reminding you to put a numeric value. This time add a numeric value and save the record. You'll see the new product appears on the Products page among others with the image you uploaded. Edit this record and see the image appearing in the defined region. Change the category of this product, switch availability to the other option and apply changes. Call the product again and observe that the product now reflects the changes you just made. Click the Remove Image button and see what happens. Click the Delete button followed by OK in the confirmation box. The product will vanish from the list. Note that the Delete button was created by the wizard with record deletion process.

Summary

In this chapter you were taught some more skills that will assist you in developing your own applications. Most importantly, you knew the techniques to handle, store, and retrieve images to and from database tables. Play around with this module by tweaking the saved attributes to see resulting effect on the two pages. This way you will learn some new things, not covered in this chapter. Of course, you can always restore the attributes to their original values by referencing the exercises provided in the chapter. An important point to consider here is that a module of this caliber would have taken plenty of time and effort to develop using conventional tools. With Oracle APEX declarative development, you created it in a couple of hours.

Chapter 7

Taking Orders

Chapter 7 – Taking Orders

7.1 About Sale Orders

This chapter will teach you how to create professional looking order forms. Orders from customers will be taken through a sequence of wizard steps. The first wizard step will allow you to select an existing customer or create a new one. In the second step, you will select ordered products. After placing the order, the last step will show summary of the placed order. Once an order is created, you can view, modify, or delete it through Order Details page using a link in orders main page. The list presented below displays the application pages you are going to create in this chapter:

Page No.	Page Name	Purpose
4	Orders	The main page to display all existing orders
29	Order Details	Display a complete order with details for modification
11	Identify Customer (Wizard Step 1)	Select an existing customer or create a new one
12	Select Order Items (Wizard Step 2)	Add products to an order
14	Order Summary (Wizard Step 3)	Show summary of the placed order

You'll build this module sequentially in the order specified above. The first two pages (Page 4 and 29) will be created initially using a new wizard option: Master Detail Form. Both these pages are not part of the Order Wizard and will be utilized for order modification and deletion, after recording an order. Page 4 is similar to the pages you created in Customer and Product modules and lists all placed orders, while Page 29 will be used to manipulate order details. For example, you can call an order in the usual way using the provided link in the master page. The called order will appear in the details page where you can:

- Add/Remove products to and from an order
- Delete the order itself

The purpose of each chapter in this book is to teach you some new features. Here as well, you'll get some new stuff. This chapter will walk you through to get detailed practical exposure to the techniques this module contains. After completing the two main pages, you will work on actual order wizard steps and will create other pages of the module. Recall that in the previous chapter you modified the main interactive report (Page 3) to create a couple of views (Icon and Detail), and used the Actions menu to select and sort table columns. The bar which carried the three icons to access these reports also carried a Search box that you used to search a customer record in chapter 5. In this chapter, you will be exposed to many other utilities provided under the Actions menu. But first, let's create the two main pages using the conventional route.

7.2 Create Order Master and Order Detail Pages

1. Click the **Create Page** button in the Application Builder.
2. Select the **Form** option and click **Next**.
3. This time select **Master Detail Form** option. A master detail form reflects a one-to-many relationship between two tables in a database. Typically, a master detail form displays a master row and multiple detail rows within a single HTML form. With this form, users can insert, update, and delete values from two tables or views. On the Master Detail page, the master record displays as a standard form and the detail records appear in a tabular form under the master section.
4. Accept your schema in Table/View Owner, select **DEMO_ORDERS (table)** in Table/View Name, select **all columns** by moving them to the right pane, and click **Next**. In this step, you selected the parent table which contains the master information for each order.

5. Accepting the default Table/View Owner select **DEMO_ORDER_ITEMS (table)** in Table/View Name, select **all columns**, and click **Next**. This is the relational child table, which carries line item information for each order.
6. Select primary key columns for the specified Master and Detail pages in the Define Primary Key page as illustrated below, and click **Next**.

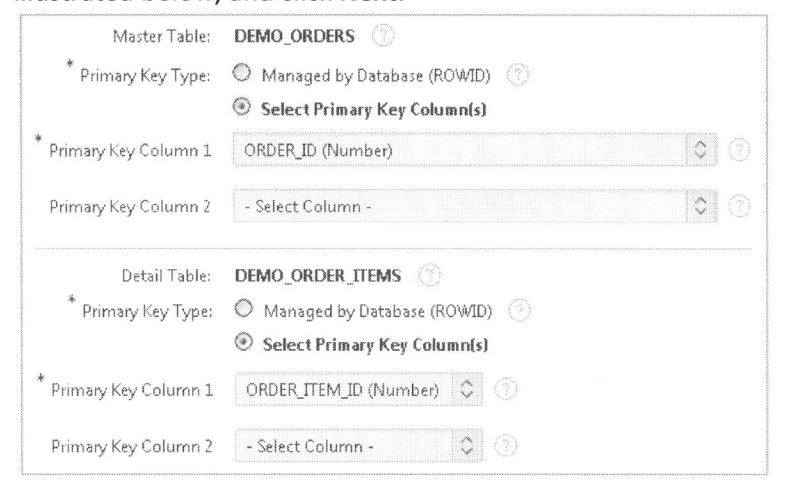

Forms perform insert, update and delete operations on table rows in the database. The rows are identified using either a primary key defined on the table, or the ROWID pseudo column, which uniquely identifies a row in a table. The first option "Managed by Database (ROWID)" is selected if you would like to use the ROWID; otherwise, select the primary key column(s) defined for your table. Forms support up to two columns in the primary key. For tables using primary keys with more than two columns, the ROWID option should be used.

7. On the Primary Key wizard page, select the **Existing Sequence** option, select **DEMO_ORD_SEQ** as Sequence, and click **Next**. In this step, you selected the method by which the master table's primary key is populated and chose the database sequence object to populate the primary key. The same option, with respective sequences, was selected in the previous two chapters.
8. Repeat the same process for the child table by selecting the **Existing Sequence** option, followed by selecting **DEMO_ORDER_ITEMS_SEQ** as its Sequence and click **Next**.
9. Do not select any option on the Master Options wizard page. Click **Next** to accept the default options. This step determines whether to include master row navigation. The default is Yes. If you include master row navigation, then you have to define navigation order column(s). If a navigation order column is not defined, the master update form will navigate by the primary key column. By default, this wizard creates a master report page. You can choose to not create master report page if you already have a report page.
10. Click **Next** to accept the default layout, *Edit detail as tabular form on same page,* which creates a two page master detail setup. The second option, *Edit detail on separate page*, comprises three pages.
11. Set master and detail page information according to the illustration, and click **Next**.
12. On the Navigation Menu page, set Navigation Preference to **Identify an existing navigation menu entry for this page**, and set Existing Navigation Menu Entry to **Orders**. Click Next.
13. Click the **Create** button on the Confirm page to finish the wizard.

Before running these pages, let's see what the wizard has done for us. The following table lists all those components that were created automatically by the wizard with complete functionalities to execute this module. The master page (Page 4) is created with an interactive report containing details of all orders. Just like previous interactive reports, created in the previous two chapters, this one is also created without any special process or validation. The details page (Page 29), on the other hand, has many things to reveal, and these are the components that I have mentioned in the following table.

Component	Name	Description
Pre-Rendering Process	Fetch Row from DEMO_ORDERS	Fetches master row from DEMO_ORDERS table.
Region	Orders	The page has two regions. The upper region (ORDERS) is a Static Content region which displays master information, such as customer name, address etc.
Buttons	GET_NEXT_ORDER_ID GET_PREVIOUS_ORDER_ID	These buttons are added to the master region to fetch next and previous orders, respectively. For example, when you click the Next button > , the page is submitted to get the next order record from the server. After retrieving the record, a process named Get Next or Previous Primary Key Value in the Pre-Rendering section of the page is triggered. Based on the currently fetched order number, which is held in the page item P29_ORDER_ID, the process dynamically obtains the next and previous order numbers and stores them in two hidden page items: P29_ORDER_ID_NEXT and P29_ORDER_ID_PREV. The visibility of these buttons is controlled by a condition (Item is NOT NULL) which says that these buttons will be visible only when their corresponding hidden items have some values.
Region	Order Items	This is the lower region that shows product details along with quantity and price in a tabular form.
Buttons	APPLY_CHANGES_ADD APPLY_CHANGES_MRD	These two buttons are also added by the wizard and are placed in the details region. The Add Row button (named APPLY_CHANGES_ADD) is there to add items to the details section. The default Action attribute of this button is set to Redirect to URL with Target set to *javascript:apex.widget.tabular.addRow();*. Using this JavaScript code, you can add multiple items at once. The code executes on the client machine so no server round trip is needed, which of course takes extra time to add items to an order. Once you complete an order and press the Save button, a wizard-generated process named ApplyMRU (in the Processing tab) comes into action to save all items' details to the database. Similarly, the second button (APPLY_CHANGES_MRD) is placed to delete all marked rows from the details section. After marking record(s) in the tabular form, when you click this button, a process named ApplyMRD is executed to removes all marked rows from order details table.
Buttons	Cancel	The Cancel button closes Page 29 and takes you back to Page 4

			without saving an order. To do so, it is associated to an auto-generated dynamic action named Cancel Dialog in the Dynamic Actions tab.
		Delete	The Delete button removes a complete order. When this button is clicked, a confirmation dialog pops up using its Target attribute, which is set to: javascript:apex.confirm(htmldb_delete_message,'DELETE'); When you confirm deletion, a process SQL DELETE action (specified in Database Action attribute of this button) is executed.
		Save	The Save button records updates to an existing order in the corresponding database table. This button is visible when you call an order for modification i.e. P29_ORDER_ID is NOT NULL. The process behind this button is controlled by SQL UPDATE action.
		Create	The Create button is used for new orders to handle INSERT operation. This button is visible when you are creating a new order i.e. P29_ORDER_ID is NULL.
Dynamic Action		Cancel Dialog	This dynamic action is associated with the Cancel button to close Page 29.
Validations		Seven Validations	Based on the two database tables definitions, the wizard auto-generates some validations to check input of data with proper data types.
Processes		Get PK	The Get PK process executes when the Create button is clicked. It contains a PL/SQL code that calculates next order id.
		Process Row of DEMO_ORDERS	The three buttons (Save, Delete, and Create discussed above) were responsible to handle DML operations on the details table (DEMO_ORDER_ITEMS). This process is generated by the wizard to handle DML operations performed on the master row of an order that gets into DEMO_ORDERS table.
		ApplyMRU	This process is associated with the details section (tabular form) to handle update and insert operations. The process executes when you click Save, Get Next, or Get Previous buttons. The execution is controlled by a condition which looks for a request from the three specified buttons. :request like ('SAVE') or :request like 'GET_NEXT%' or :request like 'GET_PREV%'
		ApplyMRD	The MRD (Multiple Row Delete) process executes when the Delete Checked button is clicked. It removes all the marked records from the details region.
		Close Dialog	It is associated with CREATE,SAVE, and DELETE buttons to close Page 29.
Branches		Go To Page 29 Go To Page 29 Go To Page 29 Go To Page 4	The first three branches are created to keep you on Page 29. Two of these branches are associated with Next and Previous buttons. The fourth one takes you back to Page 4 when you click Save, Delete, or Create buttons.

Chapter 7 – Taking Orders

Run Page 4 to check this module. The first page (Page 4) that you see is an interactive report. It is similar to those you created in the previous chapters, and opted to create here as well. It has a default Create button that is used to create a new order. Click the edit link in front of any record to call Order Details page (Page 29). Besides usual buttons, the details page has two navigational buttons (on far right) that helps you move forward and backward to browse orders. The Order Timestamp field is supplemented with a Date Picker control. The page carries two additional buttons in the details section to delete and add products. At first glance, the page looks complete, but from professional perspective it feels a bit clumsy. Execute the steps in the following sections to give these pages a more desirable look.

7.3 Modify Orders Page - Page 4

Execute the instructions provided in the following sub sections to modify the Orders page.

7.3.1 Delete and Re-Create the Default Orders Region

You need to delete the default Orders region to create a new one with the same name and with interactive functionality. The new region is being created to incorporate customers information in the interactive report.

1. Right click **Orders** region Orders and select the **Delete** option.
2. Create a new region by right clicking the main Regions node and selecting **Create Region** option.
3. Select the new region and modify it using the following table:

Attribute	Value
Title	Orders
Type	Interactive Report

SQL Query	select lpad(to_char(o.order_id),4,'0000') order_number, o.order_id,
	       to_char(o.order_timestamp,'Month YYYY') order_month,
	       trunc(o.order_timestamp) order_date,
	       o.user_name sales_rep, o.order_total,
	       c.cust_last_name||', '||c.cust_first_name customer_name,
	       (select count(*) from demo_order_items oi
	        where oi.order_id = o.order_id and oi.quantity != 0)
	       order_items
	from demo_orders o, demo_customers c
	where o.customer_id = c.customer_id

4. Expand Columns node under Order region and set Type attribute of ORDER_ID column to **Hidden Column**.
5. In Column Attributes, set meaningful **headings** for all interactive report columns as follows. Using drag and drop you can put these columns in the defined order.
   Order #, Order Month, Order Date, Customer Name, Sales Rep, Order Items, Order Total
6. Edit **ORDER_TOTAL** column and select **$5,234.10** for Format Mask.
7. Select **Order Number** column (not Order ID) and turn it into a link using the following attributes:

Attribute	Value	Attribute	Value
Type	Link	Value	#ORDER_ID#
Target Type	Page in this application	Clear Cache	29
Page	29	Link Text	#ORDER_NUMBER#
Name	P29_ORDER_ID	-	-

8. In the region's Attribute node scroll down to Actions Menu section and set Save Public Report to **Yes** to include this option in the Actions menu at runtime. By enabling this option, you will be able to create a public report in section 7.3.4.
9. Save your modifications.

7.3.2 Modify the Interactive Report

Perform the following steps to change the look and feel of the initial interactive report. After performing these steps, the interactive report will be saved as the Default Primary Report which cannot be renamed or deleted. Note that these modifications are made using the Actions menu at runtime.

1. Click the **Save and Run Page** button to run Page 4.
2. Click on **Actions** menu and then **Select Columns**.
3. Using the arrow buttons to your right, arrange columns in *Display in Report* section as follows:
   Order #, Order Month, Order Date, Customer Name, Sales Rep, Order Items, and Order Total
4. Click the **Apply** button.
5. To display most current orders on top, click the **Actions** menu | **Format** | **Sort**. In the Sort grid, select the **Order #** column in the first row, set the corresponding Direction to **Descending**, and click **Apply**.
6. Click **Actions** | **Save Report** | **As Default Report Settings**, select **Primary** and click **Apply**. Perform this step whenever you make changes to a report; otherwise, your modifications will not be reflected the next time you log in to the application. In Interactive Reports, you can apply a number of filters, highlights, and other customizations. Rather than having to re-enter these customizations each time you run the report, you tell APEX to remember them so that they are applied automatically on every next run. Every application user can save multiple reports based on the defined default primary report.

7.3.3 Create Alternative Report

Alternative report enables developers to create multiple report layouts. Only developers can save, rename, or delete an Alternative Report. This report (named Monthly Review) is based on the default primary report and will be rendered in a different layout using the Control Break utility on Order Month column. Select *1. Primary Report* in the Search bar (on Page 4), and perform the following steps to create three different views of the report.

A. Report View

1. Click **Actions** | **Save Report** | **As Default Report Setting** | select **Alternative**, in the Name box enter **Monthly Review** and click **Apply**.
2. From Reports drop down list, select the alternative report named **2. Monthly Review**.
3. Click **Actions** | **Format** | **Control Break**. Under Column, select **Order Month** in the first row, set Status to **Enabled** and click **Apply**.

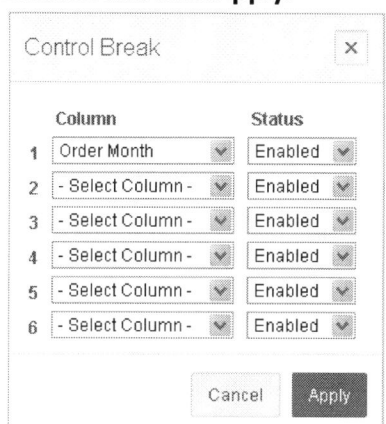

The control break feature enables grouping to be added to your report on one or more columns. The Column attribute defines which column to group on and the Status attribute determines whether the control break is active or not. When the report is run, you will see that report results are grouped by the Order Month column and the created Control Break column will be listed under the Search Bar. A checkbox is displayed next to the control break column and is used to turn the control break on or off. The control break can be deleted from the report by clicking the delete icon.

Chapter 7 – Taking Orders

4. Click **Actions | Format | Highlight**. Type **Orders > $2,000** in *Name*, set *Highlight Type* to **Cell**, click **[green]** for *Background Color*, click **[red]** for *Text Color*, in *Highlight Condition* set *Column* to **Order Total**, *Operator* to **>** (greater than), *Expression* to **2000** and click **Apply**. To distinguish important data from the rest, Oracle APEX provides you with conditional highlighting feature in interactive reports. The highlight feature in Interactive Reports enables users to display data in different colors based on a condition. You can define multiple highlight conditions for a report. In this step, you're instructing to highlight the Order Total column in the report with green background and red text color where the value of this column is greater than 2000. Since you set the Highlight Type to Cell, the condition will apply only to the Order Total column.

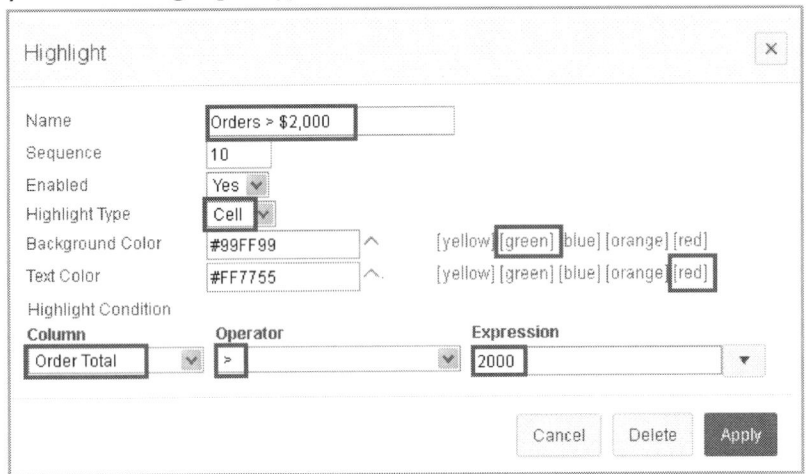

5. Click **Actions | Format | Highlight**. Type **Orders <= $900** in *Name*, set *Highlight Type* to **Row**, click **[yellow]** for *Background Color*, click **[Red]** for *Text Color*, in *Highlight Condition* set *Column* to **Order Total**, *Operator* to **<=** (less than or equal to), *Expression* to **900** and click **Apply**. This step is similar to the previous one with different parameters. In contrast to the previous action, where only a single cell was highlighted, this one highlights a complete row with yellow background and red text color and applies it to all rows in the report having Order Total equaling $900 or less.

The resulting output should resemble Figure 7-1.

Figure 7-1 Monthly Order Review Report

B. Chart View

You can generate charts in Interactive Reports based on the results of a report. You can specify the type of chart together with the data in the report you wish to chart. In the following exercise, you will create a horizontal bar chart to present monthly sales figures using the Order Month column for the chart labels and a sum of the Order Total column for the chart values.

1. Click **Actions | Format | Chart**.
2. Select the **1st option** (horizontal bar) in *Chart Type*.
3. Select **Order Month** for *Label*.
4. Enter **Period** in *Axis Title for Label*.
5. Select **Order Total** for *Value*.
6. Enter **Total Orders Amount** in *Axis Title for Value*.
7. Select **Sum** as *Function*.
8. Select **Label-Ascending** for *Sort*.
9. Click **Apply**.

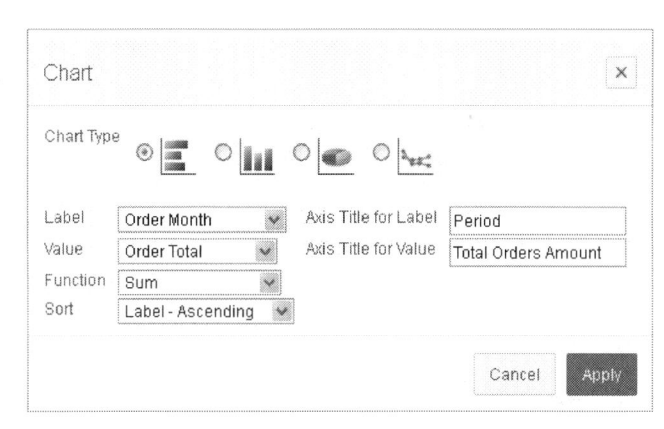

The chart should look like Figure 7-2. Note that the Search bar now has two icons: View Report and View Chart. If the chart doesn't appear, click the View Chart icon in the search bar. Move your mouse over each bar to see total amount for the month.

85

Chapter 7 – Taking Orders

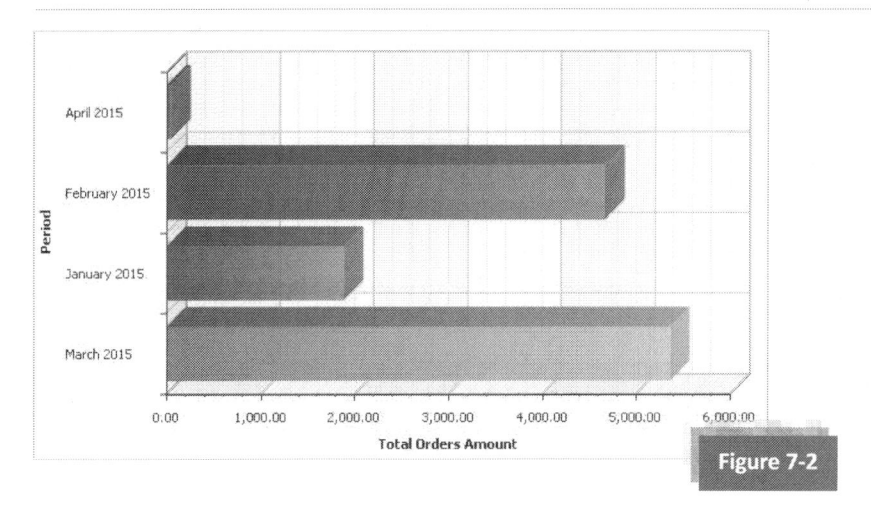

Figure 7-2

C. Group By View

Group By enables users to group the result set by one or more columns and perform mathematical computations against the columns. Once users define the group by, a corresponding icon is placed in the Search bar which they can use to switch among the three report views.

1. Click the View Report icon to switch back to the report view interface.
2. Click **Actions | Format | Group By**.
3. Set attributes as show in the following figure and click **Apply**.

4. Click on the **Actions** menu and select **Save Report**.

The output should look like the figure illustrated below. Note that a third icon - *View Group by* - will be added to the main report bar.

Order Month	Average Order Total	Number of Orders
April 2015	$50.00	1
February 2015	$1,556.67	3
January 2015	$1,890.00	1
March 2015	$895.00	6
		1 - 4

7.3.4 Create Public Report

This type of report can be saved, renamed, or deleted by end users who created it. Other users can view and save the layout as another report. Follow the instructions below to create the three views: Report, Chart, and Group by of a public report.

A. Report View

1. Select the default **1. Primary Report** from the Reports drop-down list.
2. From the **Actions** menu, select **Save Report**.
3. From the Save dropdown list select **As Named Report**. Users can create multiple variations of a report and save them as named reports, for either public or private viewing.
4. For report Name, enter **Customer Review**, put a check on **Public** and click the **Apply** button. A new report group (Public) will be added to the Reports list in the Search bar, carrying a new report named Customer Review. When you click the **Apply** button, the report is displayed on your screen.
5. With report **1. Customer Review** appearing on your screen, click **Actions | Format | Control Break**.
6. Select **Customer Name** in the first row under Column, set Status to **Enabled** and click **Apply** to see the following output.

Customer Name : Bradley, Eugene					
Order #	Order Month	Order Date	Sales Rep	Order Items	Order Total
0010	March 2015	31-MAR-2015	DEMO	3	$870.00
0001	January 2015	26-JAN-2015	DEMO	3	$1,890.00

Customer Name : Dulles, John					
Order #	Order Month	Order Date	Sales Rep	Order Items	Order Total
0002	February 2015	09-FEB-2015	DEMO	9	$2,160.00

B. Chart View

1. Click **Actions | Format | Chart**.
2. Fill in the Chart parameters as shown below:

   - Label: Customer Name
   - Value: Order Total
   - Function: Average
   - Sort: Label - Ascending
   - Axis Title for Label: Customer
   - Axis Title for Value: Average Order Total

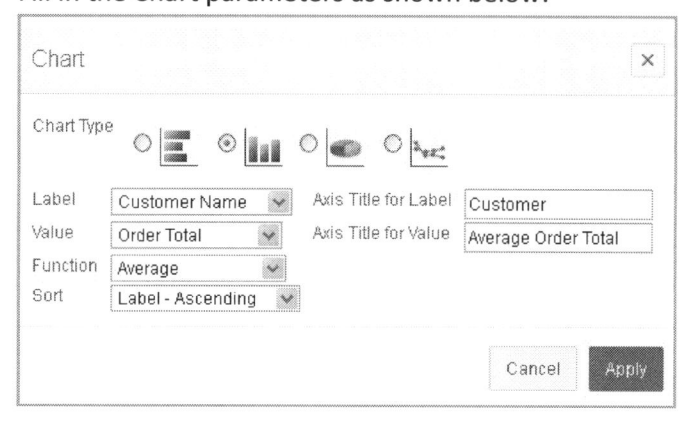

3. Click the **Apply** button to see an output similar to Figure 7-3.

Chapter 7 – Taking Orders

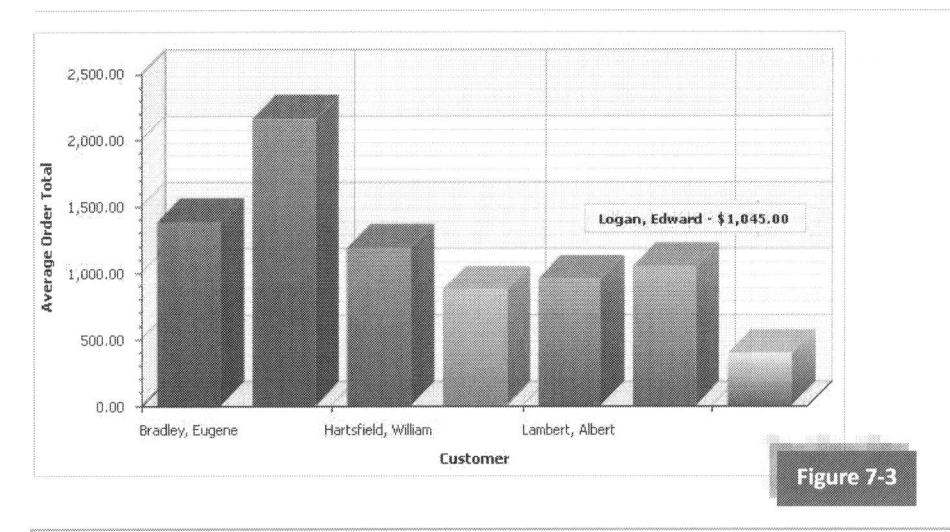

Figure 7-3

NOTE: The chart uses an Average function (as compared to the Sum function used in the previous exercise). A customer (Edward Logan) has placed two orders amounting to $2,090. The average for this customer comes to $1,045 (2,090/2) and this is what you see when you move your mouse over the bar representing this customer.

C. Group By View

1. Click on the **View Report** icon to switch back.
2. Click **Actions | Format | Group By**.
3. Set attributes as show in the following illustration. Don't forget to put check marks in the Sum columns to produce grand totals on the page.
4. Click **Apply**.

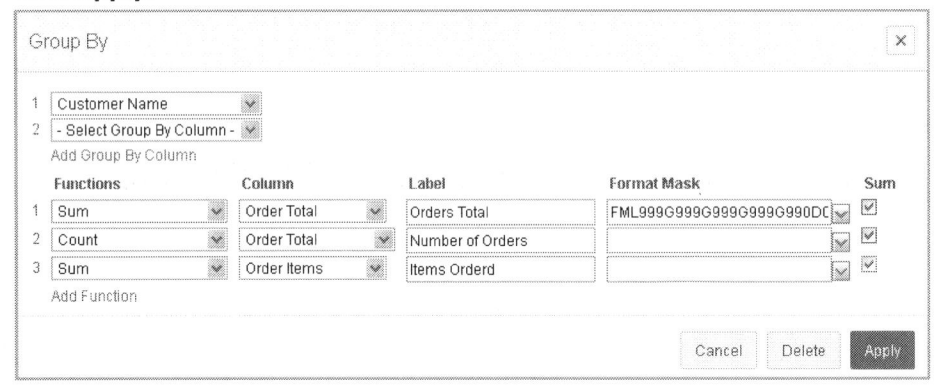

The following is the output for the selections you just made. In this view, you utilized Sum and Count functions on two columns: Order Total and Order Items. This view displays total amount of orders placed by each customer with number of orders and the total number of items ordered.

Customer Name	Orders Total	Number of Orders	Items Orderd
Dulles, John	$2,160.00	1	9
OHare, Frank	$780.00	2	4
Logan, Edward	$2,090.00	2	10
Lambert, Albert	$950.00	1	5
Hartsfield, William	$2,370.00	2	8
LaGuardia, Fiorello	$870.00	1	4
Bradley, Eugene	$2,760.00	2	6
	$11,980.00	**11**	**46**

Save your work using the **Actions** menu.

7.3.5 Modify Button – Create

You deleted and re-created the default region in section 7.3.1. Due to which you lost the Create button associated with it that was there to create new orders. In this section you will create a new button for the same purpose.

In **Page 4 | Rendering** tab right click the Breadcrumb region and click on Create Button. Set the following attributes for the new button:

Attribute	Value	Attribute	Value
Button Name	ENTER_NEW_ORDER	Action	Redirect to Page in this Application
Label	Enter New Order	Target Type	Page in this Application
Button Template	Text with Icon	Page	11
Hot	Yes	Name	P11_CUSTOMER_OPTIONS
Icon CSS Classes	fa-chevron-right	Value	EXISTING
-	-	Clear Cache	11

7.3.6 Delete Computation – P29_ORDER_ID

Once an order is generated, the Order Details page (Page 29) is used to modify or delete the order. This page was created by the Master/Detail Form wizard and was associated with DEMO_ORDER_ITEMS table. The primary key of this table is ORDER_ITEM_ID, whereas the column ORDER_ID is the foreign key to associate an order with its headers in the master table (DEMO_ORDERS). To associate the two tables, the wizard created a computation item: P29_ORDER_ID. The purpose of this computation was to assign the order ID value to the identified item and pass it on to Page 29. This computation is being deleted because we intend to process new orders with the help of a wizard.

1. In the Processing tab, expand After Submit | Computations nodes.
2. Right click P29_ORDER_ID and select **Delete** from the context menu.

Chapter 7 – Taking Orders

7.4 Modify Order Details Page - Page 29
7.4.1 Modify Master Region Attributes

Page 29 contains two regions. The master region is of Static Content type which carries order header information, while the second region is a tabular form which contains line item details. Modify the master region using the following steps:

1. In Page 29, click on Order Details Region </> Order Details and enter **Order #&P29_ORDER_ID.** (including the terminating period) for its Title. The expression consists of two parts. The first one (Order #), is a string concatenated to a page item (P29_ORDER_ID) which carries the order number. Combined together, the string would be presented as: Order # 1. In order to show this title, make sure that region's Template attribute is set to **Standard**.
2. Create a new page item in the Items node under the master region and set the following attributes. Through this item you will present customer information on each order as display only text. Note that when you enter the following query, you may get an invalid query error message. Clicking the Save button twice makes it valid. Moreover, if you keep the default Yes value for Escape Special Characters attribute, the customer information appears on a single line with <br/> tags.

Attribute	Value
Name	P29_CUSTOMER_INFO
Type	Display Only
Label	Customer
Save Session State	No
Show Line Breaks	No
Type (Source)	SQL Query (return single value)
SQL Query	select apex_escape.html(cust_first_name) || ' ' || apex_escape.html(cust_last_name) || ' ' || apex_escape.html(cust_street_address1) || decode(cust_street_address2, null, null, ' ' || apex_escape.html(cust_street_address2)) || '</br>' || apex_escape.html(cust_city) || ', ' || apex_escape.html(cust_state) || ' ' || apex_escape.html(cust_postal_code) from demo_customers where customer_id = :P29_CUSTOMER_ID
Escape Special Characters	No

Using drag and drop arrange the columns in this order: P29_CUSTOMER_INFO, P29_ORDER_TIMESTAMP, P29_ORDER_TOTAL, P29_USER_NAME, P29_TAGS, and P29_CUSTOMER_ID.

Edit the following items individually and set the corresponding attributes shown under each item.

1. **P29_ORDER_TIMESTAMP**

Attribute	Value	Attribute	Value
Type	Display Only	Format Mask	DD-MON-YYYY HH:MIPM
Label	Order Date	-	-

2. **P29_ORDER_TOTAL**

Attribute	Value	Attribute	Value
Type	Display Only	Format Mask	$5,234.10

3. **P29_USER_NAME**

Attribute	Value
Type	Select List
Label	Sales Rep
Type (List of Values)	SQL Query
List of Values	select distinct user_name d, user_name r from demo_orders union select upper(:APP_USER) d, upper(:APP_USER) r from dual order by 1
Display Extra Value	No
Display Null Value	No
Help Text	Use to change the Sales Rep associated with this order.

   In the Help Text attribute you specify help text for an item. The help text may be used to provide field level, context sensitive help. At run-time you will see a small help icon ⓘ in-front of this item which, upon click, will show the above help in a popup window.

4. **P29_TAGS**

Attribute	Value
Type	Text Field

5. **P29_CUSTOMER_ID**

Attribute	Value	Attribute	Value
Type	Hidden	Value Protected	No

6. **P29_ORDER_ID**

Attribute	Value	Attribute	Value
Type	Hidden	Value Protected	No

7.4.2 Modify Details Region Attributes

After setting the master region, let's do some more with the details region to give it a desirable look.

1. Click on **Order Details** report region *Order Details* and set its Title to **Items for Order #&P29_ORDER_ID.** (including the terminating period). Also replace existing SQL Query with the one that follows:

   ```
   select oi.order_item_id, oi.order_id, oi.product_id, oi.unit_price, oi.quantity,
       (oi.unit_price * oi.quantity) extended_price, dbms_lob.getlength(product_image) product_image,
       decode(nvl(dbms_lob.getlength(pi.product_image),0),0,null,
       '<img style="border: 4px solid #CCC; -moz-border-radius: 4px; -webkit-border-radius: 4px;" '
       ||'src="'||apex_util.get_blob_file_src('P6_PRODUCT_IMAGE',pi.product_id)||
       '" height="75" width="75" alt="Product Image" title="Product Image" />') detail_img
   from DEMO_ORDER_ITEMS oi, DEMO_PRODUCT_INFO pi
   where oi.ORDER_ID = :P29_ORDER_ID and oi.product_id = pi.product_id (+)
   ```

2. Click the **Save** button to reflect the impact of the above SQL statement in the report region.
3. Under Columns node, edit the following columns using the specified attributes. The default Type for UNIT_PRICE is Text Field, which allows end user to modify price of a product, is changed to a Plain Text type to eliminate price alteration. With this value set, the price column is displayed as text and the values contained within this column are not editable. For Product ID column, we changed two attributes. First, we set its Type attribute to Select List. Secondly, we associated an LOV (Products with Price) to it. This LOV was created in chapter 3 section 3.4.2 to display list of products along with respective prices.

Column	Attribute	Value
CHECK$01	Column Alignment	Center
UNIT_PRICE	Type	Plain Text
	Alignment	Right
	Column Alignment	Right
	Format Mask	$5,234.10
PRODUCT_ID	Type	Select List
	Heading	Product
	Alignment	Left
	Type (LOV)	Shared Components
	List of Values	Products With Price
	Display Null Value	No
	Default Sequence (Sorting)	1
QUANTITY	Width	5
	Type (Default)	PL/SQL Expression
	PL/SQL Expression	1
EXTENDED_PRICE	Heading	Price
	Alignment	Right
	Column Alignment	Right
	Format Mask	$5,234.10
	Compute Sum (Advanced)	Yes
PRODUCT_IMAGE	Type	Hidden Column
	Escape Special Characters	No
DETAIL_IMG	Heading	*Clear Heading*
	Escape Special Characters	No

4. Using drag and drop arrange the five visible columns in the following order:
    DETAIL_IMG, PRODUCT_ID, QUANTITY, UNIT_PRICE, and EXTENDED_PRICE
5. Click on the Attributes node under the Columns node. Scroll down to Break Formatting section and type **Grand Total** in Report Sum Label attribute. This attribute along with the Compute Sum attribute (set for EXTENDED_PRICE above), shows the Grand Total text and the sum of order total at the bottom of this region.
6. Save the changes.

Test Your Work

Run the application and click the Orders option in the main navigation menu. The page that comes up should look like Figure 7-4. Click on any order number to call Order Details page (Figure 7-5). Try to navigate forward and backward using Next and Previous buttons. At the moment, you can only use these two pages to manipulate existing orders. In the next sections, you will create some more pages to enter new orders.

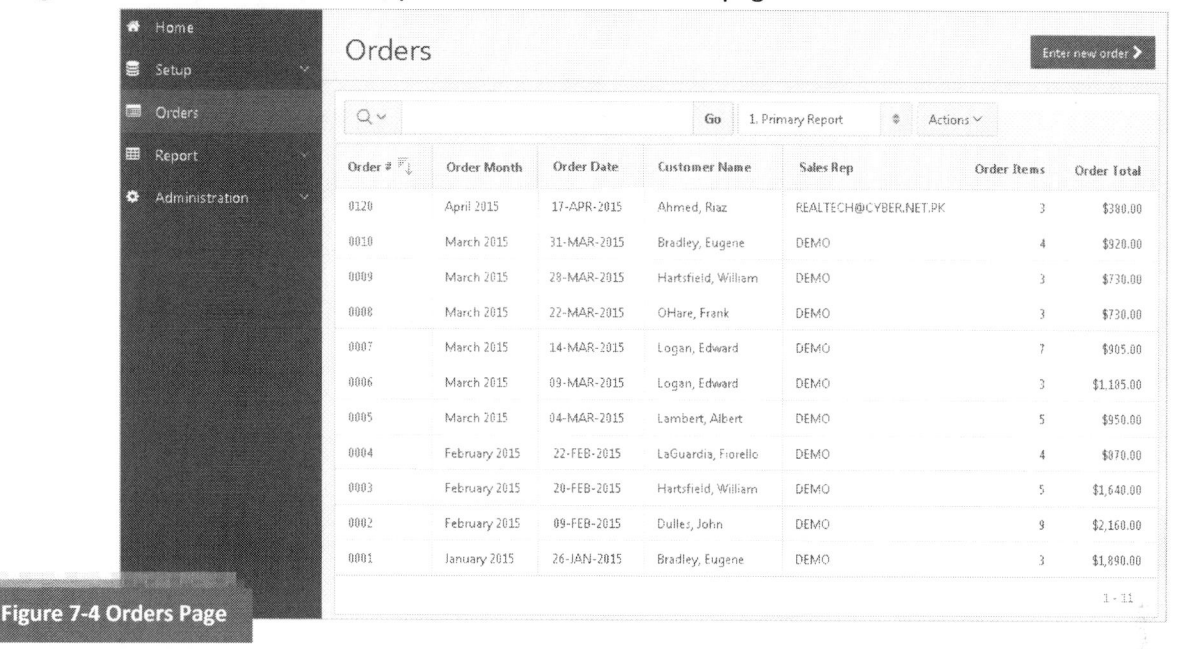

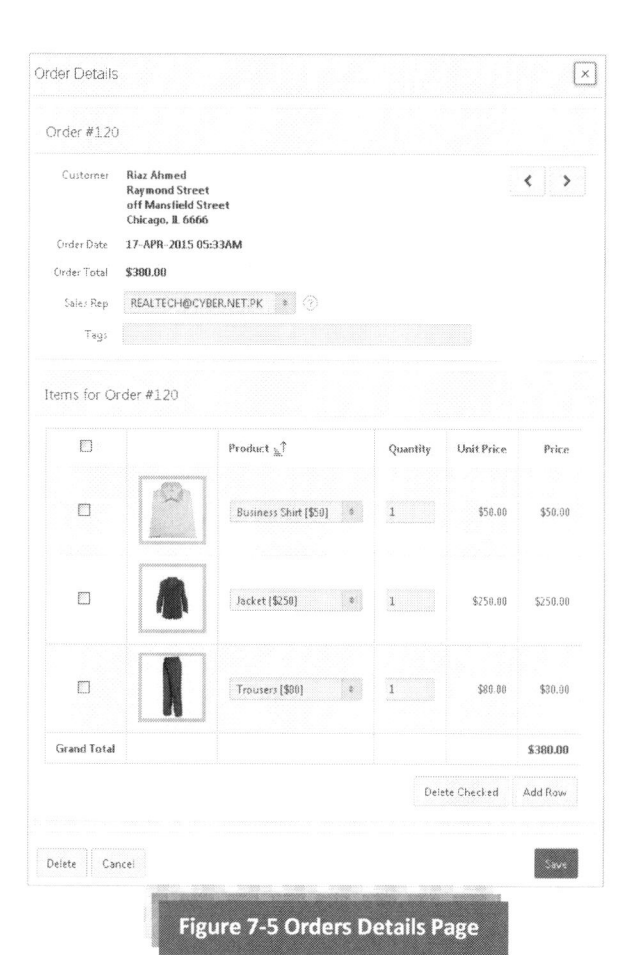

Figure 7-4 Orders Page

Figure 7-5 Orders Details Page

93

Chapter 7 – Taking Orders

7.5 Create Page Enter New Order - Page 11

As mentioned earlier, you will go through a series of steps to enter a new order. You identified and created these steps in Order Wizard list in Chapter 3 section 3.2.3. The top region in the following figure (Figure 7-6) reflects those steps. The rest of this chapter will guide you to create those three pages individually. In this exercise, you will create Page 11 - Enter New Order. The order recording process initiates when you click Enter New Order button on the Orders page (Page 4). Besides selecting an existing customer, you can also create record of a new customer on this page. The LOV button corresponding to the **Customer** box calls a list of existing customers from which you can select one for the order. If you select the **New Customer** option, a region (New Customer Details) will be shown under the existing region. By default, this region is hidden and becomes visible when you click on the New Customer option. This functionality is controlled by a dynamic action (Hide/Show Customer), which will also be created for this page. In addition to various techniques taught in this part, you'll create this page from an existing page - Customer Details (Page 7) - to generate a new customer record. Here, you'll make a copy of that page and will tweak it for the current scenario. Let's see how it is done.

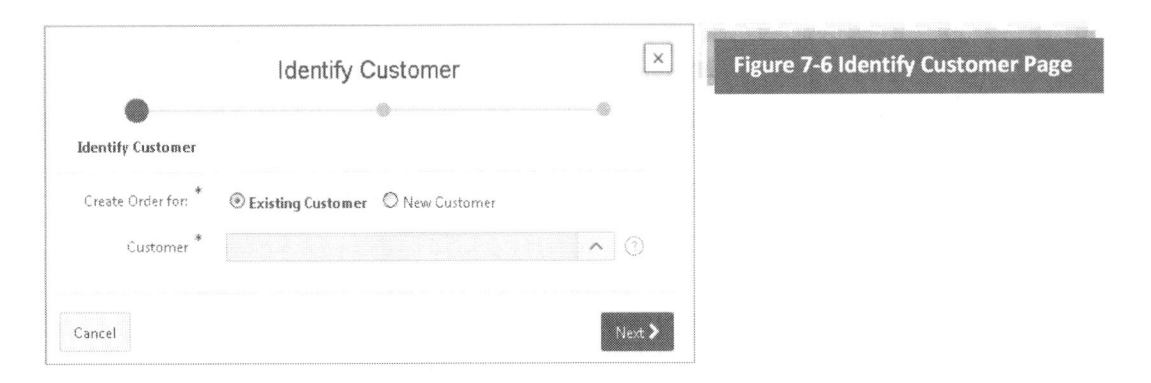

Figure 7-6 Identify Customer Page

1. In Application Builder interface, click on **Customer Details - Page 7**.
2. Click on the **Create** menu on top right and select **Page as copy**.
3. For *Create a page as a copy of*, select the option **Page in this application** and click **Next**.
4. Fill in the following values in *Page To Copy* and click **Next**.

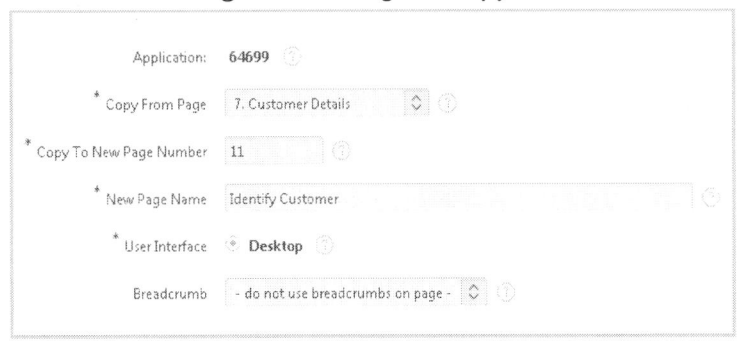

   - Application: 64699
   - Copy From Page: 7. Customer Details
   - Copy To New Page Number: 11
   - New Page Name: Identify Customer
   - User Interface: Desktop
   - Breadcrumb: - do not use breadcrumbs on page -

5. In the New Names page, do not change anything at this stage and click **Next**.
6. On Navigation Menu page select **Identify an existing navigation menu entry for this page** option, select **Orders** for Existing Navigation Menu, and click **Next.**
7. Click the **Copy** button to finish the wizard.

Look at the Page Designer. All the elements from Page 7 appeared on the new page, especially the items section, which carries all input elements to create a new customer record. This is the section we needed on our new page to spare some time.

7.5.1 Modify Page Attributes

1. In Page 11, click on the root node (Page 11: Identify Customer).
2. Set Dialog Template to **Wizard Modal Dialog**. The template creates a region (Wizard Progress Bar) to hold the order progress list, as shown in Figure 7-6, and alters the name of the main region from Content Body to Wizard Body.
3. Set Width and Height to **700** and **500**, respectively.
4. Remove variable **htmldb_delete_message** from Function and Global Variable Declaration section, and **Apply changes**. The variable (htmldb_delete_message) is an auto-generated variable and is associated with the customer record deletion process, handled transparently by APEX. It is removed because the customer record deletion process is not required here.

7.5.2 Create Region – Order Progress

Right click on the Wizard Progress Bar node and select **Create Region**. Set the following attributes for the new region. The specified list (Order Wizard) was created in Chapter 3 - section 3.2.3.

Attribute	Value
Title	Order Progress
Type	List
List	Order Wizard
Template	Blank with Attributes
List Template (under Attributes node)	Wizard Progress

7.5.3 Create Region – Identify Customer

Right click on the Wizard Body node and select **Create Region**. Drag the new region and place it above the Customer Details region. Set the following attributes for it. This region is created to act as a main container to hold a radio group item and a couple of sub regions.

Attribute	Value
Title	Identify Customer
Type	Static Content
Template	Standard

7.5.4 Create Items

Right click Identify Customer region and select **Create Page Item**. The list of value, NEW OR EXISTING CUSTOMER, specfied here was created in chapter 3 - section 3.4.5 with two static values.

Attribute	Value	Attribute	Value
Name	P11_CUSTOMER_OPTIONS	List of Values	NEW OR EXISTING CUSTOMER
Type	Radio Group	Display Null Value	No
Label	Create Order for:	Type (Source)	Static Value
Number of Columns	2	Static Value (Source)	EXISTING
Template	Required	Type (Default)	Static Value
Type (List of Values)	Shared Components	Static Value (Default)	EXISTING

Chapter 7 – Taking Orders

7.5.5 Create a Sub Region – Existing Customer

Right click on Identify Customer node and select **Create Sub Region**. This will add a sub region under the page item P11_CUSTOMER_OPTIONS. Set the following attributes from the sub region.

Attribute	Value
Title	Existing Customer
Type	Static Content
Template	Blank with Attributes

7.5.6 Modify Item – P11_CUSTOMER_ID

In the Items section, click on **P11_CUSTOMER_ID**. Set the Name attribute of this hidden item to **P11_CUSTOMER_ID_XYZ**. Set Condition Type to **Never**. This item is renamed and suppressed from being rendered because a new item (of POP LOV type) with the same name is created in the next section to display a list of customers, instead. By selecting the Never value for the Condition Type, you permanently disable a page component.

7.5.7 Add LOV

Right click Existing Customer sub-region and select **Create Page Item**. Set the following attributes for this item:

Attribute	Value
Name	P11_CUSTOMER_ID
Type	Popup LOV
Label	Customer
Template	Required
Width	70
Type (List of Values)	SQL Query
SQL Query	select cust_last_name || ', ' || cust_first_name d, customer_id r from demo_customers order by cust_last_name
Display Extra Value	No
Display Null Value	No
Type (Source)	Null
Help Text	Choose a customer using the popup selector, or to create a new customer, select the New customer option.

7.5.8 Modify Customer Details Region

Click on Customer Details node and set the following attributes for this region. By specifying the parent region you make a region child of a parent region.

Attribute	Value
Title	New Customer Details
Parent Region	Identify Customer

7.5.9 Delete Validation, Processes and Buttons

1. Under the Processing tab, click the link **Can't Delete Customer with Orders** under Validations, click the **Delete** button and confirm deletion. Using the same technique, delete **Get PK**, **Process Row of DEMO_CUSTOMERS**, and **reset page** processes.
2. Also remove **Delete**, **Save**, and **Create** buttons from the Buttons section under the Rendering tab.

7.5.10 Delete Process

Under the Rendering tab, expand Pre-Rendering | After Header | Processes node. Delete process **Fetch Row from DEMO CUSTOMERS**. This is a default process created in the Customers module and is not required in the current scenario.

7.5.11 Create Button – Next

Create a new button in the Buttons region and set the following attributes for it. After identifying a customer, you click this button to advance to the second order wizard step.

Attribute	Value	Attribute	Value
Button Name	NEXT	Hot	Yes
Label	Next	Icon CSS Classes	fa-chevron-right
Button Position	Next	Action	Submit Page (default)
Button Template	Text with Icon	-	-

7.5.12 Create Process - Create or Truncate Order Collection

When developing web applications in APEX, you often need a mechanism to store an unknown number of items in a temporary location. The most common example of this is an online shopping cart where a user adds unknown number of items. To cope with this situation in APEX, you use collections to store variable information. Before using a collection, it is necessary to initialize it in the context of the current application session. After clicking the Enter New Order button, you're brought to this page (Page 11), and this is where your collection (ORDER) is initialized using a PL/SQL process that fires Before Header when the user enters into the interface of Page 11. See sections 7.6.4 and 7.6.8 for relevant details on collections.

In the Rendering tab, expand Pre-Rendering node. Right click on Before Header node and select **Create Process**. Set the following attributes for the new process.

Attribute	Value
Name	Create or Truncate ORDER Collection
Type	PL/SQL Code
PL/SQL Code	apex_collection.create_or_truncate_collection (p_collection_name => 'ORDER');

7.5.13 Create Dynamic Action (Page Rendering)

Click on the Dynamic Actions tab. Right click on Change node and select **Create Dynamic Action**. Click on the New node and set the following attributes. The following settings inform APEX to fire the dynamic action when user changes (*Event*) the radio group item (*Selection Type*) P11_CUSTOMER_OPTIONS (*Item*), from New Customer to Existing.

Attribute	Value	Attribute	Value
Name	Hide / Show Customers	Item(s)	P11_CUSTOMER_OPTIONS
Event	Change (default)	Condition	equal to
Selection Type	Item(s)	Value	EXISTING

Click on the Show node to set the following attributes. These attributes are associated with the above settings to show Existing Customer region when the EXISTING option is selected from the radio group.

Attribute	Value	Attribute	Value
Action	Show (default)	Fire When Event Result is	True (default)
Selection Type	Region	Fire On Page Load	Yes (default)
Region	Existing Customer	-	-

Chapter 7 – Taking Orders

Right click on the Show node and select Create Action. Set the following attributes for it. This action is also assoicated with the previous two, and is added to hide New Customer Details region when the EXISTING option is selected.

Attribute	Value	Attribute	Value
Action	Hide	Fire When Event Result is	True (default)
Selection Type	Region	Fire On Page Load	Yes (default)
Region	New Customer Details	-	-

Right click on the Show node again and select Create Opposite Action. This will add an opposite Hide action under the False node, with all attributes set, to hide Existing Customer region.

Right click on the Hide node under the True node and select Create Opposite Action to add a Show node under the False node to show New Customer Details region.

If you run the page at this stage, you'll see that the item P11_CUSTOMER_ID (carried in the region Existing Customer region) is shown on the page. Now, select the New Customer option. The item P11_CUSTOMER_ID disappears from the page and the New Customer Details region becomes visible. Select the Existing Customer option again, the item becomes visible and the New Customer Details region hides.

7.5.14 Modify Validation – Check Credit Limit

In the Processing tab, click the link for **Check Credit Limit** under Validations node. Set its Sequence to **100** and save the change to place this validation in a proper sequence after the following validations.

7.5.15 Create Validation – Customer ID Not Null

Right click the Validations node and select **Create Validation**. Set the following attributes for the new validation. The validation fires when you select the Existing Customer option, and do not select a customer from the provided list. The condition (item=value) is formed like this: P11_CUSTOMER_OPTIONS=EXISTING.

Attribute	Value	Attribute	Value
Name	Customer ID Not Null	Associated Item	P11_CUSTOMER_ID
Sequence	10	Type (Condition)	Item = Value
Type (Validation)	Item is NOT NULL	Item	P11_CUSTOMER_OPTIONS
Item	P11_CUSTOMER_ID	Value	EXISTING
Error Message	#LABEL# must have some value.	-	-

7.5.16 Create Validation – First Name Not Null

Create another validation. This validation will check whether the first name of a new customer is provided. It is fired only when the New Customer option is selected.

Attribute	Value	Attribute	Value
Name	First Name is Not Null	Error Message	#LABEL# must have some value.
Sequence	20	Type (Condition)	Item = Value
Type (Validation)	Item is NOT NULL	Item	P11_CUSTOMER_OPTIONS
Item	P11_CUST_FIRST_NAME	Value	NEW

Using the steps performed in the above section, create NOT NULL validations for Last Name, State, Postal Code, and Credit Limit items.

7.5.17 Create Validation – Phone Number Format

Create the following validation to check input of proper phone numbers.

Attribute	Value
Name	Phone Number Format
Type (Validation)	Item Matches Regular Expression
Item	P11_PHONE_NUMBER1
Regular Expression	^\(?[[:digit:]]{3}\)?[-.][[:digit:]]{3}[-.][[:digit:]]{4}$
Error Message	Phone number format not recognized
Associated Item	P11_PHONE_NUMBER1
Type (Condition)	Item = Value
Item	P11_CUSTOMER_OPTIONS
Value	NEW

Create a similar validation for **P11_PHONE_NUMBER2** item. Next, set Value Required attribute to **No** for P11_CUSTOMER_ID (in Existing Customer Region), P11_CUST_FIRST_NAME, P11_CUST_LAST_NAME, P11_CUST_STATE, P11_CUST_POSTAL_CODE, and P11_CREDIT_LIMIT. The Value Required attributes for these items were inherited from Page 7 where they were set to Yes, to mark them as mandatory. In the above two sections, you used an alternate method to manually control the validation process for these items. If you don't reverse the Value Required status, then the application will throw NOT NULL errors for these items, even if you select an existing customer.

7.5.18 Create Branch

When the Next button is clicked, the defined button action (submit page) triggers after performing all validations. The submit page process executes instructions specified in this branch and moves the user to the next order wizard step. In the Processing tab, right click After Processing node and select **Create Branch**. Set the following attributes for the new branch.

Attribute	Value	Attribute	Value
Name	Go To Page 12	Value	&P11_CUSTOMER_ID.
Target Type	Page in this Application	Clear Cache	12
Page	12	When Button Pressed	NEXT
Name	P12_CUSTOMER_ID	-	-

Test Your Work

From the main menu select Orders and click Enter New Order button. Your page should look like Figure 7-6. Select Existing Customer and click the LOV button to call list of customers. Note that each customer name is displayed as a link. Click on a link to select a customer. The name of the selected customer appears in the Customer box. This is how an existing customer is selected for an order. Now, click the New Customer option, the Dynamic Action created in section 7.5.13 invokes and performs two actions. First, it hides the Customer box and LOV. Second, it shows a form similar to the one you created in chapter 5 to add a new customer record. Click the Next button without putting any value in the provided form. You'll see an inline message box appearing with five errors. This is the procedure you handled in the validation sections. After correcting all the form errors if you click Next, a Page Not Found error message will come up indicating that Page 12 doesn't exist. Your next task is to create Page 12 where you'll select products for an order.

Chapter 7 – Taking Orders

7.6 Create Select Items Page - Pages 12

Having identified the customer, the second step in the order wizard is to add products to the order. In this exercise you will create Page 12 of the application to select order items and input the required quantities.

1. Click the **Create Page** button in the Application Builder interface.
2. This time select the **Blank Page** option. In this exercise you are using a new option (blank page) to create an application page from scratch. Using this option you can create and customize a page according to your own specific needs.
3. Complete the first wizard step as show in the following figure and click **Next**.

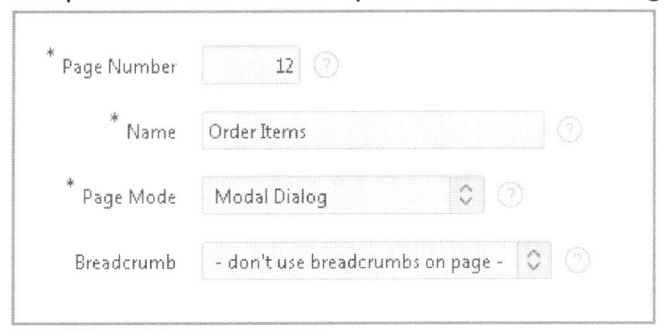

   - Page Number: 12
   - Name: Order Items
   - Page Mode: Modal Dialog
   - Breadcrumb: - don't use breadcrumbs on page -

4. On the Navigation Menu page, set Navigation Preference to **Identify an existing navigation menu entry for this page**, and set Existing Navigation Menu Entry to **Orders**. Click **Next**.
5. Click **Finish** to end the wizard.

7.6.1 Modify Page Attributes

In the previous chapter you styled Detail View of an interactive report to customize its look. Here as well, you will apply styling rules to give the page a professional touch. Previously, you added rules to a single page element: HTML table. In the following exercise you'll apply rules to the whole page. Before getting your feet wet, go through the following topic to understand Cascading Style Sheets (CSS).

Cascading Style Sheets

A cascading style sheet (CSS) provides a way to control the style of a Web page without changing its structure. When used properly, a CSS separates visual attributes such as color, margins, and fonts from the structure of the HTML document. Go through free CSS tutorials on http://www.w3schools.com/.

In this chapter, you are going to use CSS to style Page 12 (Select Items - Figure 7-7). On this page you will add class attributes to PL/SQL code and will reference them in CSS in the HTML Header section. Before moving on to understand the actual functionality, let's first take a look at a simple example on how to use class attribute in an HTML document. The class attribute is mostly used to point to a class in a style sheet. The syntax is <element class="classname">.

```html
<html>
  <head>
    <style type="text/css">
      h1.header {color:blue;}
      p.styledpara {color:red;}
    </style>
  </head>
  <body>
    <h1 class="header">Class Referenced in CSS</h1>
    <p>A normal paragraph.</p>
    <p class="styledpara">Note that this is an important paragraph.</p>
  </body>
</html>
```

The body of this page contains three sections:

1. `<h1 class="header">Class Referenced in CSS</h1>`. The text, "Class Referenced in CSS", is enclosed in h1 html tag. It is called level 1 heading and is the most important heading in a document; it is usually used to indicate the title of the document. The text is preceded by a class, named "header".
Considering the above class syntax, here, h1 is the element and header is the classname. Combined together (element.classname), this class is referenced in the style section using a CSS rule – h1.header {color:blue;} – to present the heading in blue color. A CSS rule has two main parts: a selector, and one or more declarations. The selector is normally the HTML element you want to style. Each declaration consists of a property and a value. The property is the style attribute you want to change. Each property has a value. In the above h1.header {color:blue;} rule, h1 is the selector, followed by the classname (header), followed by the declaration: {color:blue;}.
2. `<p>A normal paragraph.</p>` – A plain paragraph without any style applied to it. HTML documents are divided into paragraphs and paragraphs are defined with the `<p>` tag. `<p>` is called the start tag or opening tag while `</p>` is called the end or closing tag.
3. `<p class="styledpara">Note that this is an important paragraph.</p>`. A paragraph with a class, named "styledpara". In the style section, the selector "p" followed by the classname "styledpara" having declaration{color:red;} is referencing this section to present the paragraph text in red color.

Now that you have understood how CSS is used in web pages, let's figure out how it is used in APEX.

1. Click on the root node (Page 12: Order Items).
2. Set Dialog Template to **Wizard Modal Dialog**.
3. Set Width and Height to 500 and 600, respectively.
4. Enter the following code in the **inline** box under CSS section and **Apply Changes**. CSS rules entered in this box is applied to all the referenced elements on the current page.

Chapter 7 – Taking Orders

Rule #	Rule	PL/SQL Ref.
	A - CustomerInfo	
1	div.CustomerInfo strong{font:bold 12px/16px Arial,sans-serif;display:block;width:120px;}	11,22
2	div.CustomerInfo p{display:block;margin:0; font: normal 12px/16px Arial, sans-serif;}	12-19,23-30
	B - Products	
3	div.Products{clear:both;margin:16px 0 0 0;padding:0 8px 0 0;}	36-42
4	div.Products table{border:1px solid #CCC;border-bottom:none;}	37,47
5	div.Products table th{background-color:#DDD;color:#000;font:bold 12px/16px Arial,sans-serif;padding:4px 10px;text-align:right;border-bottom:1px solid #CCC;}	37,47
6	div.Products table td{border-bottom:1px solid #CCC;font:normal 12px/16px Arial,sans-serif; padding:4px 10px;text-align:right;}	39
7	div.Products table td a{color:#000;}	39
8	div.Products .left{text-align:left;}	37,39,47
	C - CartItem	
9	div.CartItem{padding:8px 8px 0 8px;font:normal 11px/14px Arial,sans-serif;}	53-59
10	div.CartItem a{color:#000;}	54-55
11	div.CartItem span{display:block;text-align:right;padding:8px 0 0 0;}	56-57
12	div.CartItem span.subtotal{font-weight:bold;}	58
	D - CartTotal	
13	div.CartTotal{margin-top:8px;padding:8px;border-top:1px dotted #AAA;}	65-68
14	div.CartTotal span{display:block;text-align:right;font:normal 11px/14px Arial,sans-serif;padding:0 0 4px 0;}	66
15	div.CartTotal p{padding:0;margin:0;font:normal 11px/14px Arial,sans-serif;position:relative;}	66
16	div.CartTotal p.CartTotal{font:bold 12px/14px Arial,sans-serif;padding:8px 0 0 0;}	67
17	div.CartTotal p.CartTotal span{font:bold 12px/14px Arial,sans-serif;padding:8px 0 0 0;}	67
18	div.CartTotal p span{padding:0;position:absolute;right:0;top:0;}	66

Cascading Style Sheet (CSS) Rules

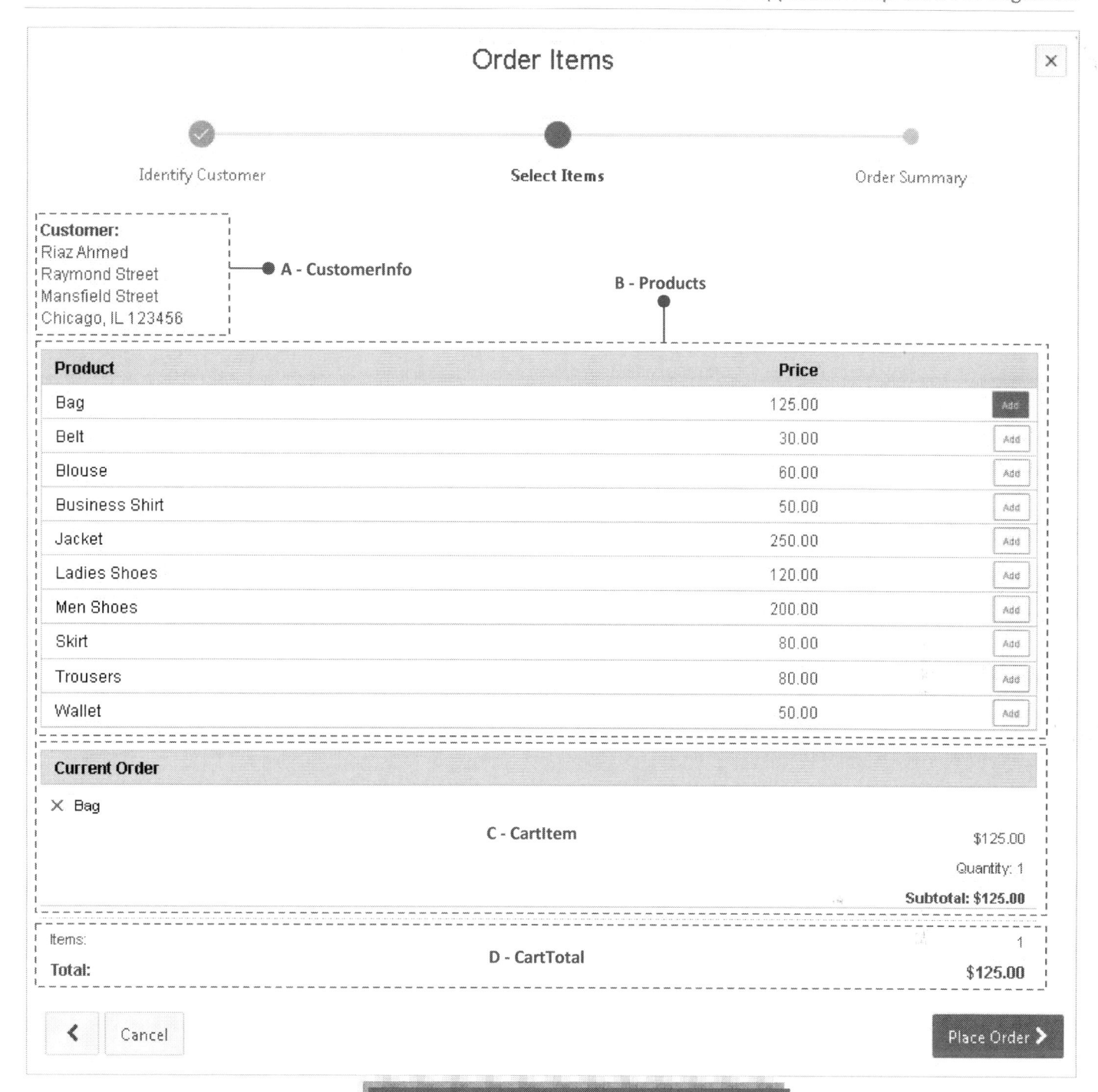

Figure 7-7 CSS Rules Applied to Select Items Page

7.6.2 Create Region – Order Progress

Right click on the Wizard Progress Bar node and select **Create Region**. Set the following attributes for the new region. A similar region was added to Page 11 to display Order Progress bar.

Attribute	Value	Attribute	Value
Title	Order Progress	Template	Blank with Attributes
Type	List	List Template (under Attributes node)	Wizard Progress
List	Order Wizard	-	-

Chapter 7 – Taking Orders

7.6.3 Create a Hidden Item

Right click Order Progress region and select **Create Page Item**. Select the new item. Enter **P12_CUSTOMER_ID** for its Name, and set its Type to **Hidden**. This item was referenced in the branch created in section 7.5.18.

7.6.4 Create Region – Select Items

The region being created in this section is based on a custom PL/SQL code. The code references CSS rules (defined in the previous section) to design the Select Items page as illustrated in Figure 7-7.

What is PL/SQL?

PL/SQL stands for Procedural Language/Structured Query Language. It is a programming language that uses detailed sequential instructions to process data. A PL/SQL program combines SQL command (such as Select and Update) with procedural commands for tasks, such as manipulating variable values, evaluating IF/THEN logic structure, and creating loop structures that repeat instructions multiple times until the condition satisfies the defined criteria. PL/SQL was expressly designed for this purpose.

The structure of a PL/SQL program block is:

>   Declare
>   Variable declaration
>   Begin
>   Program statements
>   Exception
>   Error-handling statements
>   End;

PL/SQL program variables are declared in the program's declaration section using the data declaration syntax shown earlier. The beginning of the declaration section is marked with the reserved word DECLARE. You can declare multiple variables in the declaration section. The body of a PL/SQL block consists of program statements, which can be assigned statements, conditional statements, loop statements, and so on, that lie between the BEGIN and EXCEPTION statements. The exception section contains program statements for error handling. Finally, PL/SQL programs end with the END; statement.

In a PL/SQL program block, the DECLARE and EXCEPTION sections are optional. If there are no variables to declare, you can omit the DECLARE section and start the program with the BEGIN command.

1. Under Regions, right click on Wizard Body node and click **Create Region**.
2. Enter **Select Items** for its Title, and set its Type to **PL/SQL Dynamic Content** to display the page content from PL/SQL code. PL/SQL Dynamic Content creates a region based on PL/SQL that enable you to render any HTML or text using the PL/SQL Web Toolkit.
3. Do not set any option for the Template attribute (i.e. set it to -Select-).
4. From the following table, enter the code defined in PL/SQL code column. The first column (CSS Rule) references the rules defined in the previous section. These rules are applied to the injected HTML elements in the following PL/SQL code. The second column is populated with a serial number, assigned to each PL/SQL code. These numbers are referenced in the explanation section underneath.

CSS Rule	Line No.	PL/SQL Code
	1	declare
	2	l_customer_id varchar2(30) := :P11_CUSTOMER_ID;
	3	begin
	4	--
	5	-- **display customer information**
	6	--
	7	sys.htp.p('<div class="CustomerInfo">');
	8	if :P11_CUSTOMER_OPTIONS = 'EXISTING' then
	9	for x in (select * from demo_customers where customer_id = l_customer_id) loop
	10	sys.htp.p('<div class="CustomerInfo">');
1	11	sys.htp.p('<strong>Customer:</strong>');
	12	sys.htp.p('<p>');
	13	sys.htp.p(sys.htf.escape_sc(x.cust_first_name) || ' ' || sys.htf.escape_sc(x.cust_last_name) || ' ');
	14	sys.htp.p(sys.htf.escape_sc(x.cust_street_address1) || ' ');
	15	if x.cust_street_address2 is not null then
2	16	sys.htp.p(sys.htf.escape_sc(x.cust_street_address2) || ' ');
	17	end if;
	18	sys.htp.p(sys.htf.escape_sc(x.cust_city) || ', ' || sys.htf.escape_sc(x.cust_state) || ' ' || sys.htf.escape_sc(x.cust_postal_code));
	19	sys.htp.p('</p>');
	20	end loop;
	21	else
1	22	sys.htp.p('<strong>Customer:</strong>');
	23	sys.htp.p('<p>');
	24	sys.htp.p(sys.htf.escape_sc(:P11_CUST_FIRST_NAME) || ' ' || sys.htf.escape_sc(:P11_CUST_LAST_NAME) || ' ');
	25	sys.htp.p(sys.htf.escape_sc(:P11_CUST_STREET_ADDRESS1) || ' ');
	26	if :P11_CUST_STREET_ADDRESS2 is not null then
2	27	sys.htp.p(sys.htf.escape_sc(:P11_CUST_STREET_ADDRESS2) || ' ');
	28	end if;
	29	sys.htp.p(sys.htf.escape_sc(:P11_CUST_CITY) || ', ' || sys.htf.escape_sc(:P11_CUST_STATE) || ' ' || sys.htf.escape_sc(:P11_CUST_POSTAL_CODE));
	30	sys.htp.p('</p>');
	31	end if;
	32	sys.htp.p('</div>');

Chapter 7 – Taking Orders

CSS Rule	Line	PL/SQL Code
	33	--
	34	**-- display products**
	35	--
3	36	sys.htp.p('<div class="Products" >');
4	37	sys.htp.p('<table width="100%" cellspacing="0" cellpadding="0" border="0">
		<thead>
5,8		<tr><th class="left">Product</th><th>Price</th><th></th></tr>
		</thead>
		<tbody>');
	38	for c1 in (select product_id, product_name, list_price, 'Add to Cart' add_to_order
		from demo_product_info
		where product_avail = 'Y'
		order by product_name) loop
6, 7, 8	39	sys.htp.p('<tr><td class="left">' ||sys.htf.escape_sc(c1.product_name)||'</td>
		<td>'||trim(to_char(c1.list_price,'999G999G990D00')) || '</td>
		<td><a href="'||apex_util.prepare_url('f?p=&APP_ID.:12:'||:app_session||':**ADD**:::P12_PRODUCT_ID:'|| c1.product_id)||'" class="t-Button t-Button--simple t-Button--hot"><span>Add<i class="iR"></i></span></a></td>
		</tr>');
	40	end loop;
	41	sys.htp.p('</tbody></table>');
	42	sys.htp.p('</div>');

CSS Rule	Line	PL/SQL Code
	43	--
	44	**-- display current order**
	45	--
3	46	sys.htp.p('<div class="Products" >');
4	47	sys.htp.p('<table width="100%" cellspacing="0" cellpadding="0" border="0">
		<thead>
8		<tr><th class="left">Current Order</th></tr>
		</thead>
		</table>
4		<table width="100%" cellspacing="0" cellpadding="0" border="0">
		<tbody>');
	48	declare
	49	c number := 0; t number := 0;
	50	begin
	51	-- loop over cart values
	52	for c1 in (select c001 pid, c002 i, to_number(c003) p, count(c002) q, sum(c003) ep, 'Remove' remove
		from apex_collections
		where collection_name = 'ORDER'
		group by c001, c002, c003
		order by c002)
		loop
9	53	sys.htp.p('<div class="CartItem">
10	54	<a href="'||
		apex_util.prepare_url('f?p=&APP_ID.:12:&SESSION.:**REMOVE**:::P12_PRODUCT_ID:'||sys.htf.escape_sc(c1.pid))||'"><img src="#IMAGE_PREFIX#delete.gif" alt="Remove from cart" title="Remove from cart" /></a>
10	55	'||sys.htf.escape_sc(c1.i)||'
	56	<span>'||trim(to_char(c1.p,'$999G999G999D00'))||'</span>
	57	<span>Quantity: '||c1.q||'</span>
	58	<span class="subtotal">Subtotal: '||trim(to_char(c1.ep,'$999G999G999D00'))||'</span>
11	59	</div>');
	60	c := c + 1;
12	61	t := t + c1.ep;
	62	end loop;
	63	sys.htp.p('</tbody></table>');

CSS Rule	Line	PL/SQL Code
	64	if c > 0 then
13,14	65	sys.htp.p('<div class="CartTotal">
15,16	66	<p>Items: <span>'||c||'</span></p>
17,18	67	<p class="CartTotal">Total: <span>'||trim(to_char(t,'$999G999G999D00'))||'</span></p>
	68	</div>');
	69	else
	70	sys.htp.p('<div class="alertMessage info" style="margin-top: 8px;">');
	71	sys.htp.p('<img src="#IMAGE_PREFIX#f_spacer.gif">');
	72	sys.htp.p('<div class="innerMessage">');
	73	sys.htp.p('<h3>Note</h3>');
	74	sys.htp.p('<p>You have no items in your current order.</p>');
	75	sys.htp.p('</div>');
	76	sys.htp.p('</div>');
	77	end if;
	78	end;
	79	sys.htp.p('</div>');
	80	end;

NOTE: The ELSE block (lines 70-76) executes when the user tries to move on without selecting a product in the current order. The block uses a built-in class (alertMessage info) that carries an image (f_spacer.gif) followed by a message (lines 73-74).

Table 7-1 PL/SQL

In the above PL/SQL code you merged some HTML elements to deliver the page in your browser. Before getting into the code details, let's first acquaint ourselves with some specific terms and objects used in the PL/SQL code.

Using HTML in PL/SQL Code

Oracle Application Express installs with your Oracle database and is comprised of data in tables and PL/SQL code. Whether you are running the Oracle Application Express development environment or an application you built using Oracle Application Express, the process is the same. Your browser sends a URL request that is translated into the appropriate Oracle Application Express PL/SQL call. After the database processes the PL/SQL, the results are relayed back to your browser as HTML. This cycle happens each time you either request or submit a page.

Specific HTML content not handled by Oracle Application Express (forms, reports, and charts) are generated using the PL/SQL region type. You can use PL/SQL to have more control over dynamically generated HTML within a region, as you do here. Let's see how these two core technologies are used together.

htp and htf Packages:

htp (hypertext procedures) and htf (hypertext functions) are part of PL/SQL Web Toolkit package to generate HTML tags. These packages translate PL/SQL into HTML that is understood by a Web browser. For instance, the htp.anchor procedure generates the HTML anchor tag, <a>. The following PL/SQL block generate a simple HTML document:

```
Create or replace procedure hello AS
BEGIN
    htp.htmlopen;              -- generates <HTML>
    htp.headopen;              -- generates <HEAD>
    htp.title('Hello');        -- generates <TITLE>Hello</TITLE>
    htp.headclose;             -- generates </HEAD>
    htp.bodyopen;              -- generates <BODY>
    htp.header(1, 'Hello');    -- generates <H1>Hello</H1>
    htp.bodyclose;             -- generates </BODY>
    htp.htmlclose;             -- generates </HTML>
END;
```

Oracle provided the htp.p tag to allow you to override any PL/SQL-HTML procedure or even a tag that did not exist. If a developer wishes to use a new HTML tag or simply is unaware of the PL/SQL analog to the html tag, s/he can use the htp.p procedure.

For every htp procedure that generates HTML tags, there is a corresponding htf function with identical parameters. The function versions do not directly generate output in your web page. Instead, they pass their output as return values to the statements that invoked them.

htp.p / htp.print:
Generates the specified parameter as a string

htp.p('<p>'):
Indicates that the text that comes after the tag is to be formatted as a paragraph

Customer::
Renders the text they surround in bold

htf.escape_sc:
Escape_sc is a function which replaces characters that have special meaning in HTML with their escape sequence.

converts occurrence of & to &amp
converts occurrence of " to &quot
converts occurrence of < to &lt
converts occurrence of > to &gt

To prevent XSS (Cross Site Scripting) attacks, you must call SYS.HTF.ESCAPE_SC to prevent embedded JavaScript code from being executed when you inject the string into an HTML page. The SYS prefix is used to signify Oracle's SYS schema. The HTP and HTF packages normally exist in the SYS schema and APEX relies on them.

Cursor FOR LOOP Statement

The cursor FOR LOOP statement implicitly declares its loop index as a record variable of the row type that a specified cursor returns, and then opens a cursor. With each iteration, the cursor FOR LOOP statement fetches a row from the result set into the record. When there are no more rows to fetch, the cursor FOR LOOP statement closes the cursor. The cursor also closes if a statement inside the loop transfers control outside the loop or raises an exception.

The cursor FOR LOOP statement lets you run a SELECT statement and then immediately loop through the rows of the result set. This statement can use either an implicit or explicit cursor.

If you use the SELECT statement only in the cursor FOR LOOP statement, then specify the SELECT statement inside the cursor FOR LOOP statement, as in Example A. This form of the cursor FOR LOOP statement uses an implicit cursor, and is called an implicit cursor FOR LOOP statement. Because the implicit cursor is internal to the statement, you cannot reference it with the name SQL.

Example A - Implicit Cursor FOR LOOP Statement

```
BEGIN
  FOR item IN (
    SELECT last_name, job_id
    FROM employees
    WHERE job_id LIKE '%CLERK%' AND manager_id > 120
    ORDER BY last_name
  )
  LOOP
    DBMS_OUTPUT.PUT_LINE ('Name = ' || item.last_name || ', Job = ' || item.job_id);
  END LOOP;
END;
/
```

Output:
Name = Atkinson, Job = ST_CLERK
Name = Bell, Job = SH_CLERK
Name = Bissot, Job = ST_CLERK
...
Name = Walsh, Job = SH_CLERK

If you use the SELECT statement multiple times in the same PL/SQL unit, then define an explicit cursor for it and specify that cursor in the cursor FOR LOOP statement, as in Example B. This form of the cursor FOR LOOP statement is called an explicit cursor FOR LOOP statement. You can use the same explicit cursor elsewhere in the same PL/SQL unit.

Example B - Explicit Cursor FOR LOOP Statement

```
DECLARE
  CURSOR c1 IS
    SELECT last_name, job_id FROM employees
    WHERE job_id LIKE '%CLERK%' AND manager_id > 120
    ORDER BY last_name;
BEGIN
  FOR item IN c1
  LOOP
    DBMS_OUTPUT.PUT_LINE ('Name = ' || item.last_name || ', Job = ' || item.job_id);
  END LOOP;
END;
/
```

Output:
Name = Atkinson, Job = ST_CLERK
Name = Bell, Job = SH_CLERK
Name = Bissot, Job = ST_CLERK
...
Name = Walsh, Job = SH_CLERK

TABLE 7-1 PL/SQL CODE EXPLAINED

Display Customer Information (Lines 7-32)
This procedure fetches information of the selected customer and presents it in a desirable format (as shown in Figure 7-7) using the CSS rules defined under the class CustomerInfo.

Declare (Line: 1)
This is the parent PL/SQL block. A nested block is also used under Display Current Order section on line:48.

l_customer_id varchar2(30) := :P11_CUSTOMER_ID; (Line: 2)
Assigns customer ID, retrieved from the previous order step (Page 11), to the variable l_customer_id. This variable is used ahead in a SQL statement to fetch details of the selected customer. In PL/SQL, := is called the assignment operator. The value of the variable that is being assigned the new value is placed on the left side of the assignment operator, and the value is placed on the right side of the operator.

:P11_CUSTOMER_ID is called a bind variable. Bind variables are substituion variables that are used in place of literals. You can use bind variables syntax anywhere in Oracle Application Express where you are using SQL or PL/SQL to reference session state of a specified item. For example:

SELECT * FROM employees WHERE last_name like '%' || :SEARCH_STRING || '%'

In this example, the search string is a page item. If the region type is defined as SQL Query, you can reference the value using standard SQL bind variable syntax. Using bind variables ensures that parsed representations of SQL queries are reused by the database, optimizing memory usage by the server.

The use of bind variables is encouraged in APEX. Bind variables help you protect your Oracle APEX application from SQL injection attacks. Bind variables work in much the same way as passing data to a stored procedure. Bind variables automatically treat all input data as "flat" data and never mistake it for SQL code. Besides the prevention of SQL injection attacks, there are other performance-related benefits to its use.

You declare a field item as a bind variable by prefixing a colon character (:), like this:
:P11_CUSTOMER_OPTIONS

When using bind variable syntax, remember the following rules:

- Bind variable names must correspond to an item name.
- Bind variable names are not case-sensitive.
- Bind variable names cannot be longer than 30 characters.

Although page item and application item names can be up to 255 characters, if you intend to use an application item within SQL using bind variable syntax, the item name must be 30 characters or less.

Begin (Line: 3)
Read What is PL/SQL at the beginning of this section.
The code block from line number 7 to 32 creates the first section on the page (marked as A in Figure 7-7) using the <div> HTML element, and styles it using Rule 1 and 2. The code between lines 9-20 is executed when the user selects an existing customer from the previous wizard step.

sys.htp.p('<div class="CustomerInfo">'); (Line: 7)
The <div> tag defines a division or a section in an HTML document. This is the opening tag which references the CustomerInfo class in CSS rules to format the following elements. The ending tag is defined on Line 32.

for x in (select * from demo_customers where customer_id = l_customer_id) loop (Line: 9)
Initiates the FOR loop to locate and fetch record of the selected customer from the demo_customers table.

sys.htp.p('<strong>Customer:</strong>'); (Line: 11)
Displays the label "Customer:" in bold.

sys.htp.p('<p>'); (Line: 12)
The paragraph opening tag. It ends on Line 19.

sys.htp.p(sys.htf.escape_sc(x.cust_first_name) || ' ' || sys.htf.escape_sc(x.cust_last_name) || '<br />'); (Line: 13)
Concatenates customer's first and last names using the concatenation characters (||). The <br /> tag inserts a single line break.

sys.htp.p(sys.htf.escape_sc(x.cust_street_address1) || '<br />'); (Line: 14)
Show customer's first address on a new line.

if x.cust_street_address2 is not null then (Lines: 15-17)
  sys.htp.p(sys.htf.escape_sc(x.cust_street_address2) || '<br />');
end if;
It's a condition to check whether the customer's second address is not null. If it's not, print it on a new line.

sys.htp.p(sys.htf.escape_sc(x.cust_city) || ', ' || sys.htf.escapte_sc(x.cust_state) || ' ' ||
sys.htf.escape_sc(x.cust_postal_code)); (Line: 18)
Displays city, state and postal code data on the same row separating each other with a comma and a blank space.

sys.htp.p('</p>'); (Line: 19)
The paragraph end tag.

end loop; (Line: 20)
The loop terminates here after fetching details of an existing customer from the database table.

sys.htp.p('</div>'); (Line: 32)
The div tag terminates here. The output of this section is illustrated in Figure 7-7: A - CustomerInfo. The ELSE block (line 22-30) is executed when a new customer is added to the database from the order interface. In that situation, all values on the current page are fetched from Page 11.

Display Products (Lines: 36-42)
Here you create a section on your web page to display all products along with their prices and include an option which allows users to add products to their cart.

sys.htp.p('<div class="Products" >'); (Line: 36)
Creates a division based on the Products class. HTML elements under this division are styled using rules 3-8.

sys.htp.p('<table width="100%" cellspacing="0" cellpadding="0" border="0"> (Line: 37)
Here you are initiating to draw an HTML table. The <table> tag defines an HTML table. An HTML table consists of the <table> element and one or more <tr>, <th>, and <td> elements. The <tr> element defines a table row, the <th> element defines a table header, and the <td> element defines a table cell. The Width attribute specifies the width of the table. Setting 100% width instructs the browser to consume the full screen width to display the table element.

<thead> (Line: 37)
   <tr><th class="left">Product</th><th>Price</th><th></th></tr>
</thead>
The <thead> tag is used to group header content in an HTML table. The <thead> element is used in conjunction with the <tbody> and <tfoot> elements to specify each part of a table (header, body, footer). The <tr> tag creates a row for column heading. The three <th> tags specify the headings i.e. Product, Price, and leaves the thrid column heading blank. A specific declaration (class="left") is included that points towards the CSS rule (8) div.Products .left{text-align:left;} to align the title of the first column (Product) to the left. The second column (Price) is styled using a general rule (5).

<tbody>'); (Line: 37)
The <tbody> tag is used to group the body content in an HTML table. This section spans till line 41, and is marked as B in Figure 7-7.

Chapter 7 – Taking Orders

```
for c1 in (select product_id, product_name, list_price, 'Add to Cart' add_to_order
from demo_product_info
where product_avail = 'Y'
order by product_name) loop  (Line: 38)
```
The FOR loop fetches Product ID, Product Name, and List Price columns from the products table. To display a button (Add) in the table, we appended a column aliased add_to_order and populated all rows with a constant value 'Add to Cart'. For information on FOR LOOP see Cursor FOR LOOP Statement section earlier in this section.

```
sys.htp.p('<tr><td class="left">' ||sys.htf.escape_sc(c1.product_name)||'</td>
          <td>'||trim(to_char(c1.list_price,'999G999G990D00')) || '</td>
          <td><a href="'||apex_util.prepare_url('f?p=&APP_ID.:12:'||:app_session||'
                :ADD:::P12_PRODUCT_ID:'|| c1.product_id)||'"
                class="t-Button t-Button--simple t-Button--hot">
                <span>Add<i class="iR"></i></span></a>
          </td>
        </tr>');  (Line: 39)
```
This line displays product name with respective price, in two separate columns. The product column is styled using Rule 8, while the price column is styled using Rule 5. There is a button (labeled Add) in the third column of the table, which is presented as a link using the HTML anchor tag <a> and is styled using a built-in class (t-Button). An anchor can be used in two ways:

1. To create a link to another document, by using the href attribute.
2. To create a bookmark inside a document, by using the name attribute.

It is usually referred to as a link or a hyperlink. The most important attribute of the <a> element is the href attribute, which specifies the URL of the page the link goes to. When this button is clicked, the product it represents is moved to the Current Order section with the help of a process (Add Product to the Order Collection) defined in section 7.6.8.

The c1 prefix in front of column names, points to the FOR LOOP cursor. The TRIM function in the expression, *trim(to_char(c1.list_price,'999G999G990D00'))*, takes a character expression and returns that expression with leading and/or trailing pad characters removed. This expression initially formats the list price column to add thousand separators and decimal place. Next, it converts the numeric price value to text expression using the TO_CHAR function and finally applies the TRIM function. The TO_CHAR function converts a DATETIME, number, or NTEXT expression to a TEXT expression in a specified format. The tables that follow lists the elements of a number format model that we used above, with some examples.

Element	Example	Description
0	0999	Returns leading zeros.
	9990	Returns trailing zeros.
9	9999	Returns value with the specified number of digits with a leading space if positive or with a leading minus if negative. Leading zeros are blank, except for a zero value, which returns a zero for the integer part of the fixed-point number.
D	99D99	Returns in the specified position the decimal character, which is the current value of the NLS_NUMERIC_CHARACTER parameter. The default is a period (.).
G	9G999	Returns the group separator (which is usually comma) in the specified position. You can specify multiple group separators in a number format model. Use the following SQL statement to check the current value for decimal and group separator characters: SELECT value FROM v$nls_parameters WHERE parameter='NLS_NUMERIC_CHARACTERS';

The code,
<a href="'||apex_util.prepare_url('f?p=&APP_ID.:12:'||:app_session||':ADD:::P12_PRODUCT_ID:'||
c1.product_id)||'" class="t-Button t-Button--simple t-Button--hot"> Add<iclass="iR"></i></a>,
creates a link with an ADD request. The value of REQUEST is the name of the button the user clicks. For example, suppose you have a button with a name of CHANGE, and a label Apply Change. When a user clicks the button, the value of REQUEST is CHANGE. In section 7.6.8, you will create the following process named Add product to the order collection.

```
for x in (select p.rowid, p.* from demo_product_info p where product_id = :P12_PRODUCT_ID)
loop
  select count(*)
  into l_count
  from wwv_flow_collections
  where collection_name = 'ORDER'
  and c001 = x.product_id;
  if l_count >= 10 then
    exit;
  end if;
  apex_collection.add_member(p_collection_name => 'ORDER',
    p_c001 => x.product_id,
    p_c002 => x.product_name,
    p_c003 => x.list_price,
    p_c004 => 1,
    p_c010 => x.rowid);
end loop;
```

During the process creation, you'll select Request=Value in Condition Type and will enter ADD for Value. The ADD request in the above <a> tag is referencing the same expression. When a user clicks the ADD button on the web page, the URL sends the ADD request to the above process along with the selected product ID. In turn, the process adds the product to the Current Order section. The URL generated from this code looks something like this at runtime: f?p=64699:12:13238397476902:ADD:::P12_PRODUCT_ID:10

end loop; (Line: 40)
End of FOR loop.

sys.htp.p('</tbody></table>'); (Line: 41)
Table and body closing tags.

sys.htp.p('</div>'); (Line: 42)
The closing div tag.

Chapter 7 – Taking Orders

Display Current Order (Lines: 46-79)
This section acts as a shopping cart. Products selected by users are placed in this section.

sys.htp.p('<div class="Products" >'); (Line: 46)
Defines the <div> tag and utilizes the Products class referenced in rules 3-8.

sys.htp.p('<table width="100%" cellspacing="0" cellpadding="0" border="0">
 <thead>
  <tr><th class="left">Current Order</th></tr>
 </thead>
</table> (Line: 47)
Displays section heading as follows in the first row of a separate table.

Current Order

Declare (Line: 48)
This is the nested or child block. To nest a block means to embed one or more PL/SQL block inside another PL/SQL block to have better control over program's execution.

c number := 0; t number := 0; (Line: 49)
Declared two numeric counter variables and initialized them with zero. The variable c is used to evaluate whether any product is selected in the current order while the variable t stores total value for the order.

Begin (Line: 50)

for c1 in (select c001 pid, c002 i, to_number(c003) p, count(c002) q, sum(c003) ep, 'Remove' remove
        from apex_collections
        where collection_name = 'ORDER'
        group by c001, c002, c003
        order by c001)
loop (Line: 52)
Collection enables you to temporarily capture one or more non-scalar values. You can use collections to store rows and columns currently in session state so they can be accessed, manipulated, or processed during a user's specific session. You can think of a collection as a bucket in which you temporarily store and name rows of information.

Every collection contains a named list of data elements (or members) which can have up to 50 character attributes (varchar2 (4000)), 5 number, 5 date, 1 XML type, 1 BLOB, and 1 CLOB attribute. You insert, update, and delete collection information using the PL/SQL API APEX_COLLECTION.

When you create a new collection, you must give it a name that cannot exceed 255 characters. Note that collection names are not case-sensitive and will be converted to uppercase. Once the collection is named, you can access the values (members of a collection) in the collection by running a SQL query against the database view APEX_COLLECTIONS.

The APEX_COLLECTIONS view has the following definition:

COLLECTION_NAME	NOT NULL VARCHAR2(255)
SEQ_ID	NOT NULL NUMBER
C001	VARCHAR2(4000)
C002	VARCHAR2(4000)
C003	VARCHAR2(4000)
C004	VARCHAR2(4000)
C005	VARCHAR2(4000)
...	
C050	VARCHAR2(4000)
N001	NUMBER
N002	NUMBER
N003	NUMBER
N004	NUMBER
N005	NUMBER
CLOB001	CLOB
BLOB001	BLOB
XMLTYPE001	XMLTYPE
MD5_ORIGINAL	VARCHAR2(4000)

Use the APEX_COLLECTIONS view in an application just as you would use any other table or view in an application, for example:

SELECT c001, c002, c003, n001, clob001   FROM APEX_collections WHERE collection_name = 'DEPARTMENTS'

Note that you can't read apex_collection using external tools. A collection is related to an APEX session and not available outside of it. However, using the following statement you can query WWV_FLOW_COLLECTION_MEMBERS$. It is into this table that APEX stores its collection data. Add Men Shoes to the Current Order section on the Select Items page. Connect to the SQL Command Line utility as sys/manager and issue the following statement in a SQL Command Line session:

Select c001,c002,c003,c004 from APEX_040200.wwv_flow_collection_members$;
Output:
   c001=9 (product id), c002=Men Shoes (product), c003=110 (list price), and c004=1 (quantity)

The CREATE_OR_TRUNCATE_COLLECTION method creates a new collection if the named collection does not exist. If the named collection already exists, this method truncates it. Truncating a collection empties it, but leaves it in place.

In section 7.5.12, we created a process named Create or Truncate Order Collection under page rendering section and used the following statement to create a collection named ORDER:

   apex_collection.create_or_truncate_collection (p_collection_name => 'ORDER');

In the above (For C1 in) loop, we're selecting records from the same ORDER collection. Columns from apex_collections in the SELECT statement correspond to:

Column	Corresponds To
C001 – pid	Product ID (9)
C002 – i	Product Name (Men Shoes)
C003 – p	List Price (110)
C002 - q	Quantity (1)
C003 - ep	Extended Price (110) This value will increase with each Add button click to accumulate total cost of a product.

sys.htp.p('<div class="CartItem"> (Line: 53)
This line references another class (CartItem) to style the actual Current Order section.

**<a href="'||apex_util.prepare_url('f?p=&APP_ID.:12:&SESSION.:REMOVE:::P12_PRODUCT_ID:'||sys.htf.escape_sc(c1.pid))||'"><img src="#IMAGE_PREFIX#delete.gif" alt="Remove from cart" title="Remove from cart" /> </a> ** (Line: 54)
The above <a> tag creates a link with a REMOVE request. This time it uses product ID from the collection. In section 7.6.8 (B), there is a process named Remove product from the order collection (as shown below) where the request expression is set to REMOVE.

```
for x in
 (select seq_id, c001 from apex_collections
    where collection_name = 'ORDER' and c001 = :P12_PRODUCT_ID)
loop
apex_collection.delete_member(p_collection_name => 'ORDER', p_seq => x.seq_id);
end loop;
```

In HTML, images are defined with the <img> tag. The <img> tag has no closing tag. To display an image on a page, you need to use the src attribute. Src stands for "source". The value of the src attribute is the URL of the image you want to display.

Syntax for defining an image:
<img src="url" alt="some_text"/>

The URL points to the location where the image is stored. The value of IMAGE_PREFIX determines the virtual path the Web server uses to point to the images directory distributed with Oracle Application Express. We used "delete.gif" that is displayed in front of product name. The required alt attribute specifies an alternate text for an image, if the image cannot be displayed.

When a user clicks the remove link [**X**] in the Current Order section, the above URL sends a REMOVE request to the above process along with the product ID. The DELETE_MEMBER procedure deletes a specified member from a given named collection using the p_seq => x.seq_id parameter which is the sequence ID of the collection member to be deleted.

'||sys.htf.escape_sc(c1.i)||' (Line: 55)
Displays name of the selected product in the Current Order section.

<span>'||trim(to_char(c1.p,'$999G999G999D00'))||'</span> (Line: 56)
<span>Quantity: '||c1.q||'</span> (Line: 57)
<span class="subtotal">Subtotal: '||trim(to_char(c1.ep,'$999G999G999D00'))||'</span> (Line: 58)
The above three lines display price, quantity, and sub-total of the selected product in the Current Order section as shown below:

```
            $125.00
         Quantity: 10
Subtotal: $1,250.00
```

</div>'); (Line: 59)
The ending div tag.

c := c + 1; (Line: 60)
This counter increments the value of c with 1 at the end of each loop. The variable c is used to calculate number of items selected in the current order.

t := t + c1.ep; (Line: 61)
Similar to the variable c, t is also incremented to sum up extended price **(c1.ep)** in order to calculate total order value.

```
if c > 0 then
   sys.htp.p('<div class="CartTotal">
     <p>Items: <span>'||c||'</span></p>
     <p class="CartTotal">Total: <span>'||trim(to_char(t,'$999G999G999D00'))||'</span></p>
   </div>');
else
   sys.htp.p('<div class="alertMessage info" style="margin-top: 8px;">');
      sys.htp.p('<img src="#IMAGE_PREFIX#f_spacer.gif">');
      sys.htp.p('<div class="innerMessage">');
         sys.htp.p('<h3>Note</h3>');
         sys.htp.p('<p>You have no items in your current order.</p>');
      sys.htp.p('</div>');
   sys.htp.p('</div>');
end if; (Line: 64-77)
```

The condition (IF c > 0) evaluates whether a product is selected in the current order. A value other than zero in this variable indicates addition of product(s). If the current order has some items added, show the label Total: along with the value, which is stored in the variable t. If no items are selected, show the message defined in the else block using built-in classes.

7.6.5 Create Hidden Items

Create a hidden item in Select Items region to store product ID.

Attribute	Value
Name	P12_PRODUCT_ID
Type	Hidden

7.6.6 Create Region to hold Buttons

Right click on Wizard Buttons node and select **Create Region**. Enter **Buttons** for the Title of this region, and set its Template to **Buttons Container**. The region will hold three buttons: Cancel, Previous, and Next. These buttons are created in the next section.

7.6.7 Create Buttons

All the three buttons created in this section have one thing in common, and that is the Action attribute, which is set to Submit Page. When you click any of these three buttons, the page is submitted and a corresponding branch (created in section 7.6.10) is fired to take you to the specified location. For example, if you click the Cancel button, the corresponding branch takes you back to the main Orders page (Page 4). Right click the new Buttons region node and select **Create Button**. Set the following attributes for the new button:

Attribute	Value	Attribute	Value
Button Name	CANCEL	Button Position	Close
Label	Cancel	Action	Submit Page (default)

Create another button under the Cancel button, and set the following attributes:

Attribute	Value	Attribute	Value
Button Name	PREVIOUS	Button Template	Icon
Label	Previous	Icon CSS Classes	fa-chevron-left
Button Position	Previous	Action	Submit Page (default)

Create one more button under the Previous button, and set the following attributes:

Attribute	Value	Attribute	Value
Button Name	NEXT	Hot	Yes
Label	Place Order	Icon CSS Classes	fa-chevron-right
Button Position	Next	Action	Submit Page (default)
Button Template	Text with Icon	-	-

7.6.8 Create Processes

The two processes created in this section handle the routine to either add a product to the Current Order section or remove one from it. The add_member function references the collection (ORDER created in section 7.5.12) to populate the collection with a new product. In Table 7-1, the link defined on line 39 in the PL/SQL code forwards an ADD request, which is entertained here after evaluating the request in step 4 below.

A. Add Product to the Order Collection

1. Expand Pre-Rendering node (on the Rendering tab) and create a process under Before Header node.
2. Enter **Add Product to the ORDER Collection** for the name of the new process, and set its Type to **PL/SQL Code**.
3. Enter the following code in PL/SQL Code box:

```
declare
 l_count number := 0;
begin
for x in (select p.rowid, p.* from demo_product_info p where product_id = :P12_PRODUCT_ID)
loop
  select count(*)
  into l_count
  from wwv_flow_collections
  where collection_name = 'ORDER'
  and c001 = x.product_id;
  if l_count >= 10 then
    exit;
  end if;
  apex_collection.add_member(p_collection_name => 'ORDER',
    p_c001 => x.product_id,
    p_c002 => x.product_name,
    p_c003 => x.list_price,
    p_c004 => 1,
    p_c010 => x.rowid);
end loop;
end;
```

4. In Conditions section, set Type to **Request=Value** and enter **ADD** in the Value box.

Chapter 7 – Taking Orders

The delete_member function is just opposite to the add_member function. It is called by a link (Table 7-1 line 54), which carries a REMOVE request. The request is evaluated by a condition, set in Step 3 below. If the request matches, the selected product is deleted from the ORDER collection.

B. Remove Product from the Order Collection

1. **Create** another process under the previous one. Name it **Remove Product from the ORDER Collection** and set its Type to **PL/SQL Code**.
2. Enter the following code in PL/SQL Code box:

```
for x in
  (select seq_id, c001 from apex_collections
    where collection_name = 'ORDER' and c001 = :P12_PRODUCT_ID)
loop
  apex_collection.delete_member(p_collection_name => 'ORDER', p_seq => x.seq_id);
end loop;
```

3. In Conditions section, set Type to **Request=Value** and enter **REMOVE** in the Value box.

7.6.9 Create Process – Place Order

After selecting products for an order, you click the Next button. The process defined in this section is associated with the Next button. The PL/SQL code specified in this process adds new customer and order information in relevant database tables using SQL INSERT statements. After committing the DML statement, the process truncates the ORDER collection.

1. In the Processing tab, create a new process under Processing node.
2. Enter **Place Order** for the name of the new process, and set its Type to **PL/SQL Code**. Enter the following code in PL/SQL Code box. Also select **NEXT** for When Button Pressed attribute.

```
declare
  l_order_id    number;
  l_customer_id varchar2(30) := :P11_CUSTOMER_ID;
begin
-- Create New Customer
  if :P11_CUSTOMER_OPTIONS = 'NEW' then
    insert into DEMO_CUSTOMERS (
      CUST_FIRST_NAME, CUST_LAST_NAME, CUST_STREET_ADDRESS1,
      CUST_STREET_ADDRESS2, CUST_CITY, CUST_STATE, CUST_POSTAL_CODE,
      CUST_EMAIL, PHONE_NUMBER1, PHONE_NUMBER2, URL, CREDIT_LIMIT, TAGS)
    values (
      :P11_CUST_FIRST_NAME, :P11_CUST_LAST_NAME, :P11_CUST_STREET_ADDRESS1,
      :P11_CUST_STREET_ADDRESS2, :P11_CUST_CITY, :P11_CUST_STATE,
      :P11_CUST_POSTAL_CODE, :P11_CUST_EMAIL, :P11_PHONE_NUMBER1,
      :P11_PHONE_NUMBER2, :P11_URL, :P11_CREDIT_LIMIT, :P11_TAGS)
    returning customer_id into l_customer_id;
    :P11_CUSTOMER_ID := l_customer_id;
  end if;
```

```
-- Insert a row into the Order Header table
   insert into demo_orders(customer_id, order_total, order_timestamp, user_name)
   values (l_customer_id, null, systimestamp, upper(:APP_USER))
   returning order_id into l_order_id;
   commit;
-- Loop through the ORDER collection and insert rows into the Order Line Item table
   for x in (select c001, c003, sum(c004) c004 from apex_collections
        where collection_name = 'ORDER' group by c001, c003) loop
     insert into demo_order_items(order_item_id, order_id, product_id, unit_price, quantity)
     values (null, l_order_id, to_number(x.c001), to_number(x.c003),to_number(x.c004));
   end loop;
   commit;
-- Set the item P14_ORDER_ID to the order which was just placed
   :P14_ORDER_ID := l_order_id;
-- Truncate the collection after the order has been placed
   apex_collection.truncate_collection(p_collection_name => 'ORDER');
end;
```

7.6.10 Create Branches

Create the following three branches under After Processing node in the Processing tab. The buttons referenced in these branches were created in section 7.6.7.

Attribute	Value	Attribute	Value
Name	Go To Page 14	Name	P14_CUSTOMER_ID
Target Type	Page in this Application	Value	&P12_CUSTOMER_ID.
Page	14	When Button Pressed	NEXT

Attribute	Value	Attribute	Value
Name	Go To Page 4	Page	4
Target Type	Page in this Application	When Button Pressed	CANCEL

Attribute	Value	Attribute	Value
Name	Go To Page 11	Page	11
Type (Behavior)	Page or URL (redirect)	When Button Pressed	PREVIOUS
Target	Page in this Application	-	-

Test Your Work

Navigate to the Orders page using the Home menu route and click the button **Enter New Order**. Select a customer using the Existing Customer option and click Next. Click the Add button next to Business Shirt to add this product to the Current Order pane. Click the Add button for Business Shirt again and see increase in Quantity and Total. Add few more products and observe the change in the Current Order section. Click the cross sign ✕ to remove a product from the section.

Click the Place Order button. This action will result in an error (ERR-1002 Unable to find item ID for item "P14_ORDER_ID" in application "64699") indicating missing Page 14 - the Order Summary page. In the next sections you will create this page to complete the order placement module.

Chapter 7 – Taking Orders

7.7 Create Order Summary Page - Page 14

After adding products to the Order form, you click the Place Order button. The next page, Order Summary, comes up to show details of the placed order. In this section, you are going to create this page. It is the last step in the order creation wizard.

1. Create one more **Blank Page**.
2. Complete the first wizard step as show in the adjacent figure and click **Next**.
3. On the Navigation Menu page, set Navigation Preference to **Identify an existing navigation menu entry for this page**, and set Existing Navigation Menu Entry to **Orders**. Click **Next**.
4. Click **Finish** to end the wizard.
5. Click on the root node (Page 14: Order Summary) and set Dialog Template to **Wizard Modal Dialog**.

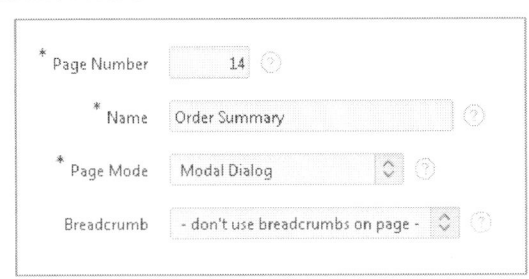

7.7.1 Create Region – Order Progress

Right click on the Wizard Progress Bar node and select **Create Region**. Set the following attributes for the new region.

Attribute	Value	Attribute	Value
Title	Order Progress	Template	Blank with Attributes
Type	List	List Template (under Attributes node)	Wizard Progress
List	Order Wizard	-	-

7.7.2 Create Region – Order Header

Right click Wizard Body node and select **Create Region**. Set the following attributes for this region. Just like section 7.6.4, you defined the region as PL/SQL Dynamic Content which is based on PL/SQL that enable you to render any HTML or text using the PL/SQL Web Toolkit.

Attribute	Value
Title	Order Header
Type	PL/SQL Dynamic Content

PL/SQL Code	begin
	for x in (select c.cust_first_name, c.cust_last_name, cust_street_address1,
	cust_street_address2, cust_city, cust_state, cust_postal_code from demo_customers c,
	demo_orders o
	where c.customer_id = o.customer_id and o.order_id = :P14_ORDER_ID)
	loop
	  htp.p('\<span style="font-size:16px;font-weight:bold;"\>ORDER #' ||
	     sys.htf.escape_sc(:P14_ORDER_ID) || '\</span\>\<br /\>');
	  htp.p(sys.htf.escape_sc(x.cust_first_name) || ' ' || sys.htf.escape_sc(x.cust_last_name) ||
	     '\<br /\>');
	  htp.p(sys.htf.escape_sc(x.cust_street_address1) || '\<br /\>');
	  if x.cust_street_address2 is not null then
	    htp.p(sys.htf.escape_sc(x.cust_street_address2) || '\<br /\>');
	  end if;
	  htp.p(sys.htf.escape_sc(x.cust_city) || ', ' || sys.htf.escape_sc(x.cust_state) || ' ' ||
	     sys.htf.escape_sc(x.cust_postal_code) || '\<br /\>\<br /\>');
	end loop;
	end;

7.7.3 Create Region – Order Lines

Add another region under Wizard Body node and set the following attributes for this region. After creating this region expand its Columns node and set appropriate headings for each column. This region will carry line item information.

Attribute	Value
Title	Order Lines
Type	Classic Report
PL/SQL Code	select p.product_name, oi.unit_price, oi.quantity, (oi.unit_price * oi.quantity) extended_price from demo_order_items oi, demo_product_info p where oi.product_id = p.product_id and oi.order_id = :P14_ORDER_ID

7.7.4 Create Item

Right click Order Lines region and select **Create Page Item**. Set the following attributes for the new item. The value for this item was set in the PL/SQL code defined in section 7.6.9, and was utilized in the codes defined in section 7.7.2 and in section 7.7.3 to fetch order information.

Attribute	Value	Attribute	Value
Name	P14_ORDER_ID	Type	Hidden

Create another item in the same region and set the following attributes. This item will carry customer's id provided to it by the branch created in section 7.6.10.

Attribute	Value	Attribute	Value
Name	P14_CUSTOMER_ID	Type	Hidden

7.7.5 Create Region – Buttons

Right click Wizard Buttons node and select **Create Region**. Enter **Buttons** for its name and set its Template to **Buttons Container**. The region will hold the following three buttons.

7.7.6 Create Button

Right click the new Buttons region node and select **Create Button**. Set the following attributes for the new button:

Attribute	Value	Attribute	Value
Button Name	BACK	Action	Redirect to Page in this Application
Label	Back To Orders	Target Type	Page in this application
Button Position	Next	Page	4
Button Template	Text	Reset Pagination	Yes
Hot	Yes	-	-

Chapter 7 – Taking Orders

Complete Testing

Congratulation! You have completed the most tiresome but interesting chapter of the book that taught you many new techniques. It is the time to test the whole work you performed in this chapter.

1. Move to the application's **Home page**.
2. Click the **Orders** menu and then click the **Enter New Order** button.
3. Select **New Customer**.
4. **Fill in the New Customer form** using your own name, address etc. and click **Next**.
5. In Select Item page **add few products** to the Current Order pane.
6. Click the **Place Order** button to see the Order Summary Page resembling Figure 7-8.

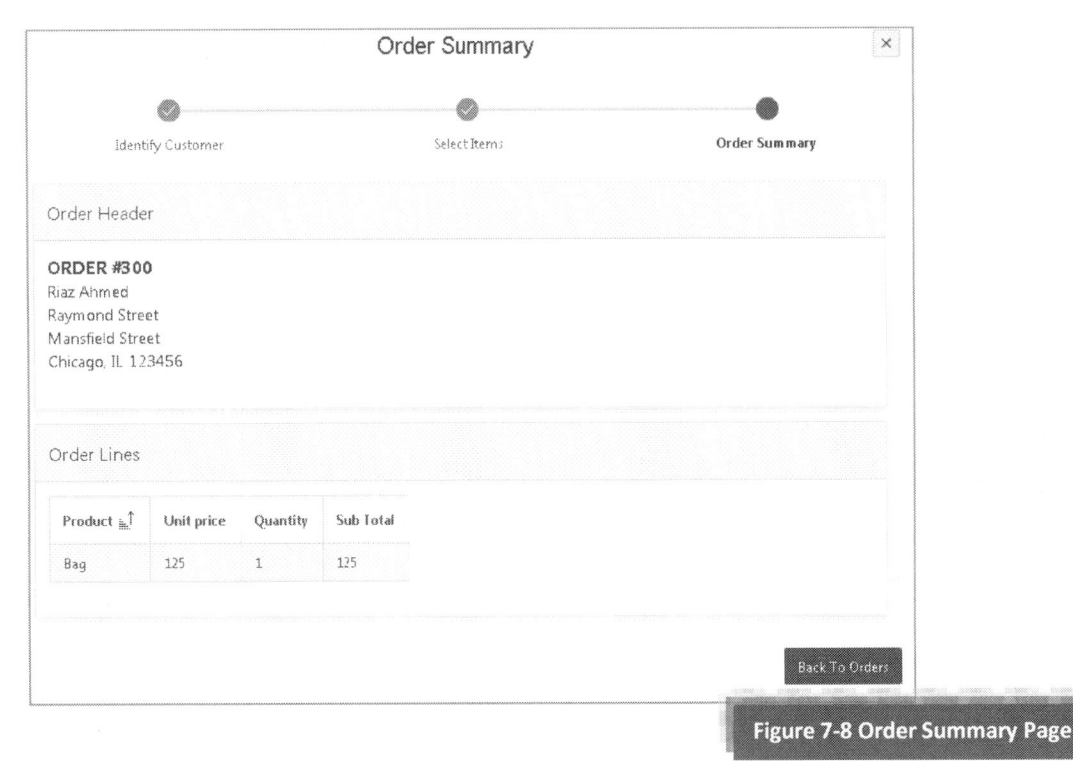

Figure 7-8 Order Summary Page

7. Click **Back To Orders** button in the Order Summary Page to return to the Orders main page. The newly created order will appear in the orders list.
8. Click the number of the new order to modify it in Order Details page (Page 29). Try to add or remove products on this page and save your modifications.
9. Also try the delete operation by deleting this new order.

Summary

I know that as a beginner you might be confused with the stuff described in section 7.5 onward. I added this stuff purposely to present something that would be helpful to you in your future endeavors. It is perfectly OK if you omit these sections at this stage and confine yourself to section 7.4.2 to manipulate order information using Page 4 and Page 29 only.

Chapter 8
Present Data Graphically

Chapter 8 – Present Data Graphically

8.1 About Oracle APEX Reports

Presenting data in Oracle APEX, either graphically or in text format, is as easy as creating the input forms. While creating the Order module in the previous chapter, you have had some glimpses of these report types and had some hands-on exposure while working on the interactive reports. Again, the wizards make it so easy to create flexible and powerful reports in Oracle Application Express. In this chapter, you will take a step forward to create the following reports to graphically present the sales application data:

Report	Purpose	Page No.
Customer Orders	Show total orders placed by each customer	17
Sales By Category and Product	Display sales for category and products	16
Sales by Category / Month	Total monthly sales for each category	5
Order Calendar	Show orders in a calendar view	10
Customer Map	Show orders in different states with the help of a map	15
Product Order Tree	Display orders data in a tree view	19

While creating the above reports, you will set the following attributes for your charts.

- **Hints** - Specify whether to display hint text on your chart. Hint text displays when a user's mouse hovers over the chart's data.
- **Values** - Specify whether to display values on your chart. Values are derived from your chart query and display next to your chart data.
- **Labels** - Specify whether to display labels on your chart. Labels are derived from your chart query and display along a chart axis.
- **Show Scrollbars** - Specify whether to display a scrollbar on your chart. Choose X-Axis to display the X-Axis scrollbar on the chart. Choose Y-Axis to display the Y-Axis scrollbar on the chart. Choose Both to display a scrollbar for both axes on the chart.
- **Show Grid** - Specify whether to display a value grid on your chart. Choose X-Axis to display the X-Axis grid on the chart. Choose Y-Axis to display the Y-Axis grid on the chart. Choose Both to display the grid for both axes on the chart.
- **Show Legend** - Specify whether to display a legend for your chart. Choose Left, Right, Top, Bottom or Float to specify where to display the legend.
- **Color Scheme** - Select a pre-built color scheme for your chart. Charts with a single series use one color for each datapoint, while charts with multiple series use one color for each series. The Look 7 scheme will use the AnyChart default palette of colors, applying a different color to each datapoint in a single series. If you wish to define your own color schemes, you can select Custom option and define your own set of colors in Custom Colors.

8.2 Create Reports List Page

Prior to creating reports, you will create a page to list all the report options available in the application. The page will appear when you click the Reports option in the main navigation menu.

1. Create a **Blank Page** and set the following attributes for it:

Attribute	Value
Page Number	26
Name	Reports
Page Mode	Normal
Breadcrumb	do not add breadcrumb...
Navigation Preference	Identify an existing navigation menu entry for this page
Existing Navigation Menu Entry	Reports

2. Right click the Body node and select **Create Region**. Set the following attributes for the new region:

Attribute	Value
Title	Reports
Type	List
List	Reports List *(created in chapter 3 section 3.2.2)*

3. Click on the Attributes node under the Reports region and set the following attributes:

Attribute	Value
List Template	Media List *(you are free to test other available options)*
Layout (Template Options)	2 Column Grid

8.3 Customer Orders Report - Page 17

This graphical report is based on a horizontal bar chart to display the amount of orders placed by each customer. Each bar in the chart has multiple slices that represent amount of different orders. When you move your mouse over these slices, a tooltip displays the corresponding amount. The chart will be created with drill-down functionality. That is, when you click a slice, you'll be taken to Page 7 where you will see profile of the selected customer.

1. Create a **Blank Page** and set the following attributes for it:

Attribute	Value
Page Number	17
Name	Customer Orders
Page Mode	Normal
Breadcrumb	do not add breadcrumb...
Navigation Preference	Identify an existing navigation menu entry for this page
Existing Navigation Menu Entry	Reports

2. Right click the Body node and select **Create Region**. Set the following attributes for the new region. Immediately after switching the region's Type, a new node named Series along with a child node (New) is added under the region.

Attribute	Value
Title	Customer Orders
Type	Chart

Chapter 8 – Present Data Graphically

3. Click on **Attributes** node under Customer Orders chart region and set the following attributes:

Attribute	Value	Attribute	Value
Type	Stacked Bar Chart	Title (X Axis)	Customers
Title	*Make it empty*	Title (Y Axis)	Order Total
Rendering	HTML5 Chart	Show (Value)	No
3D Mode	Yes	Show (Legend)	Bottom
Show Grid	Both	Title (Legend)	Categories
Width	800	Element Orientation	Horizontal
Height	500	-	-

4. Click on the **New** node under the Series node and enter the following SQL query. The first column is created as a link. As mentioned earlier, when you click a chart slice, you're drilled down to Page 7 to browse customer details.

Attribute	Value
Source Type	SQL Query
SQL Query	select 'f?p=&APP_ID.:7:'||:app_session||':::7:P7_CUSTOMER_ID:'||c.customer_id||':' link, c.cust_last_name||', '||c.cust_first_name Customer_Name, sum (decode(p.category,'Accessories',oi.quantity * oi.unit_price,0)) "Accessories", sum (decode(p.category,'Mens',oi.quantity * oi.unit_price,0)) "Men", sum (decode(p.category,'Womens',oi.quantity * oi.unit_price,0)) "Women" from demo_customers c, demo_orders o, demo_order_items oi, demo_product_info p where c.customer_id = o.customer_id and o.order_id = oi.order_id and oi.product_id = p.product_id group by c.customer_id, c.cust_last_name, c.cust_first_name order by c.cust_last_name

Save your work and run the page. You will see a chart as shown in Figure 8-1. Move your cursor over the chart bars and different portions within a particular bar. You will see a tooltip showing order amount of the corresponding customer.

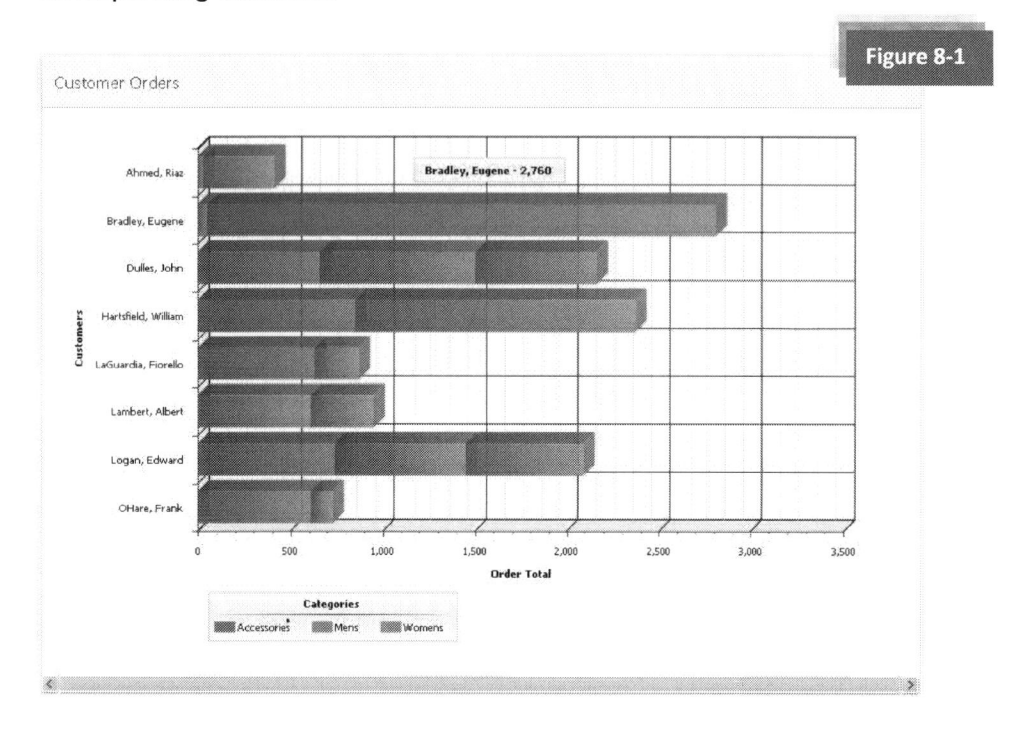

Figure 8-1

8.4 Sales by Category and Product Report - Page 16

In this report, you'll present Category and Product sales data in two different regions with different charting options.

1. Create a **Blank Page** and set the following attributes for it:

Attribute	Value
Page Number	16
Name	Sales by Category and Product
Page Mode	Normal
Breadcrumb	do not add breadcrumb...
Navigation Preference	Identify an existing navigation menu entry for this page
Existing Navigation Menu Entry	Reports

2. Right click the Body node and select **Create Region**. Set the following attributes for the new region.

Attribute	Value	Attribute	Value
Title	Sales by Category	Type	Chart

3. Click on the **Attributes** node under the Sales by Category region and set the following attributes:

Attribute	Value	Attribute	Value
Type	Pie	3D Mode	Yes
Title	*Make it empty*	Width	600
Rendering	HTML5 Chart	Height	300

4. Click on the **New** node under the Series node and enter the following SQL query.

Attribute	Value
Source Type	SQL Query
SQL Query	select null, p.category label, sum(o.order_total) total_sales from demo_orders o, demo_order_items oi, demo_product_info p where o.order_id = oi.order_id and oi.product_id = p.product_id group by category order by 3 desc

    > **NOTE:** In the SQL SELECT statement the link column is replaced with a null to follow the APEX chart syntax rule.
    > The syntax is:
    > *SELECT link, label, value*
    > *FROM ...*

5. Create another region under the Body node and set the following attributes:

Attribute	Value
Title	Sales by Product
Type	Chart

6. Click on the Attributes node under the Sales by Product region and set the following attributes:

Attribute	Value	Attribute	Value
Type	Bar Chart	Height	300
Title	*Make it empty*	Scheme	Look 7
Rendering	HTML5 Chart	Title (X Axis)	Products
3D Mode	Yes	Title (Y Axis)	Total Sales
Show Grid	Both	Show (Value)	No
Width	600	-	-

7. Click on the New node under Series and enter the following SQL query.

Attribute	Value
Source Type	SQL Query
SQL Query	select 'f?p=&APP_ID.:6:'||:app_session||':::6:P6_PRODUCT_ID:'||p.product_id||':' link, p.product_name ||' [$'||p.list_price||']' product, SUM(oi.quantity * oi.unit_price) sales from demo_order_items oi, demo_product_info p where oi.product_id = p.product_id group by p.product_id, p.product_name, p.list_price order by 3 desc, 1

Save and run the page to see the charts similar to Figure 8-2. The page has two regions, containing graphical data for category and product sales. Move the mouse cursor over each bar and see respective sales figures. Click on the bar representing Bag's data, the system will drill you down to the products page to show you the selected product's details.

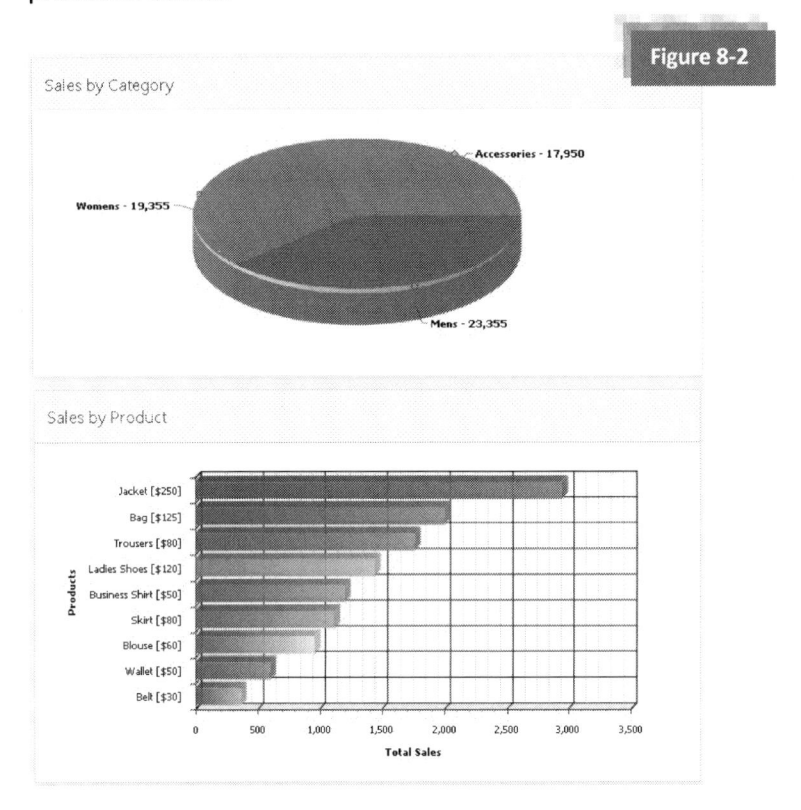

Figure 8-2

8.5 Sales by Category / Month Report - Page 5

This chart is added to present category sales in each month. In this graphical report, you will make use of Region Display Selector to display two different views of category sales data. Region Display Selector region enables you to include show and hide controls for each region on a page. This page will have two regions, containing two different chart types. After adding the Region Display Selector and the two regions, you can switch the regions using the selector appearing on top of the page – as shown in Figure 8-3.

1. Create a **Blank Page** and set the following attributes for it:

Attribute	Value
Page Number	5
Name	Sales by Category Per Month
Page Mode	Normal
Breadcrumb	do not add breadcrumb...
Navigation Preference	Identify an existing navigation menu entry for this page
Existing Navigation Menu Entry	Reports

2. Right click the Body node and select **Create Region**. Set the following attributes for the new region.

Attribute	Value
Title	Region Display Selector
Type	Region Display Selector
Template	-Select- *(i.e. no template selected)*

3. Create another region under the Body node and set the following attributes:

Attribute	Value
Title	Sales by Category (Line)
Type	D3 Line Chart [Plug-In] *(imported in Chapter 3 section 3.5.1)*

SQL Query	select trunc(o.order_timestamp) when,
	        sum (oi.quantity * oi.unit_price) sales,
	        p.category type
	from demo_product_info p, demo_order_items oi,
	        demo_orders o
	where oi.product_id = p.product_id and
	        o.order_id = oi.order_id
	group by p.category, trunc(o.order_timestamp),
	        to_char(o.order_timestamp, 'YYYYMM')
	order by to_char(o.order_timestamp, 'YYYYMM')

4. Click on the **Attributes** node under Sales by Category (Line) chart region and set the following attributes:

Attribute	Value	Attribute	Value
X Values Column	WHEN	X-Axis Data Type	Date
Y Values Column	SALES	X-Axis Tick Interval	Week
Multiple Series Column	TYPE	X-Axis Value Format Mask	12 Jan 2000
X-Axis Title	Date	Y-Axis Value Format Mask	$14,435
Y-Axis Title	Sales	Color Scheme	Modern 2
Tooltips	Check Show Series Name, Show X Value, Show Y Value		

5. Create another region under the Body node and set the following attributes:

Attribute	Value
Title	Sales by Month (Bar)
Type	Chart

6. Click on the Attributes node under Sales by Month chart region and set the following attributes:

Attribute	Value	Attribute	Value
Type	Column	Title (X Axis)	Month
Title	*Make it empty*	Title (Y Axis)	Amount
Rendering	HTML5 Chart	Show (Value)	No
3D Mode	Yes	Show (Legend)	Right
Show Grid	Both	Title (Legend)	Categories
Scheme	Look 6	-	-

Chapter 8 – Present Data Graphically

7. Click on the New node under Series and enter the following SQL query.

Attribute	Value
Source Type	SQL Query

SQL Query	select null, to_char(o.order_timestamp, 'MON RRRR') label,
	       sum (decode(p.category,'Accessories',oi.quantity * oi.unit_price,0)) "Accessories",
	       sum (decode(p.category,'Mens',oi.quantity * oi.unit_price,0)) "Men",
	       sum (decode(p.category,'Womens',oi.quantity * oi.unit_price,0)) "Women"
	from demo_product_info p, demo_order_items oi, demo_orders o
	where oi.product_id = p.product_id and o.order_id = oi.order_id
	group by to_char(o.order_timestamp, 'MON RRRR'), to_char(o.order_timestamp, 'RRRR MM')
	order by to_char(o.order_timestamp, 'RRRR MM')

The output of this graphical report is illustrated below. The two charts display comparative sales figures for each category during a month. Click all three options (individually) in Region Selector Toolbar and observe the change.

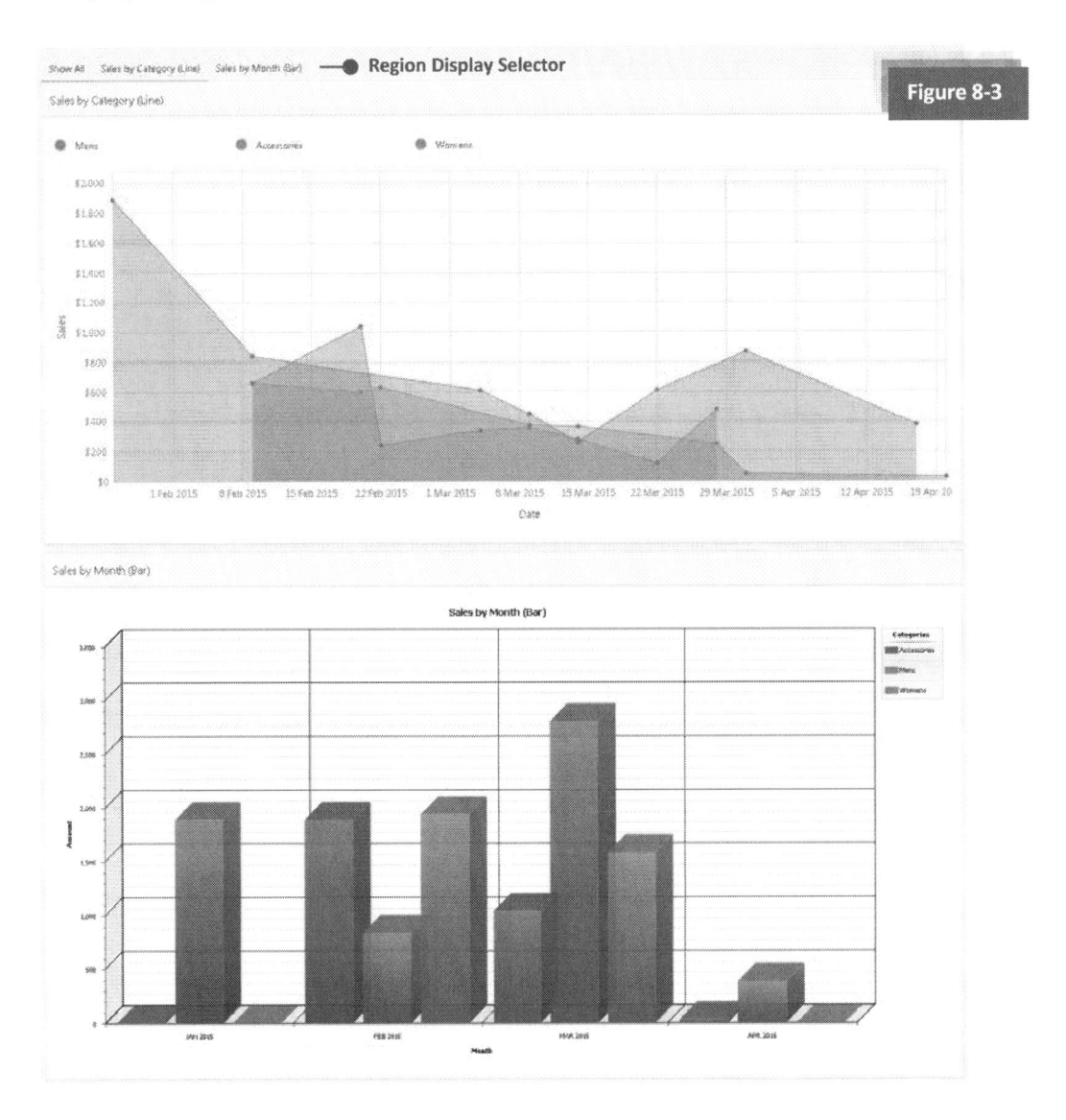

Figure 8-3

8.6 Order Calendar Report - Page 10

In this report, orders will be displayed in a calendar. APEX includes a built-in wizard for generating a calendar with monthly, daily, and list options. Execute the following steps to create a calendar report.

1. Create a new page.
2. Click on **Calendar** icon.
3. On the next page, select the **Calendar** option. The other option is Legacy Calendar, which will be deprecated in the future release.
4. Fill in the next couple of pages according to the following table and click **Next**.

Attribute	Value
Page Number	10
Name	Order Calendar
Page Mode	Normal
Region Name	Order Calendar
Breadcrumb	do not add breadcrumb...
Navigation Preference	Identify an existing navigation menu entry for this page
Existing Navigation Menu Entry	Reports

5. On the Source page, select the second option **SQL Query**, put the following query in Enter Region Source box and move on.

```
select order_id,
       (select cust_first_name||' '||cust_last_name from demo_customers c
        where c.customer_id = o.customer_id )
        ||' ['||to_char(order_total,'FML999G999G999G999G990D00')||']' customer,
       order_timestamp
from demo_orders o
```

7. Set attributes in the next screen as follows. The Date Column attribute specifies which column is used as the date to place an entry on the calendar while the Display Column specifies the column to be displayed on the calendar.

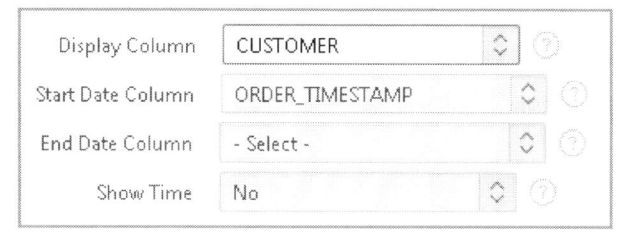

Display Column	CUSTOMER
Start Date Column	ORDER_TIMESTAMP
End Date Column	- Select -
Show Time	No

8. After completing all the wizard steps, click on the Attributes node under Order Calendar region. In the Properties pane, click on **View/Edit Link** attribute and set the following attributes to create a link. The link will drill-down to Order Details (Page 29) to show details of the selected order.

Attribute	Value	Attribute	Value
Target Type	Page in this application	Name	P29_ORDER_ID
Page	29	Value	&ORDER_ID.

9. In the Properties pane, click on **Create Link** attribute and set the following attributes to create another link. This attribute is used to create a link to call Page 11 to enter a new order.

Attribute	Value	Attribute	Value
Target Type	Page in this application	Page	11

Apply changes and run the page which should look like the following figure. Use the provided buttons to switch back and forth, if you can't see orders in the calendar. Click any name link in the calendar report to drill-down and browse order details. Click on any blank date. This will start the Order Wizard to take new order entry.

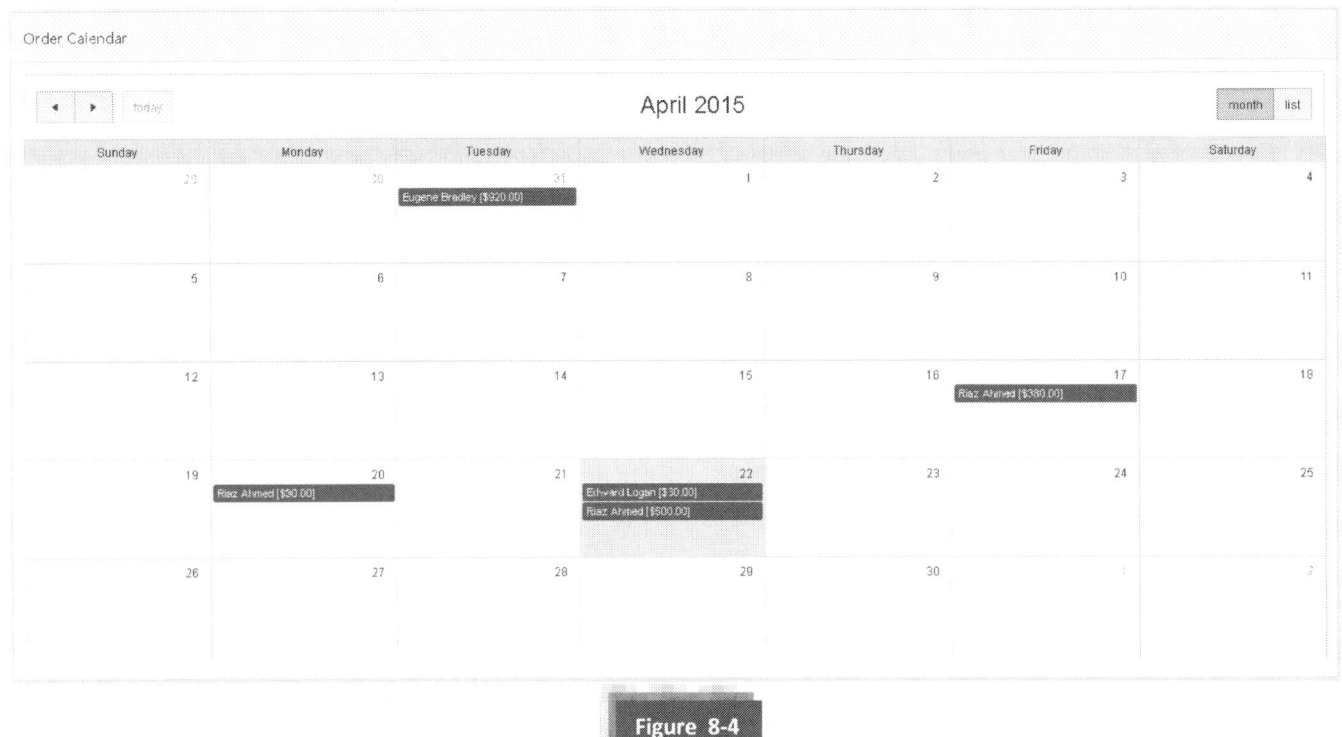

Figure 8-4

8.7 Customer Map Report - Page 15

In this exercise you'll create a map report which shows number of customers in any particular state. Clicking any state link will take you to the Customers main page (Page 2) to display records of that state's customers. You define a map in Application Builder using a wizard. For most chart wizards, you select a map type, map source, and provide a SQL query using the following syntax:

SELECT link, label, value
FROM ...

Where:
- link is an URL.
- label is the text that identifies the point on the map with which you want to associate data. The Region ID or Region Name of the map will be used as the label.
- value is the numeric column that defines the data to be associated with a point on the map.

Map support in Oracle Application Express is based on the AnyChart AnyMap Interactive Maps Component. AnyMap is a flexible Macromedia Flash-based solution that enables developers to visualize geographical related data. Flash maps are rendered by a browser and require Flash Player 9 or later. AnyChart stores map data in files with a *.amap extension, and supports 300 map files for the United States of America, Europe, Asia, Africa, Oceania, North America, and South America. To render a desired map, you select the map source in the wizard (for example, Germany) and the map XML automatically references the desired map source .amap file, germany.amap.

Figure 8-5

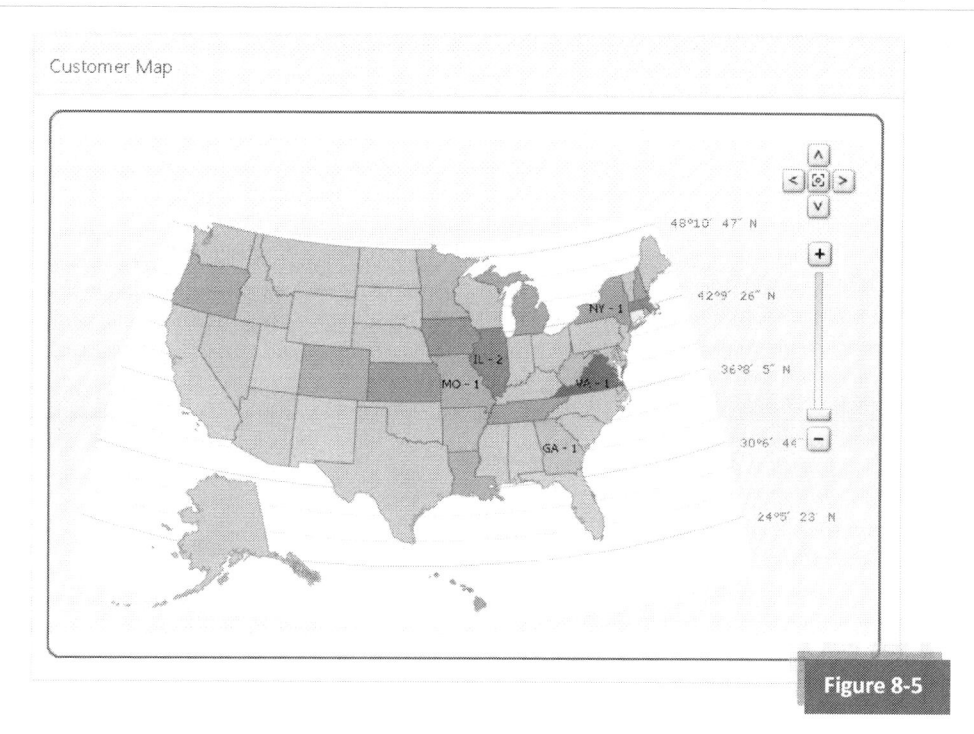

Follow the instructions listed below to create a map report.

1. Create a new page.
2. Select the **Map Chart** option.
3. For Map Type, select **United States of America**.
4. Expand Country Maps folder and click on **States** node to proceed.
5. Fill in the next screen as shown in the following table and click **Next**.

Attribute	Value
Page Number	15
Name	Customer Map
Page Mode	Normal
Region Name	Customer Map
Breadcrumb	do not add breadcrumb...
Navigation Preference	Identify an existing navigation menu entry for this page
Existing Navigation Menu Entry	Reports

6. Enter **Customer Map** for Map Title. Accept all other default attributes and click **Next**.
7. In Enter SQL Query, enter the following statement and click **Next**:

```
select apex_util.prepare_url('f?p='||:APP_ID||':2:'||:app_session||':::2,RIR:IR_CUST_STATE:'||
       cust_state) click_link, cust_state region_id, count(*) count_of_customers
 from demo_customers
group by cust_state
```

8. Click **Create** to finish the wizard.
9. Click on the Attribute node and set Map Region Column to **REGION_ID**. This attribute sets the map region column for the selected map. By default, Map Region Column is set to REGION_NAME. This is the AnyChart Map Reference column holding the data that corresponds with the information returned via the LABEL parameter of the map series query. Selecting the REGION_ID column will highlight corresponding states with number of customers, as illustrated in Figure 8-5.
10. Save the page and run it. Click the Illinois state marked as IL-2. This will call the Customers page (Page 2) carrying two customers in that state, filtered through the SQL statement defined above.

Chapter 8 – Present Data Graphically

8.8 Product Order Tree - Page 19

Application Builder includes a built-in wizard for generating a tree. You can create a Tree from a query that specifies a hierarchical relationship by identifying an ID and parent ID column in a table or view. The tree query utilizes a START WITH .. CONNECT BY clause to generate the hierarchical query.

In this exercise you'll be guided to create a tree view of orders. The root node will show the three product categories, you've been dealing with throughout this book. Level 1 node will be populated with individual categories and each category will have corresponding products at Level 2. The final node (Level 3), will hold names of all customers who placed some orders for the selected product, along with quantity.

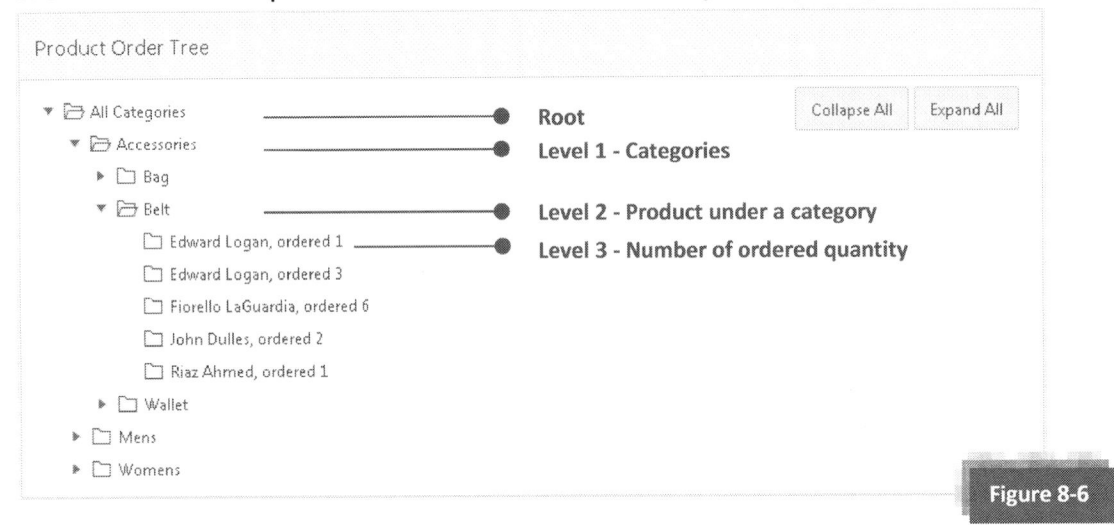

Figure 8-6

Here are the steps to create the tree view.

1. Create a new page.
2. Select the **Tree** option.
3. Complete the next screen using the following table and click **Next**.

Attribute	Value
Page Number	19
Name	Product Order Tree
Page Mode	Normal
Region Name	Product Order Tree
Breadcrumb	do not add breadcrumb...
Navigation Preference	Identify an existing navigation menu entry for this page
Existing Navigation Menu Entry	Reports

4. Accept the Table/View Owner and select **DEMO_PRODUCT_INFO** for Table Name and click **Next**.
5. Click **Next** to accept default entries in the Query page, as shown on the next page. A tree is based on a query and returns data that can be represented in a hierarchy. A *start with .. connect by* clause will be used to generate the hierarchical query for your tree. Use this page to identify the column you want to use as the ID, the Parent ID, and text that should appear on the nodes. The *Start With* column will be used to specify the root of the hierarchical query, and its value can be based on an existing item, static value or SQL query returning a single value.

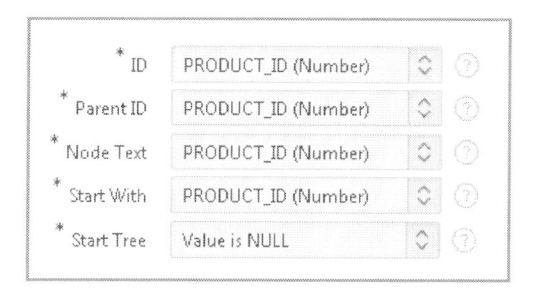

* ID	PRODUCT_ID (Number)
* Parent ID	PRODUCT_ID (Number)
* Node Text	PRODUCT_ID (Number)
* Start With	PRODUCT_ID (Number)
* Start Tree	Value is NULL

6. Click **Next** again to skip the Where Clause.
7. In the final form, put checks on **Collapse All** and **Expand All** to include these buttons on the page. Set Tooltip to **Static Assignment (value equals Tooltip Source attribute)** and enter **View Details** in Tooltip Source. The text "View Details" would appear, when you move over a tree node, to indicate a link. Click **Next**.
8. Click **Create** to finish the wizard.
9. Click the **Product Order Tree** link under Regions.
10. Replace the existing statement in **Tree Query** with the one shown below, which comprises links.

with data as (
select 'R' as link_type, null as parent, 'All Categories' as id, 'All Categories' as name, null as sub_id from demo_product_info
union
select distinct('C') as link_type, 'All Categories' as parent, category as id, category as name, null as sub_id from demo_product_info
union
select 'P' as link_type, category parent, to_char(product_id) id, product_name as name, product_id as sub_id from demo_product_info
union
select 'O' as link_type, to_char(product_id) as parent, null as id, (select c.cust_first_name ||' '|| c.cust_last_name from demo_customers c, demo_orders o where c.customer_id = o.customer_id and o.order_id = oi.order_id) ||', ordered '|| to_char(oi.quantity) as name, order_id as sub_id
from demo_order_items oi
)
select case
    when connect_by_isleaf = 1 then 0
    when level = 1 then 1
    else -1
    end as status, level, name as title, null as icon, id as value, 'View' as tooltip,
case
  when link_type = 'R'
    then apex_util.prepare_url('f?p='||:APP_ID||':3:'||:APP_SESSION||'::NO:RIR')
  when link_type = 'C'
    then apex_util.prepare_url('f?p='||:APP_ID||':3:'||:APP_SESSION||'::NO:CIR
              :IR_CATEGORY:' || name)
  when link_type = 'P'
    then apex_util.prepare_url('f?p='||:APP_ID||':6:'||:APP_SESSION||'::NO::
              P6_PRODUCT_ID:' || sub_id)

```
            when link_type = 'O'
              then apex_util.prepare_url('f?p='||:APP_ID||':29:'||:APP_SESSION||'::NO::
                            P29_ORDER_ID:' || sub_id)
        else null
        end as link
from data
start with parent is null
connect by prior id = parent
order siblings by name
```

The above custom query is used to form the tree using the following syntax:

```
SELECT status, level, name, icon, id, tooltip, link
FROM ...
WHERE ...
START WITH...
CONNECT BY PRIOR id = pid
ORDER SIBLINGS BY ...
```

Line #	Tree Query Code
1	WITH data AS (
2	select 'R' as link_type, null as parent, 'All Categories' as id, 'All Categories' as name, null as sub_id from demo_product_info
3	UNION
4	select distinct('C') as link_type, 'All Categories' as parent, category as id, category as name, null as sub_id from demo_product_info
5	UNION
6	select 'P' as link_type, category parent, to_char(product_id) id, product_name as name, product_id as sub_id from demo_product_info
7	UNION
8	select 'O' as link_type, to_char(product_id) as parent, null as id, (select c.cust_first_name || ' ' || c.cust_last_name from demo_customers c, demo_orders o where c.customer_id = o.customer_id and o.order_id = oi.order_id) || ', ordered '|| to_char(oi.quantity) as name, order_id as sub_id from demo_order_items oi
	)

The *WITH query_name AS* clause lets you assign a name to a subquery block. This statement creates the query name "data" with multiple SELECT statements containing UNION set operators. UNION is used to combine the result from multiple SELECT statements into a single result set as illustrated in Figure 8-7.

LINK_TYPE	PARENT	ID	NAME	SUB_ID
R			All Categories	
C	All Categories		Accessories	
C	All Categories		Mens	
C	All Categories		Womens	
P	Accessories	10	Wallet	10
P	Accessories	7	Belt	7
P	Accessories	8	Bag	8
P	Mens	1	Business Shirt	1
P	Mens	2	Trousers	2
P	Mens	3	Jacket	3
P	Mens	9	Mens Shoes	9
P	Womens	4	Blouse	4
P	Womens	5	Skirt	5
P	Womens	6	Ladies Shoes	6
O		1	Albert Lambert, ordered 3	5
O		10	Edward Logan, ordered 3	7
O		2	Albert Lambert, ordered 2	5
O		3	Albert Lambert, ordered 2	5
O		4	Albert Lambert, ordered 3	5
O		5	Albert Lambert, ordered 2	5
O		6	Edward Logan, ordered 3	6
O		7	Edward Logan, ordered 3	7
O		8	Edward Logan, ordered 1	7
O		9	Edward Logan, ordered 3	

- All Categories → Root Node
- Accessories, Mens, Womens → Categories
- Wallet...Ladies Shoes → Products
- Albert Lambert / Edward Logan entries → Orders

Figure 8-7

Line #	Tree Query Code
1	select case
2	when connect_by_isleaf = 1 then 0
3	when level = 1 then 1
4	else -1
5	end as status, level, name as title, null as icon, id as value, 'View' as tooltip,
6	case
7	when link_type = 'R'
8	then apex_util.prepare_url('f?p='||:APP_ID||':3:'||:APP_SESSION||'::NO:RIR')
9	when link_type = 'C'
10	then apex_util.prepare_url('f?p='||:APP_ID||':3:'||:APP_SESSION||'::NO:CIR:IR_CATEGORY:' || name)
11	when link_type = 'P'
12	then apex_util.prepare_url('f?p='||:APP_ID||':6:'||:APP_SESSION||'::NO::P6_PRODUCT_ID:'||sub_id)
13	when link_type = 'O'
14	then apex_util.prepare_url('f?p='||:APP_ID||':29:'||:APP_SESSION||'::NO::P29_ORDER_ID:' || sub_id)
15	else null
16	end as link
17	from data

The CASE statement within the SQL statement is used to evaluate the four link types (R=root, C=categories, P=products, and O=orders). It has the functionality of an IF-THEN-ELSE statement. Lines 8, 10, 12, and 14 make the node text a link. The R link type leads you to the main Products page (Page 3). The C link type also leads to Page 3 but, applies a filter on category name. The P link type calls Product Details page (Page 6) to display details of the selected product. The final O link type displays details of the selected order in the Order Details page (Page 29).

The CONNECT_BY_ISLEAF pseudocolumn, in the first CASE statement, returns 1 if the current row is a leaf of the tree. Otherwise, it returns 0. This information indicates whether a given row can be further expanded to show more of the hierarchy.

If no condition is found to be true, then the CASE statement will return the null value defined in the ELSE clause on line 15.

Run all these reports from the Graphical Reports sub-menu under the Reports menu. When you click the Graphical Reports option, a page (Page 26) comes up with a list of reports from where you can give them a test run.

Summary

Report is the most significant component of any application. It allows digging information from the data mine for making decisions. This chapter not only demonstrated the power of Oracle Application Express to graphically present the information but also exhibited how to drill-down to a deeper level to obtain detailed information.

Chapter 9

Produce Advance Reports

Chapter 9 – Produce Advance Reports

9.1 About Advanced Reporting

You have seen the use of interactive reporting feature in APEX to create professional looking on-screen reports. Interactive reports also have the ability to export reports to PDF, RTF, Microsoft Excel and Comma Separated Values (CSV) formats. However, it is not possible to define a custom report layout in interactive reports. If you download PDF version of these reports to have a hard copy, what you get is a generic report in simple row-column format without any control breaks and conditional formatting. For serious printing, you have to define an external reporting server to present data in desired format. This book will teach you how utilize Oracle BI Publisher to enjoy high level formatting.

Oracle Application Express provides the following two printing options:

Standard	Apache FOP or another XSL-FO processing engine is supported under the standard configuration. Oracle Application Express already includes support for Apache FOP that allows declarative formatting of report region and queries with basic control over page attributes such as column heading format, orientation, page size, header and footer.
Advanced	This option required Oracle BI Publisher to be configured as your print server. Besides standard configuration, Oracle BI Publisher has Word Template Plug-in to create RTF based report layouts that provides greater control over every aspect of your report and allows you to add complex control breaks, logos, charts, and pagination control. The following list contains few reports that can be created using the advance option: - Tax and Government Forms - Invoices - Ledgers - Financial Statements - Bill of Lading, using tables and barcode fonts - Operational Reports with re-grouping, conditional highlighting, summary calculations, and running totals - Management Reports having Chart with summary functions and table with detail records - Check Print, using conditional formatting and MICR fonts - Dunning Letters

To print these professional reports, you have to pay for a valid Oracle BI Publisher license that is worth the price considering the following advantages:

- Multiple Output Formats: In addition to PDF, the other supported output formats include DOC, XLS and HTML.
- Included in Export/Import: Being part of the application, RTF based layout are exported and imported along with the application.
- Robust Report Layout: Add complex breaks, pagination control, logos, header-footer, charts, and print data on pre-printed forms.
- Report Scheduling: This unique feature enables you to setup a schedule and deliver the report to the desired destinations including email, fax etc.

In order to explore the features provided by this robust reporting server, you can download and install the limited license version to use the program only for the development purpose. Once again you are protected from all the hassle of downloading, installing and configuring BI Publisher Server in your environment, because in the online development environment you can enjoy this utility for free. The following list presents the steps you will perform to produce advance reports for APEX.

Steps to Produce Advance Reports
- Install BI Publisher Desktop
- Create report query in APEX
- Create report layout in MS Word (I created my templates in Word 2003)
- Upload report layout to APEX
- Add links to run the report

9.2 Download and Install BI Publisher Desktop

In this chapter you will take hard copies of reports in Portable Document Format (PDF). You will use Microsoft Word to create templates for these reports. For this purpose, you need Oracle BIPublisher Desktop to prepare the report templates. During BIPublisher Desktop installation, you might be asked to install Java Runtime Edition (JRE) and Dot Net Framework – jre-6u11-windows-i586-p-s.exe and NetFx20SP1_x86.exe.

BI Publisher Desktop is a client side tools to aid in the building and testing of layout templates. This consists of a plug-in to MS Word for the building of RTF templates. You can downloaded this small piece of software from:
http://www.oracle.com/technetwork/middleware/bi-publisher/downloads/index.html

After the download, install the software on your PC using the .exe file. Once the installation completes, you'll see the BI Publisher plug-in as a menu item in MS Word. In newer versions it is placed under the main Add-Ins menu.

Figure 9-1 BI Publisher Desktop Plug-In in MS Word 2003

9.3 Create Monthly Order Review Report

In chapter 7 section 7.3.3, you created an on-screen alternative report named Monthly Review to see details of monthly orders. In the following exercise, you will create a PDF version of that report.

9.3.1 Create Report Query

You can print a report by defining a report query in Shared Component. A report query is an SQL statement that identifies the data to be extracted. You can associate a report query with a report layout and download it as a formatted document. If no report layout is selected, a generic layout is used. To make these reports available to end users, you integrate these reports with an application. For example, you can associate a report query with a button, list item, branch, or other navigational component that enables you to use URLs as targets. Selecting that item then initiates the printing process.

1. Go to **Shared Components** interface.
2. Click **Report Queries** under Reports Section.
3. Click the **Create** button to create a new report query.

4. Type **Monthly_Review** in Report Query Name, set Output Format to **PDF**, View File As to **Attachment**, and click **Next**. Enter the report query name as is or else you will encounter an error (*Error occurred while painting error page: ORA-01403: no data found ORA-22275: invalid LOB locator specified*) while printing this report.
5. Enter the following statement in SQL Query and click **Next**:

   select o.order_id,
       to_char(o.order_timestamp,'Month yyyy') order_month, o.order_timestamp order_date,
       c.cust_last_name || ', ' || c.cust_first_name customer_name, c.cust_state,
       o.user_name sales_rep,
       (select count(*) from demo_order_items oi where oi.order_id = o.order_id) order_items,
       o.order_total
   from demo_orders o, demo_customers c
   where o.customer_id = c.customer_id

6. Select **XML Data** for *Data Source for Report Layout*, to export your report definition as an XML file. This file contains column definitions and the data (fetched using the above SELECT statement) to populate the report. Click the **Download** button, select **Save File**, and click **OK**. A file named **monthly_review.xml** will be saved to your disk. Double click this file to see its contents.
7. Click the **Create Report Query** button to finish the process.

9.3.2 Create Report Template in MS Word

1. In **Microsoft Word**, click on **BI Publisher** menu.
2. From the Data ribbon, select **Load XML Data** to load data file. Open **monthly_review.xml** file that you created in the previous section. A message *Data Loaded Successfully* will be is displayed.
3. Select **Table Wizard** from the Insert ribbon. Select **Table** for Report Format and click **Next**.
4. Click **Next** to accept **DOCUMENT/ROWSET/ROW** for Data Set.
5. Add all fields to the report by moving them to the right pane using the double arrow button and click **Next**.
6. Select **Order Month** in the first drop down list under Group By and click **Next**. This will group the report on the selected column.
7. Select **Order Date** in the first Sort By list and select **Order ID** in the first *Then By* list to sort the report first on the Order Date column and then on the Order ID column. Click **Finish**.
8. In the label form, enter **State** for Cust State to give this column a meaningful name.
9. Move on to finish the wizard. An output similar to Figure 9-2 will be displayed.

group ROW by ORDER_MONTH

ORDER_MONTH

Order Id	Order Date	Customer Name	State	Sales Rep	Order Items	Order Total
F ORDER_ID	ORDER_DATE	CUSTOMER_NAME	CUST_STATE	SALES_REP	ORDER_ITEMS	ORDER_TOTAL E

end ROW by ORDER_MONTH

Figure 9-2 Raw Template Create in MS Word

10. Press ctrl+s (or click the Save icon) to save the template. Enter **monthly_review** in the File name, select **Rich Text Format** as its type, and click **Save**.
11. In the Preview ribbon, click on the **PDF** option. The output as show in Figure 9-3 will be displayed. With some data in XML file, you can format and preview your reports offline.
12. **Close the PDF** and switch back to MS Word.

February 2015

Order Id	Order Date	Customer Name	Cust State	Sales Rep	Order Items	Order Total
2	09-FEB-15 09.08.21.000000 AM	Dulles, John	VA	DEMO	9	2160
3	20-FEB-15 09.08.21.000000 AM	Hartsfield, William	GA	DEMO	5	1640
4	22-FEB-15 09.08.21.000000 AM	LaGuardia, Fiorello	NY	DEMO	4	870

January 2015

Order Id	Order Date	Customer Name	Cust State	Sales Rep	Order Items	Order Total
1	26-JAN-15 09.08.21.000000 AM	Bradley, Eugene	CT	DEMO	3	1890

March 2015

Order Id	Order Date	Customer Name	Cust State	Sales Rep	Order Items	Order Total
5	04-MAR-15 09.08.21.000000 AM	Lambert, Albert	MO	DEMO	5	950
6	09-MAR-15 09.08.21.000000 AM	Logan, Edward	MA	DEMO	3	1185
7	14-MAR-15 09.08.21.000000 AM	Logan, Edward	MA	DEMO	7	905
8	22-MAR-15 09.08.21.000000 AM	OHare, Frank	IL	DEMO	3	730
9	28-MAR-15 09.08.21.000000 AM	Hartsfield, William	GA	DEMO	3	730
10	31-MAR-15 09.08.21.000000 AM	Bradley, Eugene	CT	DEMO	4	920

Figure 9-3 Raw Template Output

9.3.3 Format Report

1. Place the cursor before the **ORDER_MONTH** field and type **Order Month:** in front of it to act as a label. Use MS Word standard tools to change font, color and size. Drag field width to a desired size.
2. Click the **ORDER_TOTAL** field and right-align it. Double click it to call its properties. Select **Number** for its Type and **#,##0.00** for Format. Click **OK**.
3. Insert a blank line above **group ROW by Order_Month** text to add a title to the report. Type **ABC CORPORATION** and then **Monthly Orders Review Report** on the subsequent line. You can also add a logo, page number and other options using standard MS Word tools.

Chapter 9 – Produce Advance Reports

9.3.4 Conditional Formatting

In these steps we are going to change font and background color of orders for which the amount is less than or equal to 900, as we did in the on-screen report version in chapter 7.

1. Select **Order Total** field by clicking its name.
2. Select **Conditional Format** from the Insert ribbon.
3. Perform the following steps in Properties tab:
    a. Select **ORDER_TOTAL** column for Data field.
    b. Select **Number** in the adjacent list.
    c. Put a check on **Apply to Entire Table Row** to apply the condition to the whole report.
    d. Select **Less than or equal to** in the Data field.
    e. Enter **900** in the box next to the Data field.
    f. Click the **Format button**.
    g. Put a check on the **Background Color** option.
    h. Click the **Select** button to choose different Font and Background colors
    i. Click **OK**.
4. Preview your work and see the application of conditional formatting to all the rows having Order Total less than or equal to 900.

Use the same procedure and change font and background color for orders greater than 2000. Select Greater than for the condition and enter 2000 in the value. This time, do not check the *Apply to Entire Table Row* option. This will highlight specific cells only. After completion, preview the report to check your work.

9.3.5 Summary Calculation

In this section you will add a summary to reveal average orders for the month.

1. Place your cursor on the blank line before the text **end ROW by ORDER_MONTH**.
2. Click on the **Field** option in the Insert ribbon.
3. In the Field dialog box, click on **Order Total** field, select **average** for Calculation, put a check mark on '**On Grouping**' and click the **Insert** button. A summary field, *average ORDER_TOTAL* will be added. Close the dialog box.
4. Add a label **Monthly Average:** before the field. Double click the calculated field and set Type property to **Number** and Format to **#,##0.00**. Align the whole expression to the right under the Order Total field.

9.3.6 Add a Summary Chart

1. Insert a blank row above **group ROW by ORDER_MONTH**.
2. Select **Chart** from the Insert ribbon.
3. From the Data tree, drag field **ORDER_TOTAL** to the Values box, set Aggregation to **Sum**, drag **ORDER_MONTH** to Labels, put a check on **Group Data**, select **Bar Graph - Horizontal** for Type, **April** in Style and click **OK**. The completed screen should look like Figure 9-4.
4. Right click the chart in MS Word and select Insert Caption. Type **Monthly Orders Review** in Caption.

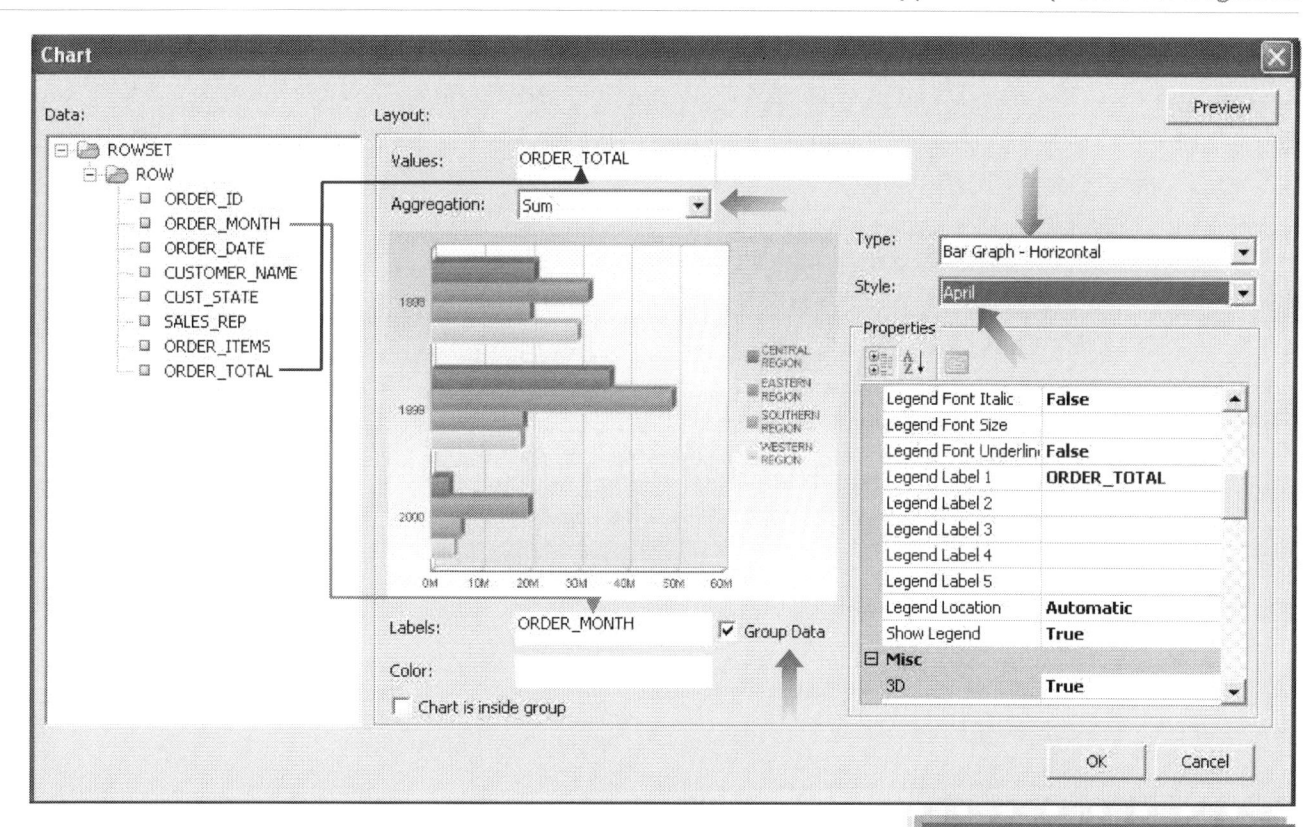

Figure 9-4 Add Chart to Template

9.3.7 Add a Pivot Table

1. In MS Word click on the line just after the text **end ROW by ORDER_MONTH**.
2. Select **Pivot Table** from the Insert ribbon.
3. Drag fields **CUST_STATE, CUSTOMER_NAME, ORDER_MONTH,** and **ORDER_TOTAL** to the layout section as shown in Figure 9-5. Click the **Preview** button to see the output within the dialog box. Click the **OK** button. Format the table using MS Word toolbar so that it matches the output shown in Figure 9-7. Browse the report in PDF. **Save the template** and close MS Word.

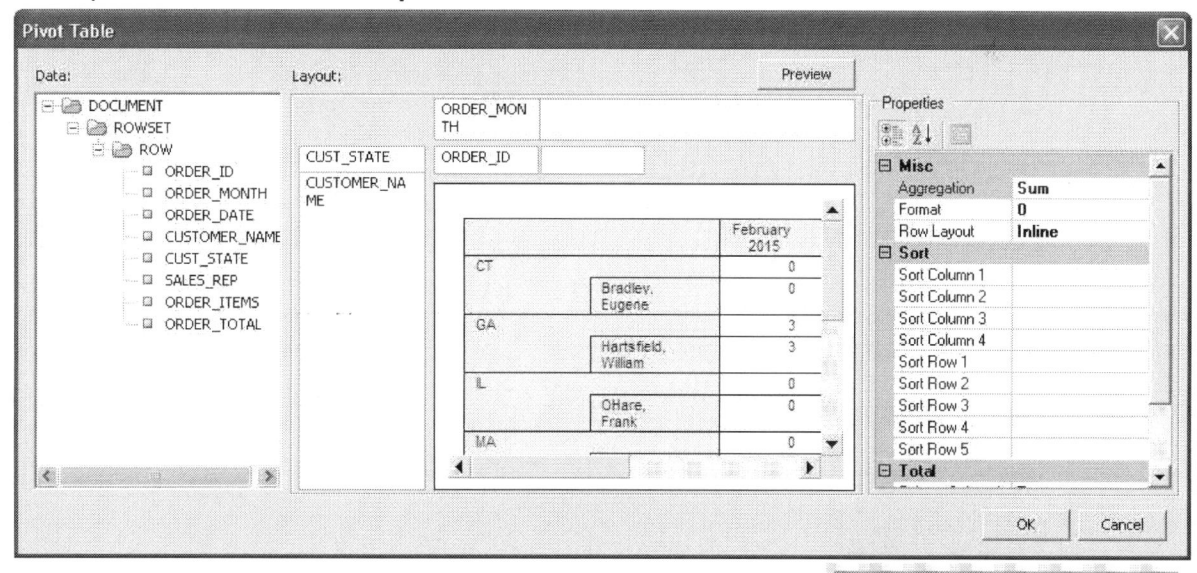

Figure 9-5 Pivot Table Settings

9.3.8 Upload Report Template to APEX

Report Layouts are used in conjunction with a report query to render data in a printer-friendly format, such as PDF, Word or Excel. A report layout has been designed using the Template Builder Word plug-in and will now be uploaded to APEX as an RTF file type.

1. In **Shared Components** interface, click **Report Layouts** under Reports.
2. Click the **Create** button.
3. Select the option **Named Columns (RTF)** and click **Next**. A named column report layout is a query-specific report layout designed to work with a defined list of columns in the query result set. This type of layout is used for custom-designed layouts when precise control of the positioning of page items and query columns is required. This layout is uploaded as an RTF file.
4. In Layout Name enter **monthly_review**, click the **Browse** button and select the MS Word template file **monthly_meview.rtf**, which was created in the previous section.
5. Click the **Create Layout** button.
6. Move back to **Shared Components**.
7. Click the **Report Queries** link under the Reports section.
8. Click on **Monthly_Review** icon.
9. In Report Query Attributes section, change Report Layout from Use Generic Report Layout to **monthly_review** to apply the layout to the report query.
10. Write down or copy the URL appearing in the Print URL box which should be:
    f?p=&APP_ID.:0:&SESSION.:PRINT_REPORT=Monthly_Review
    Report queries can be integrated with an application by using this URL as the target for buttons, navigation list entries, list items, or any other type of link. You will use this link in the next section to run the report.
11. Click **Apply Changes**.

You have created the Report Layout in APEX by uploading the MS Word Template and linked it to your Report Query. In the next section, you will create a link to run this report.

9.3.9 Run the Report

In this section you will configure Monthly Review Report menu entry in the main navigation menu to run this report.

1. Switch back to Shared Components page.
2. Click on the **Lists** link under the Navigation section and call **Desktop Navigation Menu**.
3. Click on **Monthly Review Report** entry.
4. Set Target Type to **URL** and enter or paste the URL (**f?p=&APP_ID.:0:&SESSION.:PRINT_REPORT=Monthly_Review**) in the URL Target box.
5. Save your work.
6. Run the application. Expand **Advance Reports** under **Report** menu and click on **Monthly Review Report**. Open it with Adobe Acrobat, which should look something like Figure 9-6 and Figure 9-7. I formatted the layout using standard MS Word tools, including header-footer, tables, page number, font etc.
7. The same report has a link on Page 26 that is associated with a list. Go to Shared Components and call Reports List (from Lists section). Modify Monthly Review Report entry; set Target Type to **Page in this Application**; Page to **0**; and Request to **PRINT_REPORT=Monthly_Review**. This is an alternate method to send the same print request, used in step 4 above. Save these setting and run the report through this link as well.

Congratulations! You have successfully created a professional looking report that not only matches the on-screen report of chapter 7, but also adds more value to it by incorporating a pivot table, to display the same data from a different perspective. Add a new order in the application and see its reflection in the report.

ABC CORPORATION
35-A/3, ABC House, Raymond Street off Mansfield Street, Chicago-IL, 6350, USA.

Orders Monthly Review Report

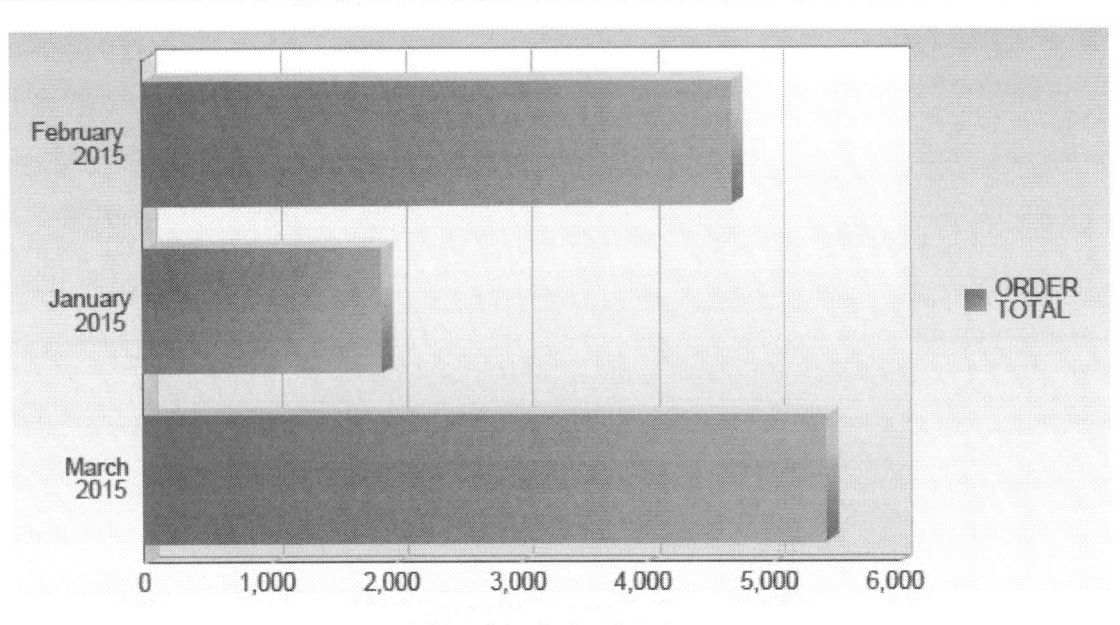

Order Month: January 2015

Order#	Order Date	Customer	State	Sales Rep	Order Items	Order Total
1	26-JAN-2015	Bradley, Eugene	CT	DEMO	3	1,890.00

Average Order: 1,890.00

Order Month: February 2015

Order#	Order Date	Customer	State	Sales Rep	Order Items	Order Total
2	09-FEB-2015	Dulles, John	VA	DEMO	9	2,160.00
3	20-FEB-2015	Hartsfield, William	GA	DEMO	5	1,640.00
4	22-FEB-2015	LaGuardia, Fiorello	NY	DEMO	4	870.00

Average Order: 1,556.67

Order Month: March 2015

Order#	Order Date	Customer	State	Sales Rep	Order Items	Order Total
10	31-MAR-2015	Bradley, Eugene	CT	DEMO	4	920.00
5	04-MAR-2015	Lambert, Albert	MO	DEMO	5	950.00
6	09-MAR-2015	Logan, Edward	MA	DEMO	3	1,185.00
7	14-MAR-2015	Logan, Edward	MA	DEMO	7	905.00
8	22-MAR-2015	OHare, Frank	IL	DEMO	3	730.00
9	28-MAR-2015	Hartsfield, William	GA	DEMO	3	730.00

Average Order: 903.33

23/04/2015 5:25:55 AM

Figure 9-6 Monthly Order Review Report

ABC CORPORATION
35-A/3, ABC House, Raymond Street off Mansfield Street,
Chicago-IL, 6350, USA.

Revenue By States

State	Customer	January 2015	February 2015	March 2015	Total
CT		1,890.00	0.00	920.00	2,810.00
	Bradley, Eugene	1,890.00	0.00	920.00	2,810.00
GA		0.00	1,640.00	730.00	2,370.00
	Hartsfield, William	0.00	1,640.00	730.00	2,370.00
IL		0.00	0.00	730.00	730.00
	OHare, Frank	0.00	0.00	730.00	730.00
MA		0.00	0.00	2,090.00	2,090.00
	Logan, Edward	0.00	0.00	2,090.00	2,090.00
MO		0.00	0.00	950.00	950.00
	Lambert, Albert	0.00	0.00	950.00	950.00
NY		0.00	870.00	0.00	870.00
	LaGuardia, Fiorello	0.00	870.00	0.00	870.00
VA		0.00	2,160.00	0.00	2,160.00
	Dulles, John	0.00	2,160.00	0.00	2,160.00
TOTAL		1,890.00	4,670.00	5,420.00	11,980.00

Figure 9-7 Pivot Table Report

9.4 Create a Commercial Invoice

In this exercise, you will generate commercial invoice for the placed Orders. You are going to use the same techniques as used in the previous section. This time you will create a parameters form to print specific orders by passing parameter values to the underlying report query.

9.4.1 Create A List of Values

Create the following LOV from scratch. It will be used in the next section to print only those orders that were recorded by the user selected from this list.

Attribute	Value
Name	Users
Type	Dynamic
Query	SELECT DISTINCT user_name d, user_name r FROM demo_orders

Chapter 9 – Produce Advance Reports

9.4.2 Create Report Parameters Page

1. Create a Blank Page using the following parameters. The page will contain report parameters.

Attribute	Value
Page Number	50
Name	Invoice Parameters
Page Mode	Normal
Breadcrumb	do not add breadcrumb...
Navigation Preference	Identify an existing navigation menu entry for this page
Existing Navigation Menu Entry	Reports

2. Create a region under the Body node and enter **Invoice Report** for its Title.

3. Add two Page Items under the Invoice Report region and set the following attributes. Using these items you can print a single order or a range of orders.

Attribute	Value	Value
Name	P50_INVOICEFROM	P50_INVOICETO
Type	Text Field	Text Field
Label	From Invoice Number:	To Invoice Number:
Template	Required	Required
Value Required	Yes	Yes
Type (Default)	Static Value	Static Value
Static Value	1	9999999999

4. Add a Select List under the two text field items and set the following attributes. It will show ids of all users from which you can select one id to print orders entered by that particular user. The expression [V('APP_USER'] displays id of the logged in user as a default value for this Select List.

Attribute	Value
Name	P50_USER
Type	Select List
Label	Entered by:
Type (List of Values)	Shared Components
List of Values	USERS
Type (Default)	PL/SQL Expression
PL/SQL Expression	V('APP_USER')

5. Right click Invoice Report region and select Create Button. Set the following attributes for the new button. When you click this button, the page is submitted and an associated branch (created in section 9.5) forwards a print request to the print server.

Attribute	Value
Name	PRINT
Label	Print Invoice
Button Position	Next
Hot	Yes
Action	Submit Page

6. Save your work.

9.4.3 Associate Page to Menu

The parameters page created above will be called from the main navigation menu. Follow the instructions mentioned below to associate it to the menu entry named Customer Invoice.

1. Go to Shared Components | Lists | Desktop Navigation menu.
2. Call properties of Customer Invoice menu entry.
3. Set Target Type to **Page in this Application** and enter **50** for Page.
4. Apply the changes.
5. Similarly, call Reports List and modify Customer Invoice entry that appears on Page 26, to call the same report from that page.

9.4.4 Create Query for the Invoice

1. Go to **Shared Components**.
2. Click **Report Queries** under Reports Section.
3. Click the **Create** button to create a new report query.
4. Type **Invoice** in Report Query Name, set Output Format to **PDF**, View File As to **Attachment**, and click **Next**.
5. Enter the following statement in SQL Query and click **Next**. As you can see, the SQL query filters data using the three parameters passed to it from Page 50. You use bind variables in SQL statements to reference parameter values.

    Select o.order_id, o.Order_timestamp, o.user_name,
        c.cust_first_name || ' ' || c.cust_last_name as customer, c.cust_street_address1,
        c.cust_street_address2, c.cust_city, c.cust_state, c.cust_postal_code,
        oi.ORDER_ITEM_ID, pi.PRODUCT_NAME, oi.UNIT_PRICE,
        oi.QUANTITY, oi.Unit_Price * oi.Quantity as Amount
    from   DEMO_ORDERS o, DEMO_ORDER_ITEMS oi, DEMO_PRODUCT_INFO pi, DEMO_CUSTOMERS c
    where o.ORDER_id = oi.ORDER_id and pi.PRODUCT_ID = oi.PRODUCT_ID and
        o.customer_id = c.customer_id and o.ORDER_id BETWEEN :P50_INVOICEFROM and
        :P50_INVOICETO and o.user_name = :P50_USER

6. Select **XML Data** for *Data Source for Report Layout* to export your report definition as an XML file. Click the **Download** button, select **Save File**, and click **OK**. A file named **invoice.xml** will be saved to your disk.
7. Click the **Create Report Query** button. Unlike the previous xml file, this one doesn't contain any data due to the involvement of parameters. Therefore, you cannot test the invoice report offline.

9.4.5 Create Invoice Template in MS Word

Perform the following steps in MS Word to create a template for the invoice report. For you convenience, I have provided both XML and RTF files with the book code.

1. Select **A4** size page and set margins.
2. From Data ribbon, select **Load XML Data**, select **invoice.xml** and click **Open** to load the xml file.
3. From the Insert ribbon choose **Table Wizard** to add a table. This table will be used to output order details. Set *Report Format* to **Table** and *Data Set* to **DOCUMENT/ROWSET/ROW**.
4. Move **Order Id, Product Name, Unit Price, Quantity,** and **Amount** columns to the right pane.
5. Select **Order Id** in *Group By* to group the report according to order numbers.
6. Do not select any field for *Sort By*.
7. Add appropriate **labels** (Product, Price, Quantity and Amount).
8. Click **Finish**.

Chapter 9 – Produce Advance Reports

9.4.6 Template Formatting

1. Double click the group field titled **group ROW by ORDER_ID** and on the Properties tab, set *Break* to **Page**. This will print each new invoice on a separate page.
2. From the **Insert** ribbon select **Field**. Select **ORDER_ID** field and click the **Insert** button to add this field to the next row just after the group titled *group Row by ORDER_ID*. Similarly, add ORDER_TIMESTAMP, CUSTOMER, CUST_STREET_ADDRESS1, CUST_STREET_ADDRESS2, CUST_CITY, CUST_STATE, CUST_POSTAL_CODE, and USER_NAME on subsequent line. I inserted a table to place these fields accordingly.
3. Double click **AMOUNT** field in the table. Set its *Type* to **Number** and *Format* to **#,##0.00**. Right align the field using standard alignment tool in MS Word.
4. Add a **blank row** to the details table. Select **Field** from the Insert ribbon. In the *Field* dialog box, select **AMOUNT**. From **Calculation** list, select **sum**, put a **check** on '*On Grouping*', and click **Insert**. Put a label **Total** and then format and align the field as shown in the template. This step will add a new row (just after the last transaction) to display a sum of Amount column.
5. Save the report to your hard drive as **invoice** and select **Rich Text Format (RTF)** as its *type*.
6. Close MS Word.

9.4.7 Upload Template to APEX

1. Call **Shared Components** interface and click **Report Layouts** under Reports.
2. Click the **Create** button.
3. Select the option **Named Columns (RTF)** and click **Next**.
4. In Layout Name enter **invoice**, click the **Browse** button and select the template file **invoice.rtf**.
5. Click the **Create Layout** button.
6. Move back to **Shared Components**.
7. Under Reports section, click on **Report Queries** link.
8. Click on **Invoice** icon.
9. In Report Query Attributes section, change Report Layout from Use Generic Report Layout to **invoice** to apply the layout.
10. Click **Apply Changes**.

9.5 Create Branch

Call Page 50 to create the following branch to send a print request when the Print Invoice button is clicked. Go to Processing tab. Right click After Submit node and select **Create Branch**. Set the following attributes for the new branch. Note that the letter I in the word Invoice (in the Request attribute) should be in caps.

Attribute	Value
Name	Run Invoice Report
Point	After Submit
Type (Behavior)	Page or URL (Redirect)
Target Type	Page in this Application
Page	0
Request (under Advance)	PRINT_REPORT=Invoice
When Button Pressed	PRINT

Test Your Work

From the main navigation menu, select Customer Invoice under the Report menu. This will bring up parameters form page (Page 26). For the time being, accept all the default values in the form, including the default user, and hit the Print Invoice button. Open the report with Adobe Acrobat, which should resemble the one show in Figure 9-8. Also try to get this report using different parameters to test your work.

> **NOTE:**
> For RTF templates created in MS Word 2007 you may get the following error when you try to open the PDF: *Acrobat could not open 'invoice-1.pdf' because it is either not a supported file type or because the file has been damaged (for example, it was sent as an email attachment and wasn't correctly decoded)*. This error message is also displayed when there is no data for the given criteria. I ran my reports successfully, created in MS Word 2003, without any problem. To cope with the second scenario, you can add a validation to check for the existence of data prior to calling the report.

Chapter 9 – Produce Advance Reports

ABC CORPORATION
35-A/3, ABC House,
Raymond Street Off
Mansfield Street, NJ 07901
Phone #(908) 316-5599
info@abccorp.com

COMMERCIAL INVOICE

Customer:
John Dulles
45020 Aviation Drive
Sterling
VA 20166

Order Number	2
Order Date	09-FEB-2015 09:08AM
Sales Rep.	DEMO

Product Name	Unit Price	Quantity	Amount
Business Shirt	50	3	150.00
Trousers	80	3	240.00
Jacket	150	3	450.00
Blouse	60	3	180.00
Skirt	80	3	240.00
Ladies Shoes	120	2	240.00
Belt	30	2	60.00
Bag	125	4	500.00
Wallet	50	2	100.00
TOTAL			**2,160.00**

Make all checks payable to ABC Corporation
THANK YOU FOR YOUR BUSINESS!

Figure 9-8 Commercial Invoice

Chapter 10

Develop A Mobile Version For Smartphones

Chapter 10 – Develop A Mobile Version For Smartphones

10.1 About Mobile Development

In the last few years there has been an eruption in the market for smartphones and mobile devices demand. As the sales are touching new heights every day, smartphone vendors are trying hard to provide the excellent product with latest technology. Things that used to be done traditionally by people on their laptops are now being done increasingly on mobile devices. Feeling the heat, application development companies are under pressure to quickly deliver web applications for smartphone and mobile platforms. For this, they need tools and frameworks to roll out new mobile enabled applications and adapt existing applications to mobile devices. The good news is that just like traditional web applications, mobile web applications are also developed using the same core technologies - HTML, CSS, and JavaScript.

With mobile web usage increasing every year, there is a huge demand in the market for applications supported on smartphones and tablets. To help develop new applications and extend existing web applications for mobile use, the APEX development team has enhanced the product with mobile development features. Probably the most significant new feature incorporated in APEX is the ability to build applications specifically aimed at mobile devices. Now you can easily build applications for modern smartphones and tablets, such as iPhone, iPad, Android, and BlackBerry using Oracle APEX. The jQuery Mobile framework is integrated to render an application for the vast majority of mobile devices. Besides, a new mobile-specific theme is incorporated to support touch input and gestures such as swipe, tap, and orientation change. Another theme takes care of responsive design, to automatically adjust the interface according to different screen dimensions, which aids in using the same interface on desktop, tablet, and smartphone devices.

Types of Mobile Applications

Mobile Applications are split into two broad categories:

Web-Based: The application you'll be creating in this chapter is known as a web-based application or simply a mobile web application. These types of applications are accessed using browsers in mobile devices. In this chapter, you'll declaratively build a mobile web application. APEX 4.2 allows you to rapidly build applications that can be accessed on the desktop, a mobile device, or both. The mobile development interface uses a collection of templates based on the jQuery Mobile framework. This framework is designed to seamlessly run and correctly deliver mobile web application on various mobile devices with different operating systems. For you, as a developer, the good news is that you develop such applications with the tools you're already familiar with. To build a mobile application, you use the same application builder, the same SQL and PL/SQL code, and with similar methods that you applied while developing the desktop version. Because of a single codebase, a mobile web application can be accessed from any mobile device, irrespective of operating system. The process of accessing such applications is very simple. All that is needed is to have the correct URL that you put into the mobile browser, and respective id with password. The application code is not stored on the device but is delivered by the application server. This way you can easily handle application updates. You only need to update the application on the server, allowing potentially thousands of users to enjoy the latest version. The second advantage to this approach is that you are not required to send updates to every client (as required in native applications), which ensures that the accessed application is current with all provided features. Here are some pros and cons to web-based applications:

Pros:
- Updates are uploaded only to the application server and become instantly available for all platforms and devices.
- Same application code for all browser-enabled mobile devices.
- Use of same application building procedures and core web technologies.
- Doesn't need app store approval.

Cons:
- To access these applications you need a reasonable Internet connection.
- Slower than native applications because these applications are based on interpreted code rather than compiled code.
- Not available in the app stores.
- Cannot interact with device hardware such as camera, microphone, compass, file uploading etc.

Native (On-Device): These applications are on the other side and are built for a specific mobile operating system, such as Windows Mobile, Android, iOS, or BlackBerry. Native mobile applications are written for a specific target operating system in its own supported language. For instance, to develop an application for a Windows device, you'll use C# (C Sharp), for iOS devices it is Objective-C, and for Android, you need to be a master of Java. This means that your app is tied to a specific platform and won't run on another. Native applications are downloaded and stored locally on the device. Because of this capability, these applications are considered better performers. Additionally, these applications have the biggest advantage of being able to interact with different device hardware (camera, compass, accelerometer, and more). Using a local data store (SQLite), these applications can even work when disconnected from the Internet. As a developer you have to handle version discrepancies because updates of these applications are downloaded manually. Let's see what pros and cons this category has:

Pros:
- Being native, it performs better than its counterpart.
- Offline availability.
- Complete access to device's hardware.
- Can be added to and searched in an app store.

Cons:
- Expensive to develop.
- Single platform support. Need to build a separate app for a different OS, which means additional time and cost.
- To get space on the device's app store, your app is required to undergo an approval process.

Chapter 10 – Develop A Mobile Version For Smartphones

10.2 Create Interface for Mobile Application

Oracle APEX allows you to create two types of interfaces: Desktop and jQuery Mobile Smartphone. Each page in an application is associated with one user interface. If a user logs into the application with a mobile device, the pages created with jQuery Mobile Smartphone interface will be rendered; if a desktop is used, the desktop user interface is delivered. You created and used the desktop interface in previous chapters. Here, you'll use jQuery Mobile interface for your mobile application.

1. Click on **Edit Application Properties** button in the main Sales Web Application interface.
2. Click on the **User Interface** tab.
3. Click the button labeled **Add User Interface**.
4. On the User Interface Page, set the attributes as follows and click **Next**.

Attribute	Value
Type	Mobile
Display Name	Mobile Specifies a display name for the user interface. The display name is shown in wizards.
Auto Detect	Yes
Home URL	f?p=&APP_ID.:HOME_JQM_SMARTPHONE:&SESSION. Specifies the home page of the application for the current user interface.
Login URL	f?p=&APP_ID.:LOGIN_JQM_SMARTPHONE:&SESSION. Points towards the login page of the application for the current user interface.

5. On the Identify Theme page, select **Standard Themes** as Theme Type, and **Mobile (Theme 51)** as the mobile application theme. Click **Next**.
6. Click **Create**.

Recall that when you initially created the desktop application, the application wizard created two pages for you: Home and Login. The mobile interface too, creates two default pages: Home (Page 30 in my scenario) and Login (Page 1001). In addition to these pages, the wizard creates a third one: Global Page - Mobile (Page 0). The Global page of your application functions as a master page. You can add a separate Global page for each user interface. The Application Express engine renders all components you add to a Global page on every page within your application.

NOTE: In chapter 3 section 3.3.1, you created a navigation bar entry to access mobile application, and entered 30 for the mobile home page id. In order to point to the correct mobile home page, you have to replace that id with the one created here.

Run the Login Page 1001 that will look like the following figure:

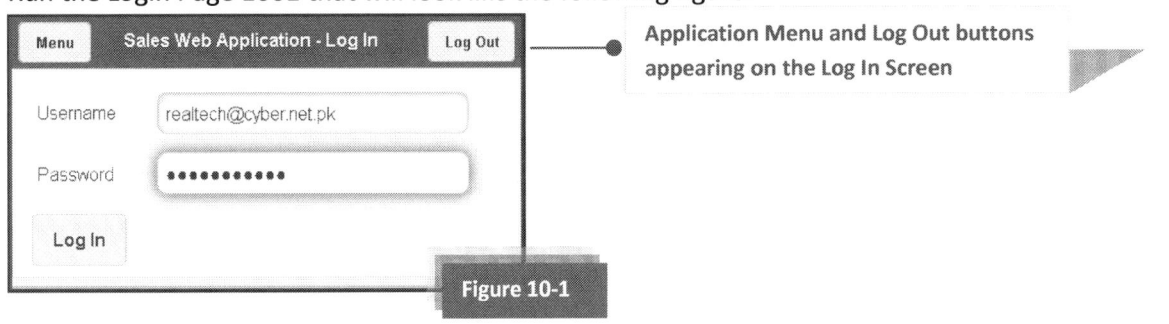

Figure 10-1

Application Menu and Log Out buttons appearing on the Log In Screen

Enter the credentials you've been using so far, and hit the Login button. A blank mobile home page will appear resembling the one illustrated on the next page.

Oracle Application Express 5 For Beginners

| Menu | Home | Log Out |

Figure 10-2

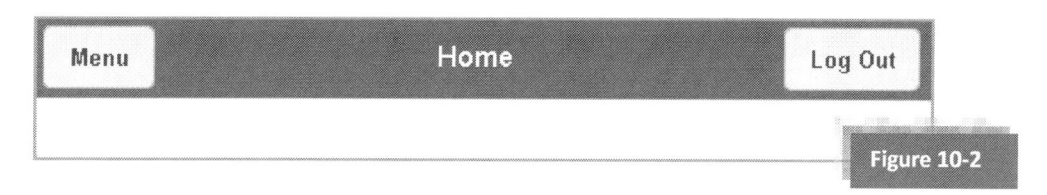

Click the Logout link. You'll land on to the desktop login page, which is not correct. Call definitions of the Global Page. Select the **Logout** button in the Region Buttons section. Scroll down to **Behavior** section. Set Action to **Redirect to Page in this Application**. Click the Target link and enter **1001** in Page. Save these settings to inform APEX where to land the user when s/he clicks the Logout button. Call and run the mobile Home page again; enter your credentials to login; and click the Logout button. This time you'll see the correct login page i.e. Page 1001.

Let's move on to fine tune the auto-generated pages by changing some attributes, starting with the Global Page.

10.3 Modify the Global Page - Page 0
10.3.1 Modify Region - Header

1. Click on the **Global Page** to call its definitions.
2. Click the **Header** region in the Regions section.
3. In Pages attribute (under Condition), enter **1001**. The region is created with a default condition (Current Page Is NOT in comma delimited list). By supplementing the condition with the mobile login page number, you suppressed this region from appearing on the login page. See Figure 10-1 where the two buttons under this region (Menu and Logout) appear on the login page.
4. Just like the desktop version, the mobile version too is created with a navigation menu that appears in a special panel on the left side. You can access the menu using the Menu button (see Figure 10-2). The Global Page contains a default dynamic action named *open panel* which is responsible for showing the menu panel. By default, the Button attribute of this dynamic action is set to LOGOUT, which prevents the menu from appearing. Click on the **Dynamic Actions** tab. Expand the **Click** node and click on **open panel**. In the Properties pane, change the Button attribute from LOGOUT to **MENU** to open the panel when this button is clicked.
5. Apply the change and test your work. This time the login screen should not display the two buttons.

10.3.2 Create List - Footer Control

This static list carries two options (Full Site and Logout) and will be displayed at the bottom in the Footer Controls region. The first option will take you to the Home page of the desktop version, while the second one will log you out of the mobile application and will show the mobile login page. Go to **Shared Components**. In the Navigation section, click the **Lists** link and then click the **Create** button to create a new list from scratch. Enter **Footer Controls** in Name and select **Static** as Type. Fill in the Static Values as shown below:

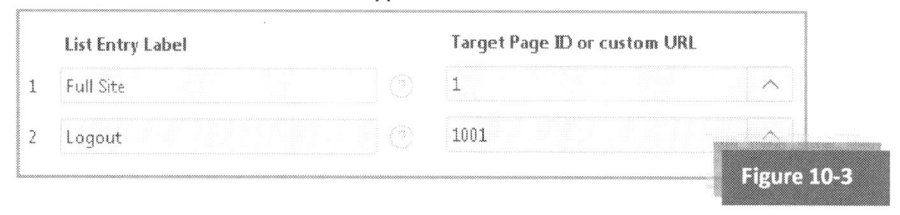

	List Entry Label	Target Page ID or custom URL
1	Full Site	1
2	Logout	1001

Figure 10-3

163

Chapter 10 – Develop A Mobile Version For Smartphones

10.3.3 Create Region - Footer Controls

The list, created in the previous section, will be displayed in this region. Call the Global Page again. Create a new region by right clicking the Header Regions node and selecting **Create Region** option. Select the new region and modify it using the following table:

Attribute	Value
Title	Footer Control
Type	List
List (Source)	Footer Control
Template	Footer Bar (Fixed)
Custom Attribute	style="text-align:center" *(to centralize the list carrying the two buttons)*
Type (Condition)	Current page is not in comma delimited list
Pages	1001 *(prevents it from appearing on the mobile login page)*
List Templates (under Attributes)	Button Control Group

10.3.4 Create Region - Mobile Styles

Create another region. Enter **Mobile Styles** in Title and set its Type to **Static Content**. Enter the following style rules in the Text box under Source. Note that these rules were created and described earlier in the desktop version to style the *Select Items* page (Page 12), and were defined in the inline page attribute. Here, you added it to the global page to test another approach to style Select Items page (Page 217) of the mobile version. Since the classes defined in these rules are referenced only in Page 217; therefore, other pages in the application are not affected. See section 10.11.1.

```
<style>
  div.CustomerInfo strong{font:bold 12px/16px Arial,sans-serif;display:block;width:120px;}
  div.CustomerInfo p{display:block;margin:0; font: normal 12px/16px Arial, sans-serif;}
  div.Products{clear:both;margin:16px 0 0 0;padding:0 8px 0 0;}
  div.Products table{border:1px solid #CCC;border-bottom:none;}
  div.Products table th{background-color:#DDD;color:#000;font:bold 12px/16px Arial,sans-serif;padding:4px 10px;text-align:right;border-bottom:1px solid #CCC;}
  div.Products table td{border-bottom:1px solid #CCC;font:normal 12px/16px Arial,sans-serif;padding:4px 10px;text-align:right;}
  div.Products table td a{color:#000;}
  div.Products .left{text-align:left;}
  div.CartItem{padding:8px 8px 0 8px;font:normal 11px/14px Arial,sans-serif;}
  div.CartItem a{color:#000;}
  div.CartItem span{display:block;text-align:right;padding:8px 0 0;}
  div.CartItem span.subtotal{font-weight:bold;}
  div.CartTotal{border-top:1px solid #FFF;margin-top:8px;padding:8px;border-top:1px dotted #AAA;}
  div.CartTotal span{display:block;text-align:right;font:normal 11px/14px Arial,sans-serif;padding:0 0 4px 0;}
  div.CartTotal p{padding:0;margin:0;font:normal 11px/14px Arial,sans-serif;position:relative;}
  div.CartTotal p.CartTotal{font:bold 12px/14px Arial,sans-serif;padding:8px 0 0 0;}
  div.CartTotal p.CartTotal span{font:bold 12px/14px Arial,sans-serif;padding:8px 0 0 0;}
  div.CartTotal p span{padding:0;position:absolute;right:0;top:0;}
</style>
```

10.4 Modify the Mobile Home Page

10.4.1 Modify the Page attributes

1. Call the mobile **Home** page.
2. Set the Name of this page to **Mobile Home Page**. Make sure that Page Alias shows HOME_JQM_SMARTPHONE. An alias is a nick name. You can enter an alphanumeric alias for a page. It is used to reference a page instead of a page number. For example, if you were working on page 1 of application 100, you could create an alias called "home" which could then be accessed from other pages using a URL like this: f?p=100:home
3. Enter **Sales Web Application** in Title and save the amendments.

10.4.2 Modify Mobile Navigation Menu

Go to **Shared Components** and click on **Navigation Menu** under Navigation section. Click on **Mobile Navigation Menu**. It's a default menu created for the mobile application and carries just one entry: Home. Using the **Create List Entry** button, add the following four entries to this menu:

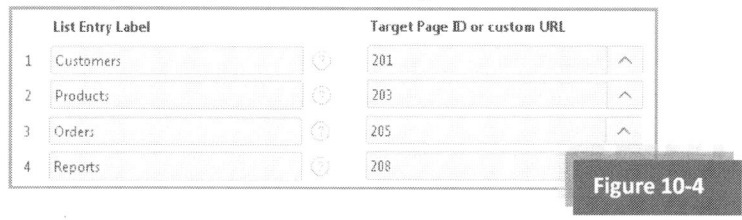

#	List Entry Label	Target Page ID or custom URL
1	Customers	201
2	Products	203
3	Orders	205
4	Reports	208

Figure 10-4

10.4.3 Mobile Reports List

Create another list named Mobile Reports for the mobile application. APEX provides a utility that lets you make a copy of an existing component. Here are the steps to create Mobile Reports list by making a copy of Reports List, you created in Chapter 3.

1. In Shared Components, click on the **Lists** link under Navigation.
2. Click on the **Copy** button.
3. In the first wizard step, select **List in this application** and move on.
4. In Copy List, select **Reports List**. Enter **Mobile Reports** for New List Name and click the **Copy** button.
5. In the Lists page, click on **Mobile Reports** you just copied. In the mobile version we will create four reports as shown in the following table, because maps, trees and PDF are not supported on this platform. Click each link individually and set the Page attribute in the Target section as follows. Delete all other report options.

List Entry	Page	List Entry	Page
Customer Orders	209	Order Calendar	211
Sales by Category and Product	210	Reflow Report	212

Test Your Work

The three default mobile pages created by APEX wizard are ready for a test. You might have noticed that we didn't work on the mobile login page 1001 (we didn't work on the desktop login page either). Application Express is smart enough to create these pages with basic functionalities, suffice to cope with our needs. Access the mobile application from the Mobile navigation bar entry. Click on the Menu button, which should open a panel carrying the mobile navigation menu. Click on the **Full Site** button at the bottom to call the Home page of the desktop version. Also try the Logout button in the mobile version.

Chapter 10 – Develop A Mobile Version For Smartphones

10.5 Create Customers Page - Page 201

1. As usual, click on the **Create Page** button to create the first mobile application page yourself.
2. Note that for User Interface you now have two options: Desktop and Mobile. This time select the Mobile option and click on **Report** icon to move ahead.
3. Select the **List View** option. One of the main differences between an APEX desktop application and a mobile application is the presence of the List View in the mobile world. Due to non-availability of an interactive report for the mobile platform, you'll use this option instead.
4. Type **201** in Page Number and **Customers** in Page Name and Region Name. Leave Page Mode to Normal and move on.
5. Set Navigation Preference to **Identify an existing navigation menu entry for this page** and select **Customers** for Existing Navigation Menu Entry.
6. For Source Type, select SQL Query and enter the following query in Region Source:
   select a.ROWID as "PK_ROWID", a.* from "#OWNER#"."DEMO_CUSTOMERS" a
   For each row in the database the ROWID pseudocolumn returns the address of the row. Oracle Database rowid values contain information necessary to locate a row.

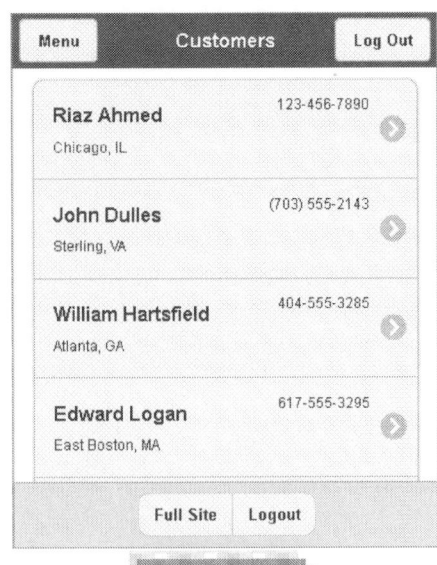

   Figure 10-5

   NOTE: Mobile pages created in Oracle APEX do not support constructs such as interactive reports, tabular forms, and master-detail pages.

7. Do not select anything on the Settings page and move on to finish the wizard.
8. In the Customers page, click on Attributes node under Customers region to set the following attributes. Put checks on **Advanced Formatting** and **Inset List** features. If lists are embedded in a page with other types of content, an inset list packages the list into a block that sits inside the content area with a bit of margin and rounded corners. Fill in the other attributes as shown in the following table:

Attribute	Value
Text Formatting	`<h3>&CUST_FIRST_NAME. &CUST_LAST_NAME.</h3>` `<p>&CUST_CITY., &CUST_STATE.</p>`
Supplemental Informational Formatting	&PHONE_NUMBER1.
Target Type	Page in this Application
Page	202
Name	P202_ROWID
Value	&PK_ROWID.
Clear Cache	202

The *Advanced Formatting* option enables you to style your list even further. The first option, *List Attributes*, is used to style the list by overriding the standard list or divider theme. The *List Entry Attributes* can be set to pick an icon other than the standard right arrow (you'll test these two options in the Product module). The mandatory option, *Text Formatting*, gives you the opportunity to show more in the list than just the Customer Name. In this example, you wrapped customer's first and last names in an HTML <h3> heading element. Besides, you can add more stuff to the list with the help of *Supplemental Information* as you did here by presenting customer's phone number. The Supplemental Information appears on the right side of the list item. Each customer record will become a link through the *Target* attribute. To display a record of the selected customer (on Page 202), the link forwards two parameters. The first one, P202_ROWID, is an item on Page 202 that will receive a primary key value from the second one that is based on PK_ROWID, selected in the SQL query. Note that rather than creating a blank page and adding main region to it later, we created the page, added a region with its source, and set attributes to display the required information, all at once.

10.5.1 Add Button - Create

Right click on Customers region and select **Create Button**. Set the following attributes for this button:

Attribute	Value	Attribute	Value
Name	CREATE	Action	Redirect to Page in this Application
Label	Create	Target Type	Page in this application
Button Position	Bottom of Region	Page	202
Hot	Yes	Clear Cache	202

Save and test the page, which should look like Figure 10-5.

10.6 Create Maintain Customer Page - Page 202

1. Create another mobile page and this time select the **Form** option followed by **Form on a Table or View**.
2. Accept the default schema and select **DEMO_CUSTOMERS** table from Table/View Name.
3. Enter **202** in Page Number. **Maintain Customer** in Page Name and Region Title. Leaving Region Template to the default value Plain (No Title), click **Next**.
4. Set Navigation Preference to **Identify an existing navigation menu entry for this page** and select **Customers** for Existing Navigation Menu Entry.
5. For Primary Key Type, select **Managed by Database (ROWID)** option and move forward. You've been using the second option (Select Primary Key Column) in the desktop application exercises to select a primary key for the selected table. This time, you're using the alternate method, which is usually selected for tables with multiple primary key columns (more than two).
6. Select **all** columns from the table and click **Next**.
7. Keep **all** the default options on the Buttons page and click **Next**.
8. On the Branching page, enter **201** for both Submit and Cancel buttons to move back to the main customers' page.
9. Click **Create** on the Confirm page.

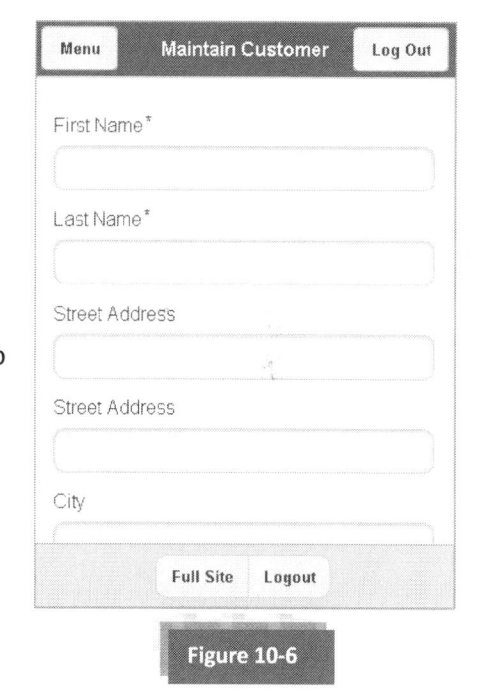

Figure 10-6

Chapter 10 – Develop A Mobile Version For Smartphones

10.6.1 Modify Items

Modify attributes of the page items as shown in the following table:

ITEM	ATTRIBUTE:VALUE	ATTRIBUTE:VALUE	ATTRIBUTE:VALUE
P202_CUSTOMER_ID	Type : Hidden	-	-
P202_CUST_FIRST_NAME	Label : First Name	-	-
P202_CUST_LAST_NAME	Label : Last Name	-	-
P202_CUST_STREET_ADDRESS1	Label : Street Address	-	-
P202_CUST_STREET_ADDRESS2	Label : Line 2	-	-
P202_CUST_CITY	Label : City	-	-
P202_CUST_POSTAL_CODE	Label : Postal Code	Template : Required	Value Required : Yes
P202_CUST_EMAIL	Label : Email	-	-
P202_PHONE_NUMBER1	Label : Phone Number	-	-
P202_PHONE_NUMBER2	Label : Alternate Number	-	-
P202_URL	Label : URL	-	-
P202_CREDIT_LIMIT	-	Template : Required	Value Required : Yes
P202_TAGS	Type : Text Field	-	-

Click on **P202_CUST_STATE** item. Change its Type from Text Field to **Select List**; enter **State** in Label; set Template to **Required**; Value Required to **Yes**; List of Values Type to **Shared Component**; and LOV to **STATES**. Save your work.

From the mobile menu select Customers. Click on any customer's record to see how the page looks like. Click the Cancel button to move back to the main customers' page. Click the Create Customer button, located at the bottom of the main Customers page. A new form will be presented with two buttons: Cancel and Create. Create a new customer record and click the Create button to store it in DEMO_CUSTOMERS table. Call the new record and try to modify and save some information. Finally, delete this record. Using the instructions provided in the desktop version, add two validations: check credit limit and prevent customer's record deletion having orders.

10.7 Create Main Products Page - Page 203

1. Create a new page by clicking on the **Create Page** button.
2. Select **Mobile** for User Interface and click on the **Report** icon to move ahead.
3. Once again select the **List View** option.
4. Type **203** in Page Number and enter **Products** for Page and Region names. Keep the Normal page mode and click **Next**.
5. Set Navigation Preference to **Identify an existing navigation menu entry for this page** and select **Products** for Existing Navigation Menu Entry. Click **Next**.
6. After selecting **SQL Query** as Source Type, enter the following SQL statement in Region Source. This statement is similar to the one you used to fetch customers records on Page 201.

    select a.ROWID as "PK_ROWID", a.*
    from "#OWNER#"."DEMO_PRODUCT_INFO" a
    order by a.product_name

7. Set attributes on the Settings page as shown below.

Figure 10-7

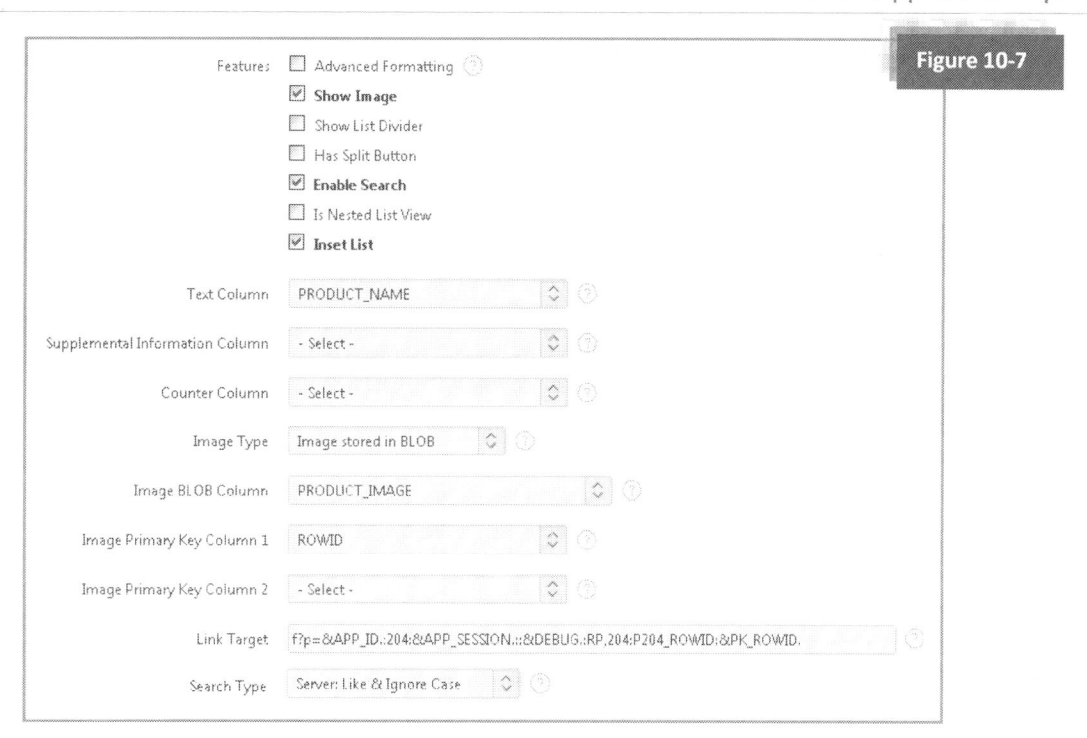

When you click the option *Show Image*, some more relevant attributes appear on your screen. The same behavior applies to the *Enable Search* option. The first option is checked because we need to display products images, while the second option is checked to add search functionality. The selected Text Column, PRODUCT_NAME, will appear next to the image at runtime. The *Image Type* attribute specifies what kind of image is displayed and where it is read from. The displayed image can be an icon with a size of 16x16 or a thumbnail with a size of 80x80. The source for the image can be a database BLOB column or a URL to a static file. After setting the *Image Type* attribute, you're required to provide the *Image BLOB Column* which, in our case, is PRODUCT_IMAGE. The *Image Primary Key* attribute specifies the primary key or a unique database column that is used to lookup the image. The value for this attribute (ROWID) is selected by the wizard. In the Customers module we set link target through the Property Editor, here we entered a link manually (f?p=&APP_ID.:204:&APP_SESSION.::&DEBUG.:RP,204:P204_ROWID:&PK_ROWID.) that you can verify by accessing the Target property. The *Search Type* attribute defines how a search will be performed. The selected option, *Server: Like & Ignore Case*, will use Oracle's LIKE operator (LIKE %UPPER([search value])%) to query the result.

After creating the page, click on Attributes node under Products region. Set *Search Column* to **PRODUCT_DESCRIPTION** and enter **Search Product Description** in *Search Box Place holder* attribute. The *Search Column* specifies an alternative database column used for the search. The text added to the *Search Box Placeholder* will appear in the search box at runtime, to inform users what to put in the search box.

10.7.1 Add Button - Create

Right click on Products region and select **Create Button**. Set the following attributes for this button:

Attribute	Value	Attribute	Value
Name	CREATE	Action	Redirect to Page in this Application
Label	Create	Target Type	Page in this application
Button Position	Bottom of Region	Page	204
Hot	Yes	Clear Cache	204

Chapter 10 – Develop A Mobile Version For Smartphones

Save the page and run the application. From the mobile menu, click on the Products option. You'll see the main Products page. Enter **shoes** in the search box and hit enter. Two shoe products (Ladies Shoes and Men Shoes) should appear. Enter **low heel** in the search box. The page will be refreshed with one record, displaying Ladies Shoes. This is because the word low heel exists in the description for this product only. Type **lower lace** in the search box. This time Men Shoes will be displayed. Click the Clear Text icon in the search box. All the products will re-appear.

Make this page more meaningful by performing the following steps:
1. Click on the region's Attribute node.
2. In the Property pane, put a check on **Advanced Formatting**.
3. In List Attributes, type: **data-divider-theme="b"**. The theme for list dividers can be set by adding the data-divider-theme to the list and specifying a swatch letter. We set swatch "b" on the dividers.
4. Enter **data-icon="plus"** in List Entry Attributes, to change the default right arrow icon with a plus icon.
5. In Text Formatting, type:
   <h3>&PRODUCT_NAME.</h3><p>&PRODUCT_DESCRIPTION.</p>
6. In Supplemental Information, type:
   <strong>Price:</strong>$&LIST_PRICE..
7. Enter **&CATEGORY.** in List Divider Formatting attribute to show the category of each product. Apply changes and run the page to see an output similar to Figure 10-8.

Figure 10-8

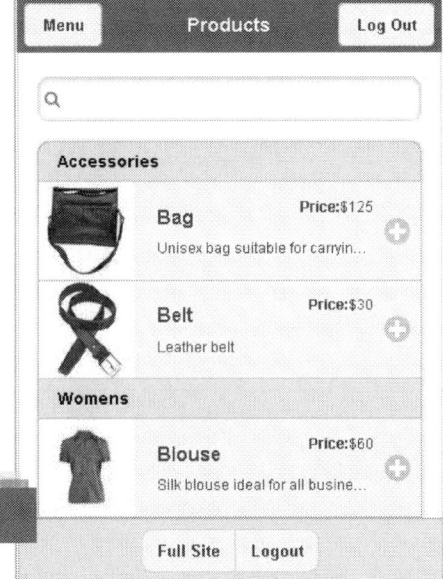

10.8 Create Maintain Product Page - Page 204

1. Create another mobile page and select the **Form** option followed by **Form on a Table or View**.
2. Accept the default schema and select **DEMO_PRODUCT_INFO** table from Table/View Name.
3. Enter **204** in Page Number and **Maintain Product** in Page Name and Region Title. Accepting the default Page Mode and Region Template, click **Next**.
4. Set Navigation Preference to **Identify an existing navigation menu entry for this page** and select **Products** for Existing Navigation Menu Entry.
5. For Primary Key Type, select the **Managed by Database (ROWID)** option and move forward.
6. Select **all** columns from the table except MIMETYPE, FILENAME, IMAGE_LAST_UPDATE, and PRODUCT_IMAGE. Click **Next**.
7. Accept all default options on the Buttons page and click **Next**.
8. On the Branching page, enter **203** for both Submit and Cancel buttons to move back to the main products page.
9. Click **Create** on the Confirm page.

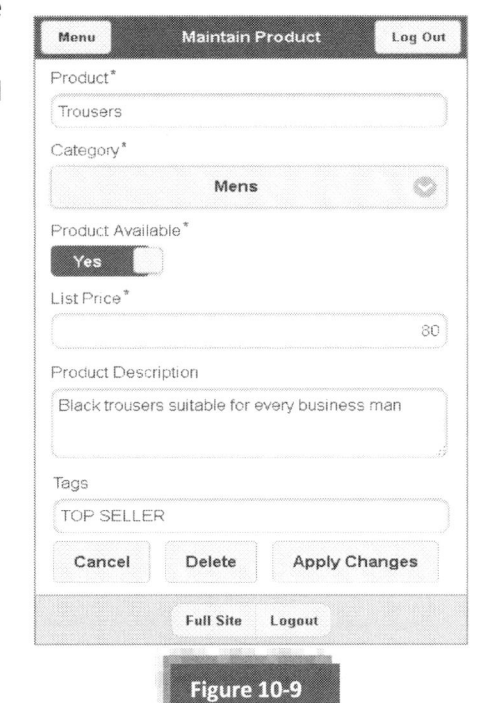

Figure 10-9

170

10.8.1 Modify Items

Modify attributes of the page items as shown in the following table:

ITEM	ATTRIBUTE:VALUE	ATTRIBUTE:VALUE	ATTRIBUTE:VALUE
P204_PRODUCT_ID	Type : Hidden	-	-
P204_PRODUCT_NAME	Label : Product	Template : Required	Value Required : Yes
P204_LIST_PRICE	Label : List Price	Template : Required	Value Required : Yes
P204_TAGS	Type : Text Field	-	-

Call **P204_CATEGORY** item's attributes. Change its Type from Text Field to **Select List**, set Label to **Category**, Template to **Required**, Value Required to **Yes**, LOV Type to **Shared Components**, and LOV to **CATEGORIES**.

Call **P204_PRODUCT_AVAIL** attributes. Change Type from Text Field to **Yes/No**, Label to **Product Available**, Template to **Required**, and Value Required to **Yes**. Recall that in chapter 6 we attached the Y or N LOV to the Product Available item in the desktop application. This time, we have used a built-in alternate.

Test Your Work

Save your work and run the module using the Products link in the main mobile menu. On the Products page, click on any product to see an output similar to Figure 10-9.

10.9 Create Orders Page 205

For desktop version you used the Master Detail Form option to simultaneously create Orders (Page 4) and Order Details (Page 29) pages. Since Master-Detail option is not available for mobile platform, you will use a new feature called Column Toggle Report provided in APEX 5. By setting a region to Column Toggle Report type, you build reports that display all of your data on any mobile device. Column toggle enables you to specify the most important columns, and those which will be hidden as necessary on smaller screens.

1. Click the **Create Page** button. Set User Interface to Mobile and select **Report** option in the initial screen followed by **Column Toggle Report** option.
2. Enter **205** in Page Number and **Orders** in Page and Region names. Keeping the default Page Mode to Normal, click **Next**.
3. Set Navigation Preference to **Identify an existing navigation menu entry for this page** and select **Orders** for Existing Navigation Menu Entry.
4. After selecting **SQL Query** as Source Type, enter the following SQL statement in Region Source.

    ```
    select o.rowid,
        o.order_id,
        to_date(to_char(o.order_timestamp,'mm yyyy'), 'mm yyyy') order_month,
        o.order_timestamp order_date,
        o.user_name sales_rep,
        o.order_total,
        c.cust_last_name || ',' || c.cust_first_name customer_name,
        (select count(*) from demo_order_items oi where oi.order_id = o.order_id) order_items,
        o.tags tags
    from  demo_orders o, demo_customers c
    where o.customer_id = c.customer_id
    ```

5. On the final wizard page click the **Create** button to end the process.

Chapter 10 – Develop A Mobile Version For Smartphones

10.9.1 Add Button - Create

Right click on Orders region and select **Create Button**. Set the following attributes for this button:

Attribute	Value	Attribute	Value
Name	CREATE	Action	Redirect to Page in this Application
Label	Create	Target Type	Page in this application
Button Position	Create	Page	216
Hot	Yes	Clear Cache	216

Save and run the page. Initially the page will display all the columns defined in the above query. Click on the columns button. In the ensuing columns list, remove checks from all columns, except Order Id, Order Month, and Customer Name to show these three columns in the main report, which should resemble Figure 10-10.

10.10 Create Order Page 216

In the desktop version we created a wizard to record customer orders. Here too, you'll adopt the same process to enter an order sequentially. In the desktop module, the first page that appeared after clicking the Enter New Order button was Page 11, where you allowed users to select an existing customer, or to create a new one. To save some time, you'll copy that page for the mobile module. Let's see how it is done.

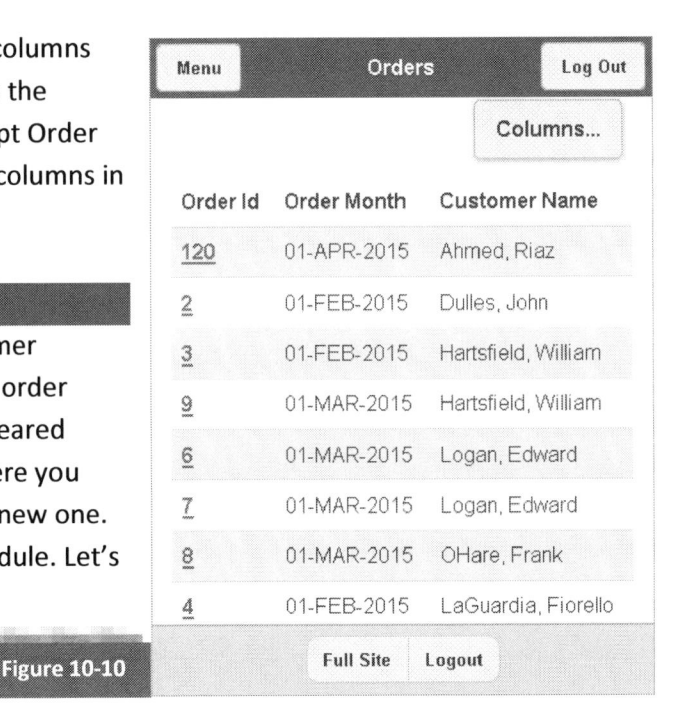

Figure 10-10

1. Call **Identify Customer** page (Page 11).
2. Click the **Create** menu button to your right and select **Page as copy**. Recall that you used this technique earlier to create Page 11 from Page 7.
3. Select the option **Page in this application**.
4. In Page to Copy, set the following attributes. Note that this time we are using Mobile option for the User Interface.

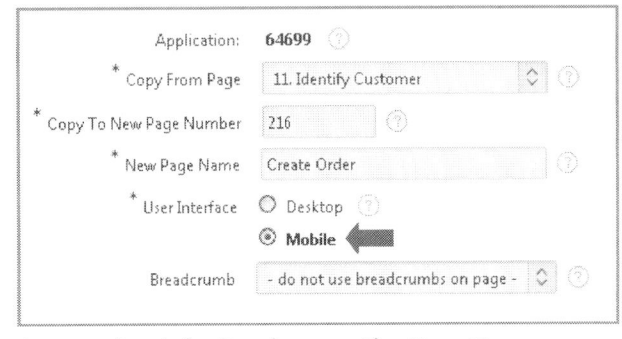

5. Accept the default values on the New Names page and click **Next**.
6. Click **Copy** to create the page.

If you run the page at this stage, you'll see an error message: *Application 64699 Dialog page 216 cannot be rendered successfully*. This is because the Page Mode attribute of the new page is set to Modal Dialog. Set it to **Normal** to prevent the error. After this major amendment, you need to modify other elements of the page to make it appropriate for mobile devices.

172

10.10.1 Delete/Modify Regions

1. Delete **Order Progress** region, because it is not supported under mobile platform.
2. Modify the **Buttons** region. Its Position attribute will be displaying REGION_POSITION_03 (Invalid). Change it to **Body3**.

10.10.2 Modify Buttons

1. Click on **Cancel** Button and set the following attributes:

Attribute	Value	Attribute	Value
Button Position	Bottom of Region	Action	Redirect to Page in this Application
Horizontal Alignment	Left	Page (Target)	205
Button Template	Standard Button	-	-

2. Select the **Next** Button and set the following attributes:

Attribute	Value	Attribute	Value
Button Position	Bottom of Region	Button Template	Standard Button
Horizontal Alignment	Right	Hot	Yes

10.10.3 Modify Items

1. Modify the first item **P216_CUSTOMER_OPTIONS** and set the following attributes:

Attribute	Value
Template	Required
Value Required	Yes
Display Extra Values	No

2. Modify **P216_CUSTOMER_ID** and set these attributes:

Attribute	Value	Attribute	Value
Type	Select List	Display Null Values	Yes
Template	Required	Null Display Value	- Select a Customer -
Display Extra Values	No	-	-

3. Set Template to **Required** for the following five items. You can use Ctrl+Click to select all these items and set the attribute at once.

    P216_CUST_FIRST_NAME, **P216_CUST_LAST_NAME**, **P216_CUST_STATE**, **P216_CUST_POSTAL_CODE** and **P216_CREDIT_LIMIT**.

4. Set Template to **Optional** for:

    P216_CUST_STREET_ADDRESS1, **P216_CUST_STREET_ADDRESS2**, **P216_CUST_CITY**, **P216_CUST_EMAIL**, **P216_URL** and **P216_TAGS**.

5. Modify **P216_PHONE_NUMBER1** and **P216_PHONE_NUMBER2** as follows:

Attribute	Value
Type	Text Field
Subtype	Phone Number
Template	Optional

6. Set Start New Row attributes of all the above items (mentioned in steps 3, 4, and 5) to **Yes** to place them vertically upon each other.

Chapter 10 – Develop A Mobile Version For Smartphones

10.10.4 Modify Branch

Modify the sole branch (Go To Page 12) under Page Processing like this:

Attribute	Value
Name	Next
Target Type	Page in this Application
Page	217 (Also clear page value from Clear Cache and remove entries from Name and Value)
When Button Pressed	Next

Save and run the page using the mobile menu route. After clicking the Create button, you'll see Figure 10-11. Click the second option, New Customer, to see an output shown in Figure 10-12.

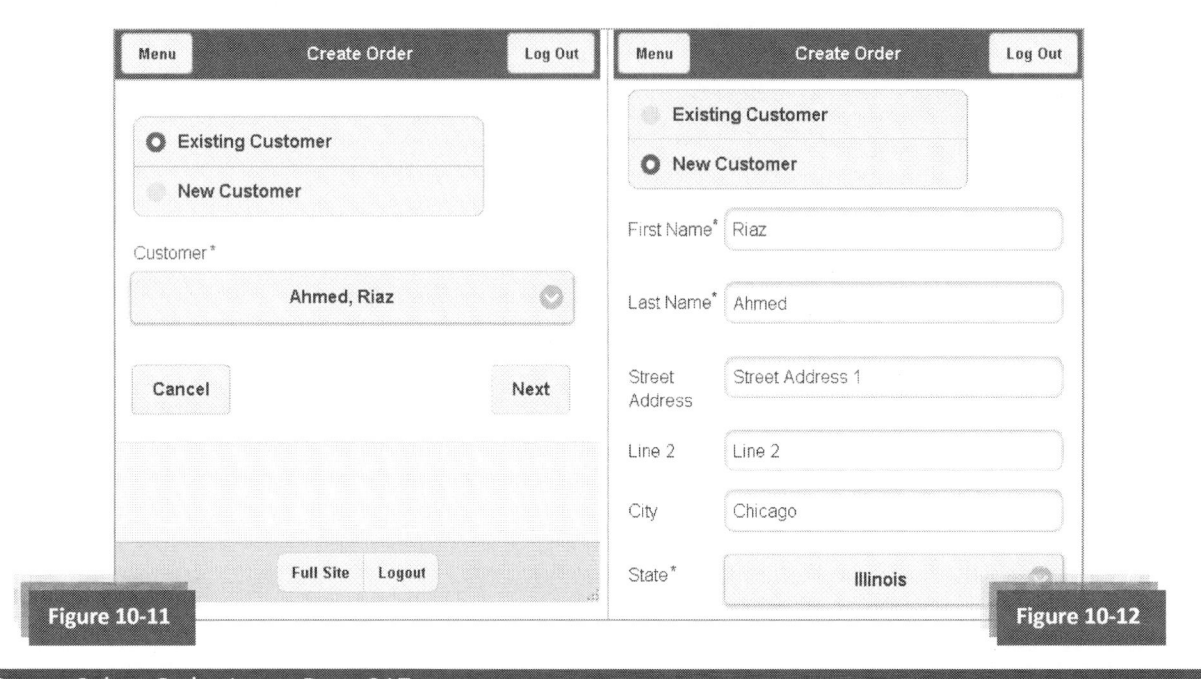

Figure 10-11

Figure 10-12

10.11 Create Select Order Items Page 217

Using the same copy utility, you'll create this page as well, to select order items. In the desktop version you created Page 12 for this purpose and this is the page you'll use as the source for your mobile application. The copied page will inherit all items and processes from the source.

1. Call **Order Items** page (Page 12).
2. Once again, click the **Create** menu button to your right and select **Page as copy**.
3. Select the option **Page in this application**.
4. In Page to Copy, set attributes as shown in the adjacent screen shot. Don't forget to select the Mobile option for the User Interface.
5. Accept the default values on the New Names page and click **Next**.
6. Click **Copy** to create the page.
7. Set Page Mode attribute to **Normal** for the new page (217).

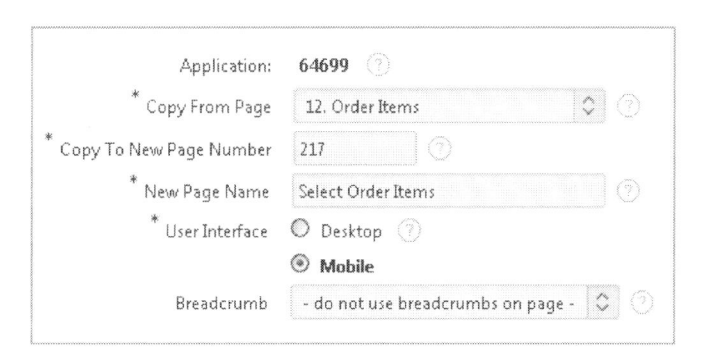

10.11.1 Modify Regions

1. Click on **Select Items** region and change its Template attribute from Plain (No Title) to **Region (With Title)**. This will add a title (Select Items) at the top of this region.
2. Delete **Order Progress** region.
3. Modify **Buttons** region by switching its Position attribute from REGION_POSITION_03 (Invalid) to **Body3**.

Replace Select Items region's Source PL/SQL Code with the following. Note that this code is similar to the desktop version (section 7.6.4) except for the items marked in bold, which are modified to represent mobile version page items.

```
declare
 l_customer_id varchar2(30) := :P216_CUSTOMER_ID;
begin
-- display customer information
sys.htp.p('<div class="CustomerInfo">');
if :P216_CUSTOMER_OPTIONS = 'EXISTING' then
 for x in (select * from demo_customers where customer_id = l_customer_id) loop
   sys.htp.p('<div class="CustomerInfo">');
   sys.htp.p('<strong>Customer:</strong>');
   sys.htp.p('<p>');
   sys.htp.p(sys.htf.escape_sc(x.cust_first_name)||' '||sys.htf.escape_sc(x.cust_last_name)||'<br/>');
   sys.htp.p(sys.htf.escape_sc(x.cust_street_address1) || '<br />');
   if x.cust_street_address2 is not null then
     sys.htp.p(sys.htf.escape_sc(x.cust_street_address2) || '<br />');
   end if;
   sys.htp.p(sys.htf.escape_sc(x.cust_city) || ',' || sys.htf.escape_sc(x.cust_state) || ' ' ||
   sys.htf.escape_sc(x.cust_postal_code));
   sys.htp.p('</p>');
 end loop;
else
 sys.htp.p('<strong>Customer:</strong>');
 sys.htp.p('<p>');
 sys.htp.p(sys.htf.escape_sc(:P216_CUST_FIRST_NAME)||' '||sys.htf.escape_sc(:P216_CUST_LAST_NAME)
 || '<br />');
 sys.htp.p(sys.htf.escape_sc(:P216_CUST_STREET_ADDRESS1) || '<br />');
 if :P216_CUST_STREET_ADDRESS2 is not null then
   sys.htp.p(sys.htf.escape_sc(:P216_CUST_STREET_ADDRESS2) || '<br />');
 end if;
 sys.htp.p(sys.htf.escape_sc(:P216_CUST_CITY) || ',' ||
 sys.htf.escape_sc(:P216_CUST_STATE) || ' ' ||
 sys.htf.escape_sc(:P216_CUST_POSTAL_CODE));
 sys.htp.p('</p>');
end if;
```

```
sys.htp.p('</div>');
-- display products
sys.htp.p('<div class="Products" >');
sys.htp.p('<table width="100%" cellspacing="0" cellpadding="0" border="0">
<thead>
<tr><th class="left">Product</th><th>Price</th><th></th></tr>
</thead>
<tbody>');
for c1 in (select product_id, product_name, list_price, 'Add to Cart' add_to_order
from demo_product_info
where product_avail = 'Y'
order by product_name) loop
sys.htp.p('<tr><td class="left">' ||
sys.htf.escape_sc(c1.product_name)||'</td><td>'||trim(to_char(c1.list_price,'999G999G990D00'))||
'</td><td><a
        href="'||apex_util.prepare_url('f?p=&APP_ID.:217:'||:app_session
        ||':ADD:::P217_PRODUCT_ID:'||c1.product_id)||'"
        class="t-Button"><span>Add</span>
  </a></td></tr>');
end loop;
sys.htp.p('</tbody></table>');
sys.htp.p('</div>');
-- display current order
sys.htp.p('<div class="Products" >');
sys.htp.p('<table width="100%" cellspacing="0" cellpadding="0" border="0">
<thead>
<tr><th class="left">Current Order</th></tr>
</thead>
</table>
<table width="100%" cellspacing="0" cellpadding="0" border="0">
<tbody>');
declare
   c number := 0; t number := 0;
begin
-- loop over cart values
for c1 in (select c001 pid, c002 i, to_number(c003) p, count(c002) q, sum(c003) ep, 'Remove' remove
from apex_collections
where collection_name = 'ORDER'
group by c001, c002, c003
order by c002)
loop
sys.htp.p('<div class="CartItem"><a href="'||
apex_util.prepare_url('f?p=&APP_ID.:217:&SESSION.:REMOVE:::P217_PRODUCT_ID:'||sys.htf.escape_sc(c1.pid))|
|'"><img src="#IMAGE_PREFIX#delete.gif" alt="Remove from cart" title="Remove from cart" /></a>  
```

```
'||sys.htf.escape_sc(c1.i)||'
<span>'||trim(to_char(c1.p,'$999G999G999D00'))||'</span>
<span>Quantity: '||c1.q||'</span>
<span class="subtotal">Subtotal: '||trim(to_char(c1.ep,'$999G999G999D00'))||'</span>
</div>');
   c := c + 1;
   t := t + c1.ep;
end loop;
sys.htp.p('</tbody></table>');
if c > 0 then
   sys.htp.p('<div class="CartTotal">
   <p>Items: <span>'||c||'</span></p>
   <p class="CartTotal">Total: <span>'||trim(to_char(t,'$999G999G999D00'))||'</span></p>
</div>');
else
   sys.htp.p('<p class="CartTotal">You have no items in your current order.</p>');
end if;
end;
sys.htp.p('</div>');
end;
```

10.11.2 Modify Buttons

1. Click the **Cancel** Button to set the following attributes:

Attribute	Value	Attribute	Value
Button Position	Bottom of Region	Action	Redirect to Page in this Application
Horizontal Alignment	Left	Page (Target)	205
Button Template	Standard Button	-	-

2. Click the **Next** Button link and set the following attributes:

Attribute	Value	Attribute	Value
Button Position	Bottom of Region	Button Template	Standard Button
Horizontal Alignment	Right	Hot	Yes

Chapter 10 – Develop A Mobile Version For Smartphones

10.11.3 After Submit Process

Go to Processing tab. Click on Place Order process and replace existing Source PL/SQL code with the following. This one too is the same PL/SQL procedure used in section 7.6.9 in the desktop module. Items marked in bold are modified in the code to reflect mobile page elements.

```
declare
  l_order_id   number;
  l_customer_id varchar2(30) := :P216_CUSTOMER_ID;
begin
  -- Create New Customer
  if :P216_CUSTOMER_OPTIONS = 'NEW' then
    insert into DEMO_CUSTOMERS (
       CUST_FIRST_NAME, CUST_LAST_NAME, CUST_STREET_ADDRESS1,
       CUST_STREET_ADDRESS2, CUST_CITY, CUST_STATE, CUST_POSTAL_CODE,
       CUST_EMAIL, PHONE_NUMBER1, PHONE_NUMBER2, URL, CREDIT_LIMIT, TAGS)
     values (
       :P216_CUST_FIRST_NAME, :P216_CUST_LAST_NAME, :P216_CUST_STREET_ADDRESS1,
       :P216_CUST_STREET_ADDRESS2, :P216_CUST_CITY, :P216_CUST_STATE,
       :P216_CUST_POSTAL_CODE, :P216_CUST_EMAIL, :P216_PHONE_NUMBER1,
       :P216_PHONE_NUMBER2, :P216_URL, :P216_CREDIT_LIMIT, :P216_TAGS)
     returning customer_id into l_customer_id;
     :P216_CUSTOMER_ID := l_customer_id;
  end if;
  -- Insert a row into the Order Header table
  insert into demo_orders(customer_id, order_total, order_timestamp, user_name)
  values(l_customer_id, null, systimestamp, upper(:APP_USER)) returning order_id into l_order_id;
  commit;
  -- Loop through the ORDER collection and insert rows into the Order Line Item table
  for x in (select c001, c003, sum(c004) c004 from apex_collections
            where collection_name = 'ORDER' group by c001, c003)
  loop
    insert into demo_order_items(order_item_id, order_id, product_id, unit_price, quantity)
    values (null, l_order_id, to_number(x.c001), to_number(x.c003),to_number(x.c004));
  end loop;
  commit;
  -- Set the item P218_ORDER_ID to the order which was just placed
  :P218_ORDER_ID := l_order_id;
  -- Truncate the collection after the order has been placed
  apex_collection.truncate_collection(p_collection_name => 'ORDER');
end;
```

10.11.4 Modify Branch

1. Modify the first branch (Go To Page 14) using the following attributes:

Attribute	Value	Attribute	Value
Name	Go To Page 218	Name	P218_CUSTOMER_ID
Target Type	Page in this Application	Value	&P217_CUSTOMER_ID.
Page	218	-	-

2. Delete the other two branches.

Save your work. Call this page from the mobile menu route. The page should look like the following screen shot.

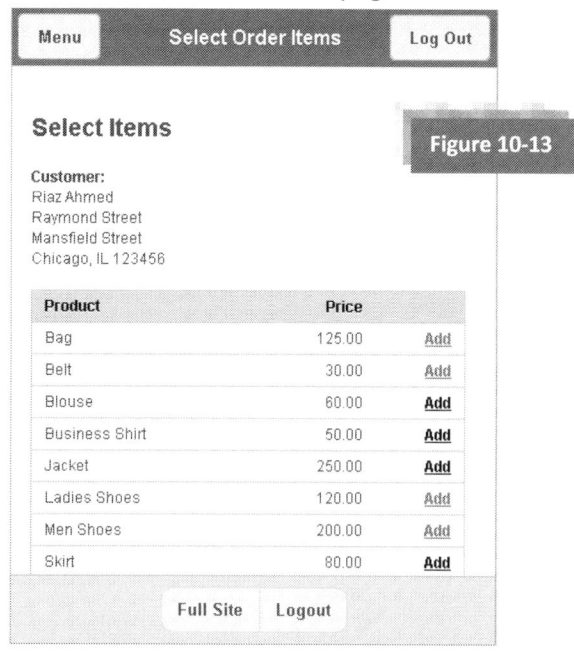

Figure 10-13

10.12 Create Order Summary Page 218

Once again, use the page copy utility to create Order Summary page from Page 14 of the desktop application using the following screen shot. After creating the page, set its Page Mode attribute to **Normal**.

10.12.1 Modify Regions

1. Click on **Order Lines** region to change its Template attribute to **Region (With Title)**.
2. Delete **Order Progress** region.
3. Modify **Buttons** region by switching its Position attribute from REGION_POSITION_03 (Invalid) to **Body3**.
4. Expand Columns node under Order Lines region. Click on EXTENDED_PRICE column. Set its Compute Sum attribute to **Yes**. This will add a row labeled Report total to show order total.

Chapter 10 – Develop A Mobile Version For Smartphones

10.12.2 Modify Button

Click the **Back** button and set the following attributes:

Attribute	Value	Attribute	Value
Button Position	Bottom of Region	Hot	Yes
Horizontal Alignment	Right	Action	Redirect to Page in this Application
Button Template	Standard Button	Page	205

Test Your Work

Run the module using the Orders link in the mobile menu. Click the Create button to enter a new order. Select an existing customer and click Next. Select some items using the Add link and click the Place Order button. The Order Summary page as illustrated in Figure 10-14 should come up displaying summary of the most recent order. Click the Back To Orders button to move back to the main orders listing where you'll see this order added to the list. Also create an order using the New Customer option.

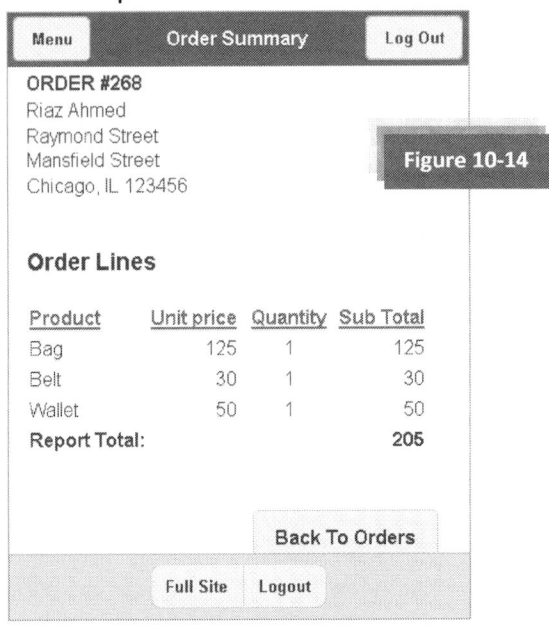

Figure 10-14

Display Reports on Smartphones

10.13 List of Reports Page 208

This is the main reports navigation page for smartphone platform carrying a list of available reports. It is almost similar to the one you went through in the desktop version.

1. Create a Blank Page using Mobile User Interface option.
2. Enter **208** in Page Number, and **Reports** for its Name. Click **Next**.
3. On the Navigation Menu page, set Navigation Preference to **Identify an existing navigation menu entry for this page**, and set Existing Navigation Menu Entry to **Reports**. Click **Next**.
4. Click **Finish** to end the wizard.
5. Create a new region on this page and set the following attributes for it. The region will carry the Mobile Reports list, created in section 10.4.3.

Attribute	Value
Title	Reports
Type	List
List	Mobile Reports

10.14 Customer Orders Report - Page 209

The reports you'll be creating in this section are the same you created earlier in chapter 8. Starting with the Customer Orders Report, let's see how graphical reports are created for smartphones.

Figure 10-15

1. Create another **Blank Page** using Mobile Interface. Set its number to **209** and enter **Customer Orders** for its name. Select **Reports** for navigation menu entry.
2. Create a new region on this page and set the following attributes:

Attribute	Value
Title	Customer Orders
Type	Chart

3. Click on the **Attributes** node under Customer Orders chart region to set the following attributes:

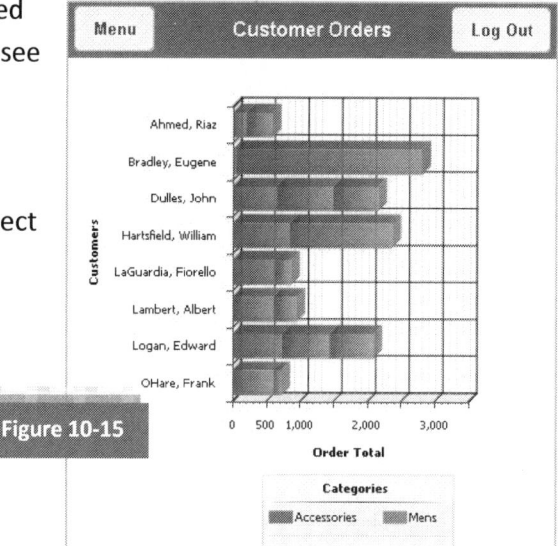

Attribute	Value	Attribute	Value
Type	Stacked Bar Chart	Title (Y Axis)	Order Total
Title	*Make it empty*	Show (Value)	No
Rendering	HTML5 Chart	Show (Legend)	Bottom
3D Mode	Yes	Title (Legend)	Categories
Show Grid	Both	Element Orientation	Horizontal
Title (X Axis)	Customers	-	-

4. Click on the **New** node under Series and enter the following SQL query.

Attribute	Value
Source Type	SQL Query
SQL Query	select c.rowid **link**, 　　　c.cust_last_name||', '||c.cust_first_name Customer_Name, 　　　sum (decode(p.category,'Accessories',oi.quantity * oi.unit_price,0)) "Accessories", 　　　sum (decode(p.category,'Mens',oi.quantity * oi.unit_price,0)) "Men", 　　　sum (decode(p.category,'Womens',oi.quantity * oi.unit_price,0)) "Women" from demo_customers c, demo_orders o, demo_order_items oi, demo_product_info p where c.customer_id = o.customer_id and o.order_id = oi.order_id and 　　　oi.product_id = p.product_id group by c.rowid, c.customer_id, c.cust_last_name, c.cust_first_name order by c.cust_last_name
Link Type	Link to Custom Target
Type	Page in this Application
Page	202
Name	P202_ROWID
Value	#LINK#
Clear Cache	202

    NOTE: The #LINK# value in the Value attribute, references the first column named **link** in the SELECT statement. This chart is created with drill-down functionality. Clicking a bar takes you to Maintain Customer page (Page 202).

Chapter 10 – Develop A Mobile Version For Smartphones

10.15 Sales by Category and Product - Page 210

This report was created earlier in the desktop version as well.

1. Create another **Blank Page** using Mobile Interface. Set its number to **210** and enter **Sales by Category and Product** for its name. Select **Reports** for navigation menu entry.
2. Create a new region on this page and set the following attributes:

Attribute	Value
Title	Sales by Category
Type	Chart
Template	Region (With Title Bar)

3. Click on the **Attributes** node under Sales by Category chart region and set the following attributes:

Attribute	Value
Type	Pie
Title	*Make it empty*
Rendering	HTML5 Chart
3D Mode	Yes
Scheme	Look 2
Show (Value)	No

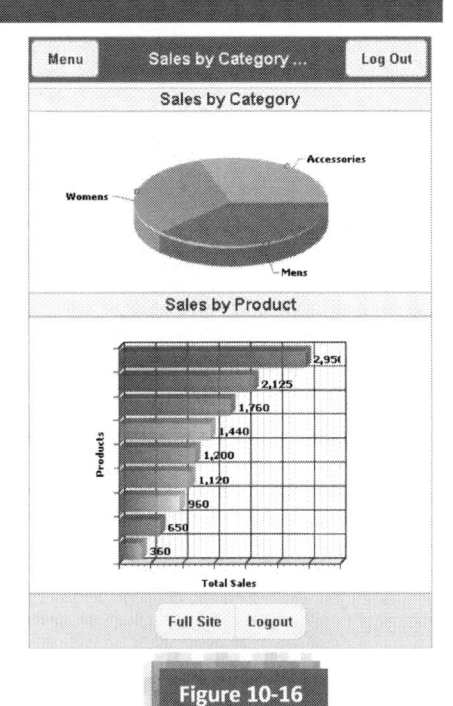

4. Click on the **New** node under Series and enter the following SQL query.

Attribute	Value
Source Type	SQL Query
SQL Query	select null, p.category label, sum(o.order_total) total_sales from demo_orders o, demo_order_items oi, demo_product_info p where o.order_id = oi.order_id and oi.product_id = p.product_id group by category order by 3 desc

5. Create another region under the Body node and set the following attributes:

Attribute	Value	Attribute	Value
Title	Sales by Product	Template	Region (With Title Bar)
Type	Chart	-	-

6. Click on the Attributes node under Sales by Product chart region and set the following attributes:

Attribute	Value	Attribute	Value
Type	Bar Chart	Scheme	Look 7
Title	*Make it empty*	Title (X Axis)	Products
Rendering	HTML5 Chart	Title (Y Axis)	Total Sales
3D Mode	Yes	Show (Value)	Yes
Show Grid	Both	-	-

Figure 10-16

7. Click on the New node under Series and enter the following SQL query.

Attribute	Value
Source Type	SQL Query
SQL Query	select p.rowid link, p.product_name||' [$'||p.list_price||']' product, SUM(oi.quantity * oi.unit_price) sales from demo_order_items oi, demo_product_info p where oi.product_id = p.product_id group by p.rowid, p.product_id, p.product_name, p.list_price order by sales desc, 1
Link Type	Link to Custom Target
Type	Page in this Application
Page	204
Name	P204_ROWID
Value	#LINK#
Clear Cache	204

10.16 Order Calendar - Page 211

1. Create a new mobile page.
2. Click on **Calendar** icon.
3. On the next page, select the **Calendar** option.
4. Fill in the next couple of page according to the following table and click **Next**.

Attribute	Value
Page Number	211
Name	Order Calendar
Page Mode	Normal
Region Name	Order Calendar
Navigation Preference	Identify an existing menu entry...
Existing Navigation Menu Entry	Reports

5. On the Source page, select the second option **SQL Query** and type the following query in Enter Region Source box and move on.

   select order_id,
        (select cust_first_name\|\|' '\|\|cust_last_name from demo_customers c
          where c.customer_id = o.customer_id)
        \|\|' ['\|\|to_char(order_total,'FML999G999G999G999G990D00')\|\|']' customer,
        order_timestamp
   from demo_orders o

6. Set the attributes in the next screen as follows. The Start Date Column attribute specifies which column is used as the date to place an entry on the calendar while the Display Column specifies the column to be displayed on the calendar.

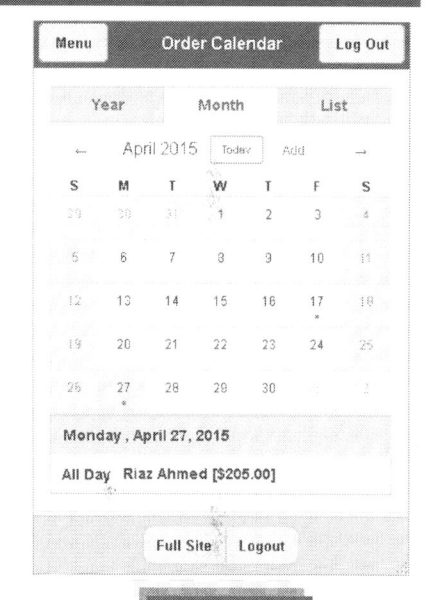

Figure 10-17

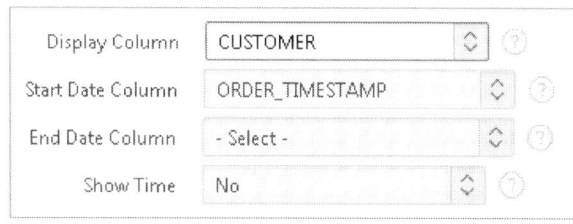

Save and run the page. The small blue circles in date columns indicate some orders. Clicking the circled date will show orders under the calendar.

183

Chapter 10 – Develop A Mobile Version For Smartphones

10.17 Reflow Table - Page 212

In this exercise you will create a responsive report for mobile applications using Reflow Report feature. Reflow table wraps each column or changes to displaying multiple lines on very small screens. When there is not enough space available to display the report horizontally, the report works by collapsing the table columns into a stacked presentation that looks like blocks of label and data pairs for each row.

1. Create a new mobile page.
2. Select the **Report** option and click **Next**.
3. Click on the **Reflow Report** icon.
4. Enter **212** for Page Number, **Reflow Report** for Page and Region names, and click **Next**.
5. For navigation menu entry, select **Reports**.
6. Enter the following SQL statement for Region Source:

   Select a.ROWID as "PK_ROWID",
          product_id, product_name, product_description, category, product_avail, list_price
   From demo_product_info a
   Order by a.product_id

7. Click the **Create** button to finish the wizard.
8. Expand Columns node, and click on **PRODUCT_NAME** column. Set the following attributes for this column:

Figure 10-18

Attribute	Value	Attribute	Value
Type	Link	Value	&PK_ROWID.
Target Type	Page in this application	Clear Cache	204
Page	204	Link Text	&PRODUCT_NAME.
Name	P204_ROWID	-	-

Save the page and run it using Menu | Reports | Reflow Report route. That's it! You have successfully created mobile version of your sales web application. In the remaining chapters of this book, we will setup a security module for our application.

Chapter 11

Define Application Segments For Security

Chapter 11 – Define Application Segments For Security

Application Segments is a hierarchical representation of all the segments included in the application. Just like a site map created for web sites, it is a tree view of our application, created to implement application security. There are three main components in the application that you would like to apply security on. These are: Menus (including main and sub menus), Pages, and Items (such as buttons and drop down lists).

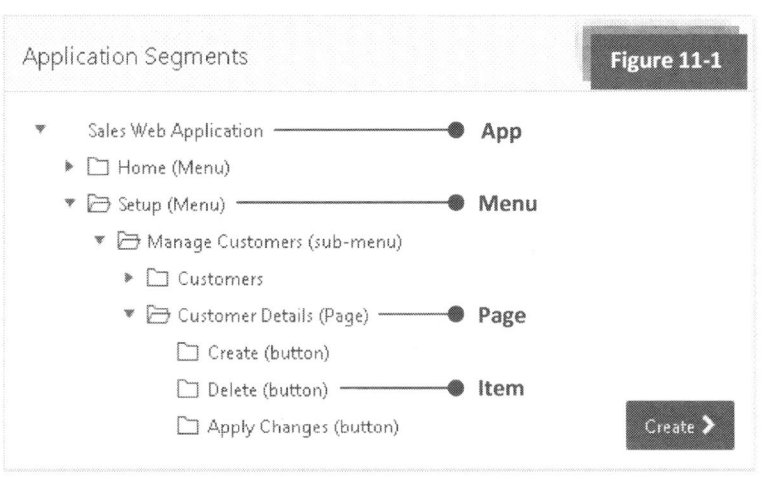

Figure 11-1

The fourth one (App) is there just to identify the application. It is the root node which is used to distinguish segments of multiple applications. After creating all the application segments here, you will use them in the next chapter to enforce application access rules. It's a flexible module, which is designed in such a way to accommodate future application enhancements.

11.1 Create Segments Table

Go to **SQL Workshop | SQL Commands** interface and enter the following two statements and click the **Run** button to create Segments table and the corresponding sequence that will auto generate primary keys for the table. The two statements are provided in the book code (Chapter11\Database Table.txt).

CREATE TABLE app_segments
(segmentID NUMBER, segmentTitle VARCHAR2(50), segmentParent NUMBER, segmentType VARCHAR2(4), pageID NUMBER(4), itemRole VARCHAR2(10), CONSTRAINT app_segments_pk PRIMARY KEY (segmentID) ENABLE);

CREATE SEQUENCE app_segments_seq MINVALUE 1 START WITH 1 INCREMENT BY 1 CACHE 20;

11.2 Create LOVs

Create two static LOVs from scratch using the following tables. The values included in these LOVs will be utilized in segment creation form to identify the type of segments, and the roles performed by page items, respectively.

Segment Type LOV	
Display Value	Return Value
App	App
Menu	Menu
Page	Page
Item	Item

Item Role LOV	
Display Value	Return Value
Create	Create
Modify	Modify
Delete	Delete

11.3 Create Segments Setup Pages

Using the following steps, create two pages for this setup. On the first wizard page, select **Form** and on the next page, select **Form on a Table with Report**. Note that all pages (including this one) in upcoming exercises relate to the desktop application. Therefore, select the Desktop interface for all the pages created hereinafter.

1. On the next wizard page (Report), set the following attributes and click **Next**.

Attribute	Value
Implementation	Interactive
Page Number	60
Page Name	Application Segments
Page Mode	Normal
Region Title	Application Segments
Region Template	Interactive Report
Breadcrumb	do not add breadcrumb...

2. On Data Source page, accept the default schema in Table/View Owner, select **APP_SEGMENTS** for Table/View Name and click **Next**.
3. On the Navigation Menu page, set Navigation Preference to **Identify an existing navigation menu entry for this page**, and set Existing Navigation Menu Entry to **Administration**. Click **Next**.
4. Select all columns from the table and click **Next**.
5. Select an edit link image and click **Next**.
6. On the **Form Page**, set the following attributes and click **Next**.

Attribute	Value
Page Number	61
Page Mode	Modal Dialog
Page Name	Application Segments
Region Title	Application Segments
Region Template	Standard

7. For Primary Key Type, select the second option **Select Primary Key Column(s)** and set Primary Key Column 1 attribute to **SEGMENTID**. Click **Next**.
8. Select the option Existing sequence, set Sequence to **APP_SEGMENTS_SEQ**, and click **Next**.
9. Add all columns from the table and click **Next**.
10. Select **Yes** for *Insert, Update,* and *Delete* options and click **Next**.
11. On the final confirmation page, click the **Create** button. The wizard creates the two pages to handle the module.

Chapter 11 – Define Application Segments For Security

11.4 Modify Segments Form

Amend the segment form (Page 61) items as follows. The P61_SEGMENTPARENT item is being transformed into a popup LOV. It will display title and type columns from the segments table to select a parent for a new entry. Since the Item type doesn't have any child, therefore, the LOV will exclude these records.

Action	Attribute	Value
Modify Items Title, Parent, & Type	Template	Required
	Value Required	Yes
Modify Item P61_SEGMENTPARENT	Type	Popup LOV
	LOV Type	SQL Query
	SQL Query	SELECT segmentTitle||' ('||segmentType||')' d, segmentID r FROM app_segments WHERE segmentType != 'Item' ORDER BY pageID,segmentID,segmentParent
	Default Type	Static Value
	Static Value	0
Modify Item P61_SEGMENTTYPE	Type	Select List
	LOV Type	Shared Component
	List Of Values	SEGMENT TYPE
Modify Item P61_PAGEID	Width	4
	Maximum Length	4
Modify Item P61_ITEMROLE	Type	Select List
	LOV Type	Shared Component
	List Of Values	ITEM ROLE

11.5 Add Tree View Region

Right now the report page (Page 60) contains an interactive report region to display all segments in a matrix report. In this section you will change this appearance to display all the segments in a tree view. First of all, **delete** the interactive report region (**Application Segments**) from page 60. Now, add a new region to Page 60 and set its Type to Tree. Set the attributes listed in the following table and **save** your work.

Attribute	Value
Title	Application Segments
Type	Tree
SQL Query	select case when connect_by_isleaf = 1 then 0 when level = 1 then 1 else -1 end as status, level, segmenttitle as title, NULL as icon, segmentid as value, 'View' as tooltip, apex_util.prepare_url('f?p='||:APP_ID||':61:'||:APP_SESSION|| '::NO::P61_SEGMENTID:'||segmentid) As link from app_segments start with segmentparent = 0 connect by prior segmentid = segmentparent order siblings by segmentid

11.6 Add Button

Add a button to Application Segments region. It will be used to create a new application segment.

Attribute	Value	Attribute	Value
Button Name	CREATE	Hot	Yes
Label	Create	Icon CSS Classes	fa-chevron-right
Region	Application Segments	Action	Redirect to Page in this Application
Button Position	Create	Page	61
Button Template	Text with Icon	Clear Cache	61

Save Page 60. After saving the page call Page 61 to add a couple of validations.

11.7 Create Validations

In Page 61, go to the Processing tab and right click Validating node. Select **Create Validation** from the context menu. Set the following attributes for this new validation. Note that the first validation below (Check Segment) will be effective after completing Chapter 12, because the table GROUPS_DETAIL used in the SELECT query will be created in that chapter.

Attribute	Value
Name	Check Segment
Type	PL/SQL Function (returning Error Text)

PL/SQL Function	declare
	  Vutilized number := 0;
	  Verrortext varchar2(60);
	begin
	  select count(*) into Vutilized from groups_detail where segmentId=:P61_SEGMENTID;
	  if Vutilized > 0 then
	    Verrortext := 'Cannot delete this segment because it is utilized';
	  end if;
	  return rtrim(Verrortext);
	end;

Error Message	Cannot delete this segment because it is utilized
When Button Pressed	DELETE

Create another validation as follows:

Attribute	Value
Name	Check Child Segment
Type	PL/SQL Function (returning Error Text)

PL/SQL Function	declare
	  VchildExist number := 0;
	  Verrortext varchar2(60);
	begin
	  select count(*) into VchildExist from app_segments where segmentParent=:P61_SEGMENTID;
	  if VchildExist > 0 then
	    Verrortext := 'Cannot delete, this segment it has child entries';
	  end if;
	  return rtrim(Verrortext);
	end;

Error Message	Cannot delete this segment it has child entries
When Button Pressed	DELETE

Chapter 11 – Define Application Segments For Security

Test Your Work

Everything is set. Test your work by calling the main segments form from Administration | Application Segments menu. Click the **Create** button, and enter the following values individually one after the other in the segments form:

TITLE	PARENT	TYPE	PAGEID	ITEMROLE
Sales Web Application	0	App		
Home (Menu)	Sales Web Application	Menu		
Home (Page)	Home (Menu)	Page	1	
Add (Button)	Home (Page)	Item	1	Create

■ Application   ■ Menu   ■ Page   ■ Item

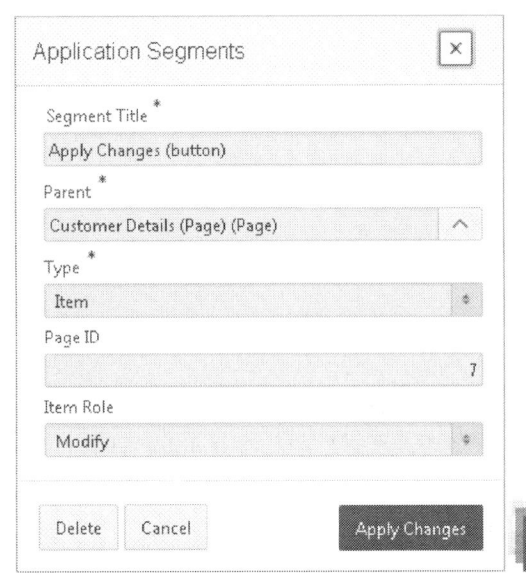

Figure 11-2 – New Segment Form

The first entry will create the application root, therefore, no parent will be assigned to it. Recall that you assigned the default value (zero) for the parent item in section 11.4. The second main menu entry will come under the application root. The first page entry defined on serial number 3 will be placed under the Home Menu, along with the corresponding page number. The last level of our application hierarchy belongs to page items (serial number 4-6). The Home page contains three buttons. So, these items are set under page 1. When you mark the Type of an entry as Item, then you must also specify its role. Roles will be used in a subsequent chapter to implement application security. The above list is a subset of a comprehensive list that covers all the application segments. You can find this list in **application_segments.xlsx** file in the book code Chapter 11 folder. Open it up, and add all application segments to complete this chapter. Note that it is not necessary to follow the defined sequence while creating new segments; you can add an entry to any level, any time. The important thing is to select the correct parent to place a new entry under it.

Chapter 12

Create Groups and Assign Privileges

Chapter 12 – Create Groups and Assign Privileges

In the previous chapter you laid the foundation of your application's security that will be imposed on menus, pages, and page items. In this chapter, you will establish a setup to create user groups, who will be assigned application rights. Allocating application rights to individual users is a tedious activity, and not recommended as well. Instead, you create a few groups and assign application privileges to these groups. Users are created afterwards and are associated with respective groups. This way each user inherits application rights from the group, s/he belongs to. For example, to handle application security for a staff of over hundred employees, comprising managers and data entry clerks, you will create just two groups (Managers and Clerks) with appropriate privileges. Any changes made to the privileges of these groups will be automatically inherited to all associated users.

12.1 Create User Group Tables

CREATE TABLE groups_master
(groupID NUMBER(4), groupTitle VARCHAR2(25), CONSTRAINT groups_pk PRIMARY KEY (groupID) ENABLE)

CREATE TABLE groups_detail
(groupID NUMBER(4) CONSTRAINT fk_Group_Details REFERENCES groups_master(groupID), segmentID NUMBER CONSTRAINT fk_user_group REFERENCES app_segments(segmentID), segmentParent NUMBER, segmentType VARCHAR2(4), pageID NUMBER(4), itemRole VARCHAR2(10), allow_access VARCHAR2(1))

In this setup you will be using two tables. The master table will hold ids and titles of groups, while the details table will contain all application privileges (specified in the segments setup) for each group.

12.2 Page & Parameters Region

Groups will be created with just one application page. This page will carry two main regions: Parameters and Group's Privileges. Using the parameters pane, you indicate whether you are creating a new group, or are willing to manipulate an existing one. Based on this selection you'll be provided with the appropriate interface. For example, if you're trying to modify or delete an existing group, then you'll select the **Existing** option, followed by a **Group** from the provided list, to show the privileges of the selected group in the second region. When you select the **New** option, the tree view will hide, and a new interface will be presented to create a new group. This module will be created using a blank page. So let's begin.

1. Create a **Blank Page** for Desktop User Interface and set the following attributes for it:

Attribute	Value
Page Number	62
Name	User Groups
Page Mode	Normal
Breadcrumb	do not add breadcrumb...
Navigation Preference	Identify an existing navigation menu entry for this page
Existing Navigation Menu Entry	Administration

2. Create a region under the Body node of Static Content type, and enter **Parameters** for its Title. Also set Column Span attribute to **4** in order to make the region four columns wide.

3. Add a page item to the Parameters region and set the following attributes.

Attribute	Value
Name	P62_EXISTINGNEW
Type	Radio Group
Label	Action:
Number of Columns	2
Page Action on Selection	Submit Page (*to show/hide Group's Privileges region*)
Template	Required
Type (LOV)	Static Values
Static Values	STATIC:New;NEW,Existing;EXISTING
Display Null Value	No
Type (Default)	Static Value
Static Value	EXISTING

4. Add another page item to the Parameters region with the following attributes:

Attribute	Value
Name	P62_GROUPID1
Type	Select List
Label	Group:
Page Action on Selection	Submit Page (*to refresh Selected Segment region*)
Type (LOV)	SQL Query
SQL Query	SELECT DISTINCT groupTitle d, groupID r FROM groups_master ORDER BY groupID
Type (Condition)	Item = Value
Item	P62_EXISTINGNEW
Value	EXISTING (*The list is displayed only when EXISTING option is on*)

5. Create a hidden page item as follows. The value held in this item will be used in section 12.8 to set title for a Tree region, created there.

Attribute	Value
Name	P62_GROUPTITLE1
Type	Hidden
Type (Source)	SQL Query (return single value)
SQL Query	SELECT groupTitle FROM groups_master WHERE groupID=:P62_GROUPID1
Used (Source)	Always, replacing any existing value in session state

6. Add a Text Field item and set the following attributes. It will carry an auto-generated ID of a new group.

Attribute	Value
Name	P62_GROUPID2
Type	Text Field
Label	Group ID:
Width/Maximum Length	4
Type (Source)	SQL Query (return single value)
SQL Query	SELECT MAX(groupID)+1 FROM groups_master
Used (Source)	Always, replacing any existing value in session state
Type (Default)	Static Value
Static Value	1
Type (Condition)	Item = Value
Item	P62_EXISTINGNEW
Value	NEW (*The item is displayed only when NEW option is on*)

Chapter 12 – Create Groups and Assign Privileges

7. Add a last page item to the Parameters region and set the following attributes. This will receive titles for new groups.

Attribute	Value
Name	P62_GROUPTITLE2
Type	Text Field
Label	Title:
Type (Condition)	Item = Value
Item	P62_EXISTINGNEW
Value	NEW

12.3 Buttons

Add the following two buttons. These buttons will be displayed on the new group creation form. Clicking the *Allow All* button will create a group with all application access privileges, while the second one will create a group without any privilege. Of course, you can amend these privileges later on.

Attribute	Button 1	Button 2
Name	Allow	Disallow
Label	Create Group - Allow All	Create Group - Disallow All
Button Position	Create	Create
Action	Submit Page	Submit Page
Type (Condition)	Item = Value	Item = Value
Item	P62_EXISTINGNEW	P62_EXISTINGNEW
Value	NEW	NEW

12.4 New Group Process

Click on the Processing tab and create a new process under the After Submit node. This process is associated with the two buttons created in the previous section. The condition says that if the request came from any of the two buttons, then execute the PL/SQL process to create the group with all or no privileges.

Attribute	Value
Name	Create New Groups
Type	PL/SQL Code

PL/SQL Code	DECLARE
	VsegmentID number := 0;
	VsegmentParent Number;
	VsegmentType varchar2(4);
	vpageID number := 0;
	VitemRole varchar2(10);
	Vallow varchar2(1);
	VmasterRow number := 0;
	
	cursor segments_cur is
	select * from app_segments order by segmentID;
	
	segments_rec segments_cur%ROWTYPE;
	
	BEGIN
	  if :request='Allow' then
	    Vallow := 'Y';
	  else
	    Vallow := 'N';
	  end if;
	  for segments_rec in segments_cur loop
	    VsegmentID := segments_rec.segmentID;
	    VsegmentParent := segments_rec.segmentParent;
	    VsegmentType := segments_rec.segmentType;
	    VpageID := segments_rec.pageID;
	    VitemRole := segments_rec.itemRole;
	    if VmasterRow = 0 then
	      insert into groups_master values (:P62_GROUPID2,:P62_GROUPTITLE2);
	      commit;
	      VmasterRow := 1;
	    end if;
	    insert into groups_detail values (:P62_GROUPID2,VsegmentID,VsegmentParent,VsegmentType,VpageID,VitemRole,Vallow);
	    commit;
	  end loop;
	END;

Point	After Submit
Success Message	Group Created Successfully
Error Message	Could not create group
Type (Condition)	Request is contained in Value
Value	Allow,Disallow *(Case Sensitive, should match with the button names provided above)*

Chapter 12 – Create Groups and Assign Privileges

12.5 Delete Group Button

Add a button to delete an existing group. On submit, the process Delete Group (created next) is executed.

Attribute	Value	Attribute	Value
Name	Delete	Action	Submit Page
Label	Delete Group	Type (Condition)	Item = Value
Button Position	Create	Item	P62_EXISTINGNEW
Hot	Yes	Value	EXISTING

12.6 Delete Group Process

Create a new process to drop a group. To avoid deletion of a group having associated users, and to present a custom error message, you can add a validation. I'm ignoring it on purpose to preserve some space. However, we'll define a constraint in the Users table (in the next chapter) on the groupID column to eliminate accidental deletion of groups. The following process will execute only when you select an existing group i.e. there is some value in P62_GROUPID1 page item.

Attribute	Value
Name	Delete Groups
Type	PL/SQL Code
PL/SQL Code	DELETE FROM groups_detail WHERE groupID=:P62_GroupID1; DELETE FROM groups_master WHERE groupID=:P62_GroupID1;
Success Message	Group Deleted Successfully
Error Message	Could not delete group
When Button Pressed	DELETE
Type (Condition)	Item is NOT NULL and NOT zero
Item	P62_GROUPID1

12.7 Group Privileges Region

It is another Static Content region that will carry a tree and a classic report region to display application access privileges of a selected group.

Attribute	Value	Attribute	Value
Title	Group's Privileges	Item	P62_EXISTINGNEW
Type (Condition)	Item = Value	Value	EXISTING

12.8 Tree Region

Add a tree region to the Group's Privileges region to display application access rights of a selected group. The query used for this tree is similar to the one used in the Segments setup chapter, except for the link column, which uses an inline JavaScript call - *'javascript:pageItemName('||apex_escape.js_literal(segmentid)||')' As link* - to a function named pageItemName, defined underneath. The APEX_ESCAPE package provides functions for escaping special characters in strings to ensure that the data is suitable for further processing. The JS_LITERAL function, of the APEX_ESCAPE package, escapes and optionally enquotes a JavaScript string.

The function (pageItemName) is called in the tree's query link. The calling procedure (in the query), passes a segment ID to the function's selectedNode parameter. The $s (which is a JavaScript function), sets the value of a hidden page item (P21_SELECTED_NODE) to the value received in the selectedNode parameter, which is then used to refresh another region (Selected Segment), to display the relevant segment along with access privilege.

Attribute	Value
Title	Group: &P62_GROUPTITLE1.
Type	Tree

SQL Query	select case when connect_by_isleaf = 1 then 0 when level = 1 then 1 else -1 end as status,
	    level, segmenttitle as title, NULL as icon, segmentid as value,
	    'View Right' as tooltip,
	'javascript:pageItemName('||apex_escape.js_literal(segmentid)||')' As link
	from app_segments
	start with segmentparent = 0
	connect by prior segmentid = segmentparent
	order siblings by segmentid

Parent Region	Group's Privileges
Select Node Page Item (Under Attributes)	P62_SELECTED_NODE (*to save the Tree state*)

Create a hidden item under the above tree region. This item is created (and is referenced in the above tree) to save the Tree state.

Attribute	Value
Name	P62_SELECTED_NODE
Type	Hidden
Value Protected	No
Region	Group: &P62_GROUPTITLE1.

Click on the root node (Page 62: User Groups) and enter the following code:

Attribute	Value

Function and Global Variable Declaration	function pageItemName(selectedNode)
	{
	  $s('P62_SELECTED_NODE', selectedNode);
	}

12.9 Add Classic Report Region

This report will show the name of the selected segment, along with its access privilege. A button will also be added to this region, which will be used to allow/revoke access rights. The report is presented using a query which is based on the value of P62_SELECTED_NODE hidden item.

Attribute	Value
Title	Selected Segment
Type	Classic Report
SQL Query	SELECT s.segmentTitle,g.allow_access FROM app_segments s, groups_detail g WHERE s.segmentID=:P62_SELECTED_NODE AND s.segmentID=g.segmentID AND g.groupID=:P62_GROUPID1
Page Items to Submit	P62_SELECTED_NODE
Parent Region	Group's Privileges
Start New Row	No
Type (Condition)	Item = Value
Item	P62_EXISTINGNEW
Value	EXISTING

Chapter 12 – Create Groups and Assign Privileges

12.10 Dynamic Action to Refresh Region

You also need to refresh the classic report region (Selected Segment) with appropriate data when the user switches from one tree node to another. The following dynamic action serves this purpose. Create this dynamic action under the Change node.

Attribute	Value	Attribute	Value
Name	Refresh Region	Action (under Show node)	Refresh
Event	Change	Selection Type	Region
Selection Type	Item(s)	Region	Selected Segment
Item(s)	P62_SELECTED_NODE	-	-

12.11 Button To Allow/Revoke Segment Access Right

This button will appear in the Selected Segment report region. When clicked, it will invoke the associated process to either allow or revoke access privilege to or from the selected group.

Attribute	Value	Attribute	Value
Name	ALLOW/REVOKE	Button Position	Next
Label	Allow/Revoke	Hot	Yes
Region	Selected Segment	Action	Submit Page

12.12 Process to Update Allow Access Table Column

Create a new process under the Delete Groups process using the following table. It is associated with the above button. When you click a node in the segments tree, the corresponding segment appears in the right pane along with its access privilege. The Allow/Revoke button also displays to the right of this pane. When clicked, the process defined below fires either to allow or to revoke the access right.

Attribute	Value
Name	Update Allow_Access Column
Type	PL/SQL Code
PL/SQL Code	```declare
VrecordExist number := 0;
Vallow varchar2(1);
Vsegmenttype varchar2(4);
Vpageid number;
Vitemrole varchar2(10);
begin
select count(*) into VrecordExist from groups_detail where groupID=:P62_GROUPID1 and
segmentID=:P62_SELECTED_NODE;
if VrecordExist = 1 then
select allow_access into Vallow from groups_detail where groupID=:P62_GROUPID1 and
segmentID=:P62_SELECTED_NODE;
if Vallow='Y' then
Vallow := 'N';
else
Vallow := 'Y';
end if;
update groups_detail set allow_access=Vallow where groupID=:P62_GROUPID1 and
segmentID=:P62_SELECTED_NODE;
commit;
else
select segmenttype,pageid,itemrole into Vsegmenttype,Vpageid,Vitemrole
from app_segments where segmentID=:P62_SELECTED_NODE;
insert into groups_detail values
(:P62_GROUPID1,:P62_SELECTED_NODE,null,Vsegmenttype,VpageID,Vitemrole,'N');
commit;
end if;
end;```
When Button Pressed	ALLOW/REVOKE

Chapter 12 – Create Groups and Assign Privileges

Test Your Work

Execute the following steps to test your work:

1. Click **User Groups** in the main navigation menu.
2. Click the **New** option in the Parameters pane.
3. Enter a title for the new group. I entered **Admins**.
4. Click the button **Create Group – Allow All**. This action will create the specified group with all application rights.
5. Click the **Existing** option, and select **Admins** from the select list. Click on different tree nodes and watch changes in the right pane. Click the **Allow/Revoke** button and note the immediate reflection.
6. Add two more groups and grant them different access rights. Name the first one as **Managers**, and the other one as **Clerks**.

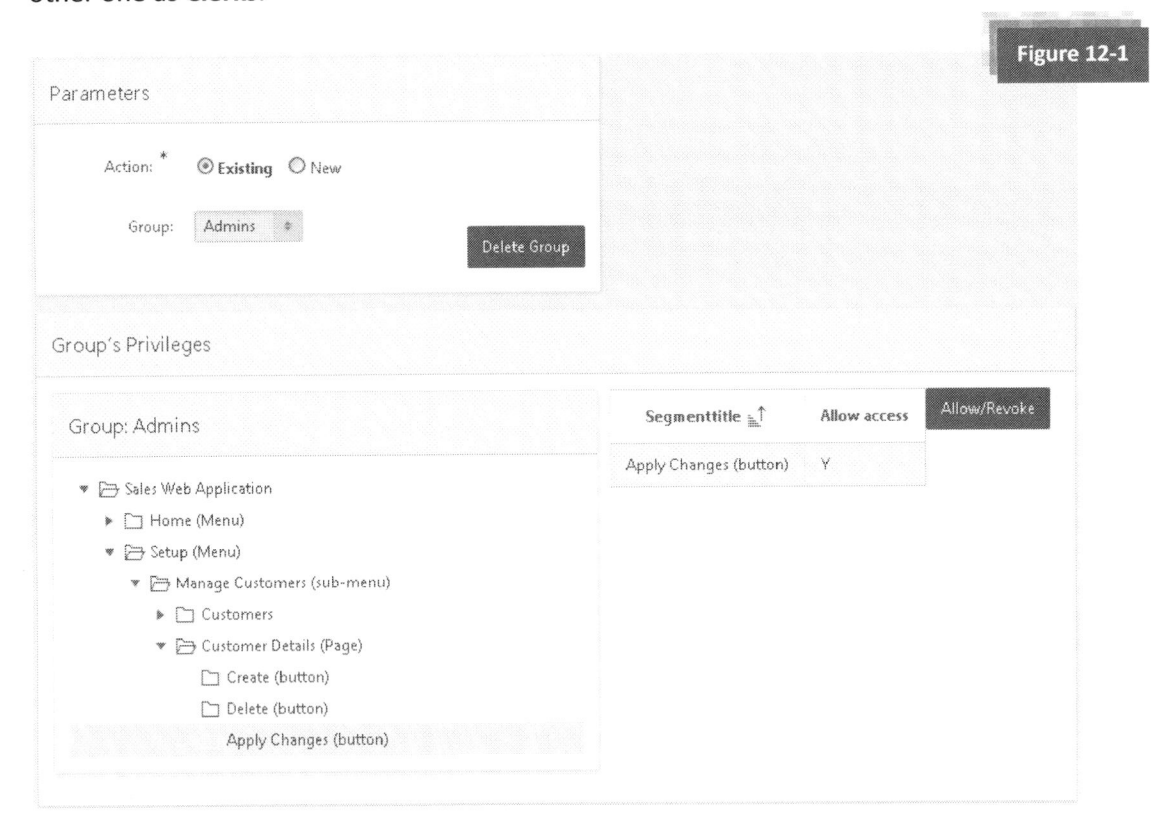

Figure 12-1

You've successfully setup application access privileges, but these privileges are not yet implemented. This is because the application is in the development phase, and only after its completion, we'll be in a position to completely deploy the security module, which will we do in chapter 14.

Chapter 13

Create Users and Assign Groups

Chapter 13 – Create Users and Assign Groups

After creating groups, you add application users and associate them to relevant groups. You input user id in a text item for new users. However, when you call an existing user's record for modification, this value is displayed as a read-only text. Besides assigning Admins group to a user, you also specify whether the user is an administrator. This is because we have a column (Admin) in the users table, which explicitly assigns administrative rights to those users marked as administrators, irrespective of the group they belong to. This explicit marking is necessary in some cases to quickly assess whether a user is an administrator. You'll see an instance of this in section 13.6.

13.1 Create Users Table

Create the following table using SQL Command utility to store users credentials. The script for this table is provided in the book code.

CREATE TABLE app_users
(userID VARCHAR2(50), groupID NUMBER(4) CONSTRAINT fk_app_users REFERENCES groups_master(groupID), password VARCHAR2(4000), admin VARCHAR2(1), CONSTRAINT app_users_pk PRIMARY KEY (userID) ENABLE)

13.2 Create Pages

Once again, create a **Form** page followed by **Form on a Table with Report** option.

1. On the next wizard screen, set the following attributes and click **Next**.

Attribute	Value
Implementation	Interactive
Page Number	63
Page Name	Application Users Report
Page Mode	Normal
Region Title	Application Users
Region Template	Interactive Report
Breadcrumb	do not add breadcrumb...

2. On Data Source page, accept the default schema in Table/View Owner, select **APP_USERS** for Table/View Name and click **Next**.
3. On the Navigation Menu page, set Navigation Preference to **Identify an existing navigation menu entry for this page**, and set Existing Navigation Menu Entry to **Administration**. Click **Next**.
4. Select all columns from the table and click **Next**.
5. Select an edit link image and click **Next**.
6. On the **Form Page**, set the following attributes and click **Next**.

Attribute	Value
Page Number	64
Page Mode	Modal Dialog
Page Name	Application User Form
Region Title	Application User
Region Template	Standard

7. For Primary Key Type, select **Managed by Database (ROWID)** and click **Next**.
8. Add three columns USERID, GROUPID, and ADMIN from the table and click **Next**.
9. Select **Yes** for *Insert, Update,* and *Delete* options and click **Next**.
10. On the final confirmation page, click the **Create** button.

After creation, modify both pages to set the following attributes. The default query in the Region Source is replaced with a custom join query to also display user groups. Also set Width and Height of Page 64 to **400** and **300**, respectively.

Action	Attribute	Value
Report Page (63) Modify Region	Region	Application Users
	Region Source	select "U"."ROWID", "U"."USERID", "G"."GROUPTITLE", "U"."PASSWORD", "U"."ADMIN" from "APP_USERS" "U", "GROUPS_MASTER" "G" where "U"."GROUPID"="G"."GROUPID"
Form Page (64) Modify Region	Region	Application User
	Title	Application User: &P64_USERID.

13.3 Create/Modify Items

Add and amend the following items on page 64. The first item (Display Only) is added (between two existing items: User ID and Group ID) to show the id of the selected user as a read-only text. The condition set for this item will display it only when you call a record of an existing user for modification. An opposite condition is set for the item P64_USERID to make it visible only for new records.

Action	Attribute	Value	Attribute	Value
Add Display Only Item	Item Name	P64_USERID2	Column Name	USERID
	Label	<b>User ID:</b>	Condition Type	Item Is NOT NULL
	Sequence	25 *(between UserID & GroupID)*	Item	P64_USERID
	Source Type	Database Column	-	-

Action	Attribute	Value	Attribute	Value
Modify Item	Item Name	P64_USERID	Value Placeholder	Enter in UPPER CASE
	Label	<b>User ID:</b>	Condition Type	Item is NULL
	Source Type	Database Column	Item	P64_USERID
	Column Name	USERID	-	-

Action	Attribute	Value
Modify Item	Item Name	P64_GROUPID
	Type	Select List
	Label	<b>Group:</b>
	Value Required	Yes
	LOV Type	SQL Query
	SQL Query	SELECT groupTitle d, groupID r FROM groups_master

Action	Attribute	Value	Attribute	Value
Modify Item	Item Name	P64_ADMIN	List of Value Type	Static Values
	Type	Radio Group	Static Values	STATIC:Yes;Y,No;N
	Label	<b>Administrator:</b>	Display Null Value	No
	No. of Columns	2	Default Type	Static Value
	-	-	Static Value	N

Chapter 13 – Create Users and Assign Groups

Test Your Work

1. Access Page 63 from Administration | Users in the main navigation menu.
2. Click the **Create** button.
3. Enter **SUPER** in UserID, set Group to **Admins**, select **Yes** for Administrator, and click **Create**. Note that the password column of the new user will be blank at this stage. You will create a setup to set users' passwords in the next section. Modify this user and have a look at the user id, which should be displayed as a read-only text.
4. Create two more users (belonging to different groups).

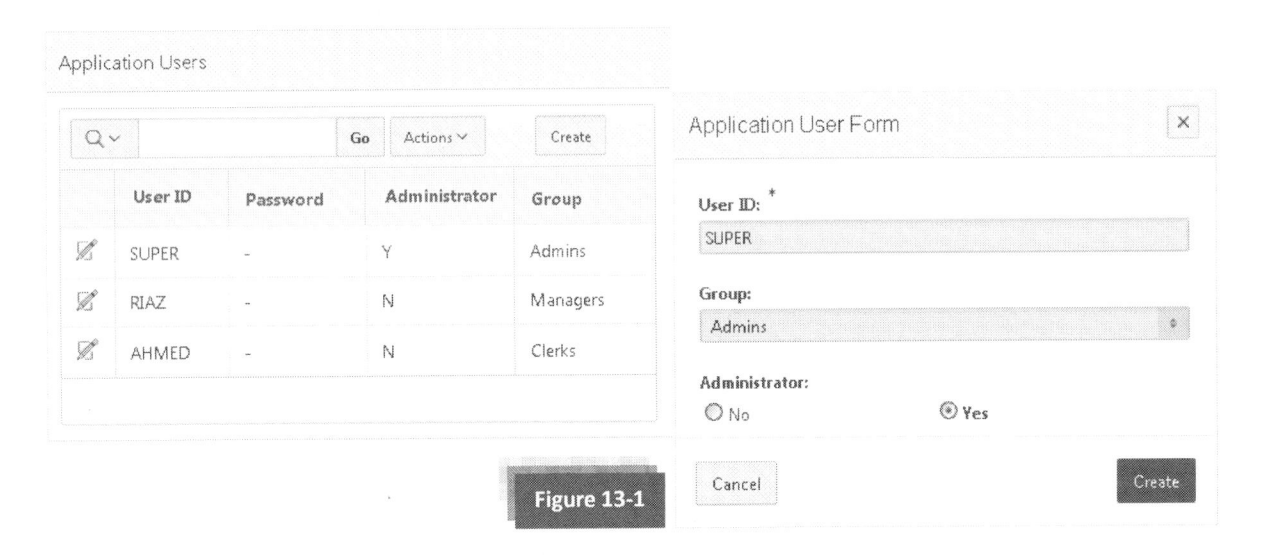

Figure 13-1

13.4 Reset Password

A user who wants to access this application can do so with a valid id and password. So far, you have created some user accounts and assigned them relevant ids and groups. In this exercise, you are going to create a setup to set initial passwords for those users, which they can alter later on using the same setup. Note that this segment will be invoked from the Setup menu. The Reset Password interface is self-explanatory. First, you select a user id and then provide a new password for it, followed by a confirmation that is added to match the actual password. As just mentioned, the same interface will be used to set initial passwords, and to reset passwords for the application users in the future. Usually, the initial password allocation task is performed by the application administrator.

13.5 Add Custom Functions

The users you created in the previous section reside in the database table (APP_USERS) without passwords, therefore, none of them can access the application at the moment. You'll create the password interface by adding a new page to the application, but first you have to add two custom functions (CUSTOM_AUTH and CUSTOM_HASH) to your database. After receiving login information, the APEX engine evaluates and executes the current authentication scheme (to be configured at the end of this chapter). The scheme makes a call to a function named CUSTOM_AUTH. In conjunction with the CUSTOM_HASH function, the CUSTOM_AUTH function authenticates users using their credentials stored in APP_USERS table. The two functions are added to the database to implement custom authentication mechanism. The CUSTOM_HASH function is a subordinate function to the CUSTOM_AUTH function and is called from the parent function to obfuscate user password using hash algorithm. Besides assisting the custom authentication scheme, it is used to obfuscate new/updated passwords. Execute the following steps to add these two functions to the database:

1. Call **SQL Commands** interface from SQL Workshop.
2. Copy/Paste the two functions available in **Chapter13\Custom Functions.txt** file, and click the **Run** button to store them in the database.
3. For verification, call the **Object Browser** interface and locate the two functions under the Functions category.

13.6 Create Page and Add Components

Create the interface using a blank page and then set the attributes mentioned in the following table. Note that this page will be called by the Reset Password option in the Setup menu. The SQL query defined for the Select List (P65_USERID) uses a condition in the WHERE clause (admin='Y') to quickly assess administrators, who are allowed to change password of any user. This is the case that I mentioned at the beginning of this chapter for the incorporation of Admin column in APP_USERS table. The condition that follows will display the Select List, carrying all user ids, only to administrators; normal users will see their own respective ids through the Display Only item (P65_USERID2).

Action	Attribute	Value
Add a Blank Page	Page Number	65
	Page Name	Reset Password
	Page Mode	Normal
	Breadcrumb	do not add breadcrumb...
	Navigation Preference	Identify an existing navigation menu entry for this page
	Menu Entry	Setup
Add Static Content Region	Title	Reset Password
	Template	Standard
Add Item - Select List	Name	P65_USERID
	Region	Reset Password
	Label	User ID:
	LOV Type	SQL Query
	SQL Query	select userid d, userid r from app_users
	Condition Type	Rows Returned
	SQL Query	SELECT 1 FROM app_users WHERE upper(userid) = upper(:APP_USER) AND admin = 'Y'

The Display Only item (P65_USERID2) will show the id of the current non-admin user using a substitution string (&APP_USER.). The Save Session State attribute is set to YES to store the current item value in the session state when the page gets submitted. Else, you'll encounter an error message: "*No user selected for the reset password process*". We also used an opposite WHERE clause in condition query, as compared to the previous one, to display non-admin ids. Next, you added two password items. The first one is used to enter a new password, whereas the other one is added for its confirmation.

Chapter 13 – Create Users and Assign Groups

Action	Attribute	Value
Add Display Only Item	Name	P65_USERID2
	Label	<b>User ID:</b>
	Save Session State	Yes
	Region	Reset Password
	Default Type	Static Value
	Static Value	&APP_USER.
	Condition Type	Rows Returned
	SQL Query	SELECT 1 FROM app_users WHERE upper(userid) = upper(:APP_USER) AND admin != 'Y'
Add Password Item	Name	P65_PASSWORD1
	Label	<b>New Password:</b>
	Region	Reset Password
	Submit When Enter Pressed	No
	Template	Required
	Value Required	Yes
Add Password Item	Name	P65_PASSWORD2
	Label	<b>Confirm Password:</b>
	Region	Reset Password
	Submit When Enter Pressed	No
	Template	Required
	Value Required	Yes
Add Button	Name	RESET_PW
	Label	Reset Password
	Region	Reset Password
	Button Position	Next
	Hot	Yes
	Action	Submit Page
	Execute Validation	Yes (default)

Upon page submission, this button will run the update password process (section 13.8).

13.7 Add Validations – Check User ID and Match Passwords

The first validation checks for the existence of user id, while the second one matches the two passwords.

Action	Attribute	Value
Add Validation	Name	Check User ID
	Type	PL/SQL Function (returning Error Text)

	PL/SQL Function	declare
		  Verrortext varchar2(100);
		begin
		  if :P65_USERID is null and :P65_USERID2 is null THEN
		    Verrortext := 'No user selected for the reset password process';
		  end if;
		  return rtrim(Verrortext);
		end;

	Error Message	No user selected for the reset password process
	When Button Pressed	RESET_PW

206

Action	Attribute	Value
Add Validation	Name	Match Passwords
	Type	PL/SQL Function Body (returning Boolean)

	PL/SQL Function	begin
		  if :P65_PASSWORD1 = :P65_PASSWORD2 then
		    return true;
		  else
		    return false;
		  end if;
		end;

	Error Message	Passwords do not match
	When Button Pressed	RESET_PW

13.8 Update Password Process

The following process will store the new password in the database table for the selected user.

Action	Attribute	Value
Add Process	Name	Update Password
	Type	PL/SQL Code

	PL/SQL Code	begin
		if :P65_USERID is not null then
		  update app_users set password = custom_hash(:P65_USERID,
		   :P65_PASSWORD1) where upper(userID) = upper(:P65_USERID);
		else
		  update app_users set password = custom_hash(:P65_USERID2,
		   :P65_PASSWORD1) where upper(userID) = upper(:P65_USERID2);
		end if;
		commit;
		end;

	Point	After Submit
	Success Message	Password changed successfully
	Error Message	Could not change password
	When Button Pressed	RESET_PW

If you run the page at this stage, you won't see the users select list. This is due to the condition set for the select list item P65_USERID that shows the list only when the currently logged in user is an administrator of the application. Since your account doesn't even exist in the APP_USERS table, therefore, the list doesn't appear as well. To make the list visible, create an admin account for yourself having the same ID you currently possess, using the Users option from the main menu. After creating your account, invoke the Password page to test your work by setting passwords for all the application users. Verify addition of passwords to the table by accessing the table either from Object Browser utility in SQL Workshop, or from the Users menu.

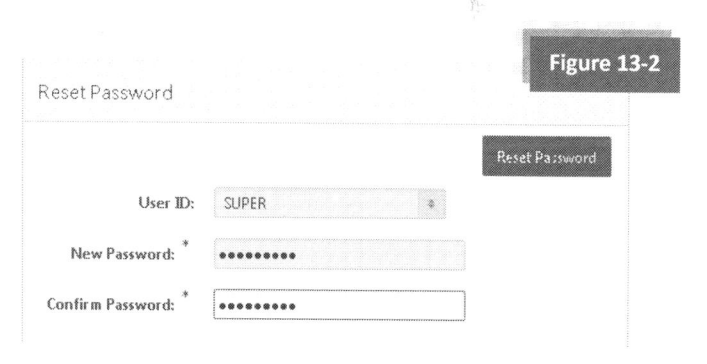

Figure 13-2

Chapter 13 – Create Users and Assign Groups

13.9 Change Authentication Scheme

At this stage you can set and browse users' passwords, but you cannot use these passwords to login. This is due to the currently implemented authentication scheme, which was set to Application Express Scheme when you initially created the workspace in chapter 2 section 2.8. In order to authenticate users with their new ids and passwords, you have to create a custom authentication scheme. Here are the steps to implement this scheme:

1. Select **Authentication Scheme** (under Security section) from Shared Components.
2. Click the **Create** button.
3. Select the option **Based on the pre-configured scheme from the gallery**, and click **Next**.
4. Enter **Custom Scheme** in the Name box, and select **Custom** as the Scheme Type. On the same page, enter **CUSTOM_AUTH** for *Authentication Function Name* attribute. This is the name of the function that you created in section 13.5 to verify a user's credentials on the login page.
5. Click the **Create Authentication Scheme** button. The new scheme will appear on the page having a check mark. Now you can access the application using the credentials stored in the APP_USERS table.

Chapter 14

Implement Application Security

Chapter 14 – Implement Application Security

After creating application segments, groups, users and setting passwords, you are now at the point where you can implement your application's security. Initially you will apply security on the main navigation menu items, followed by its pages and buttons.

14.1 Apply Security on Main Menu

1. Go to Shared Components | Navigation Menu and select **Desktop Navigation Menu**.
2. Click on the **Home** entry.
3. Set Condition Type to **PL/SQL Function Body Returning a Boolean**, enter the following code in Expression 1 box, and apply the change.

```
declare
  Vadmin varchar2(1);
  Vallow varchar2(1);
begin
  select admin into Vadmin from app_users where upper(userid)=upper(:APP_USER);
  if Vadmin = 'N' then
    select allow_access into Vallow from groups_detail
      where segmentType='Menu' and segmentID=
                            (select segmentID from app_segments where segmentTitle like
                              'Home%' and segmentType='Menu')
        and groupID=(select groupID from app_users where
                              upper(userid)=upper(:APP_USER));
    if Vallow='Y' then
      return true;
    else
      return false;
    end if;
  else
    return true;
  end if;
exception
  when NO_DATA_FOUND then return false;
end;
```

The statement on line # 5 evaluates whether the currently logged in user is an administrator. If s/he is, then the code on line # 14 is executed to return a true value. Note that admin users are exempt from restrictions and possess full access privileges to all application segments. On the contrary, if the user is not an administrator, the code specified from line # 7 through 12 is executed. This block is specified for non-admins. It checks whether the user is privileged to access the Home menu. Note that this code is specific to the Home menu entry. Call all menu entries and add the above code with the same Condition Type. The only thing that you need to replace is the 'Home%' entry (on line # 7) with the corresponding menu entry. For example, if you are entering this code for Setup menu entry, then replace the LIKE string with 'Setup%'. You can refer to the MS Excel file (application_segments.xlsx) located in Chapter 11 folder to see application menu entries.

14.2 Apply Security on Application Pages

After protecting the application main menu from unauthorized access, the next line of defense is to make application pages secure. Here are the steps to apply security on application pages.

1. Go to Shared Components and click on **Authorization Schemes** (under Security section).
2. Click the **Create** button to launch the scheme wizard.
3. Select **From Scratch** to create a new scheme from scratch.
4. On the Details wizard page, enter the following values and click the button labeled Create Authorization Scheme. The PL/SQL code defined underneath is similar to the one entered for menu items, except for the segment type, which in this case is the application Page.

Attribute	Value
Name	Page Access
Scheme Type	PL/SQL Function Returning Boolean

PL/SQL Function Body	declare
	  Vadmin varchar2(1);
	  Vallow varchar2(1);
	begin
	  select admin into Vadmin from app_users where
	      upper(userid)=upper(:APP_USER);
	  if Vadmin = 'N' then
	    select allow_access into Vallow from groups_detail
	        where pageID=:APP_PAGE_ID and segmentType='**Page**' and
	        groupID=(select groupID from app_users where
	        upper(userid)=upper(:APP_USER));
	    if Vallow='Y' then
	      return true;
	    else
	      return false;
	    end if;
	  else
	    return true;
	  end if;
	exception
	  when NO_DATA_FOUND then return false;
	end;

Error Message	You are not authorized to view this page!\<br /\> Click \<a href="f?p=&APP_ID.:999:&SESSION."\>here\</a\> to continue
Validation	Once per page view

After creating the authorization scheme, call the Home page (Sales Web Application - Page 1) in Page Designer. Click on the root node (Page 1: Sales Web Application). In the Property Editor, scroll down to Security section, and set *Authorization Scheme* attribute to **Page Access**. Click the **Save** button. The Home page is now associated with the authorization scheme. User groups who are not granted access privilege to the Home page would get the defined error message. After clicking the provided link, they will be taken to another page in the application. I created a page with 999 ID for such purpose. However, you can land them on any existing page.

Chapter 14 – Implement Application Security

14.3 Apply Security on Page Items

This is the last level of our application security where we will apply security on individual page components. APEX allows you to apply authorization scheme to every component that you create on a page. For the sake of simplicity, we just incorporated page buttons in Segments setup, and this is the only item we will be experimenting with in this section to test page item security.

1. Create another **Authorization Scheme** from scratch and set the following attributes for it:

Attribute	Value
Name	Create
Scheme Type	PL/SQL Function Returning Boolean

PL/SQL Function Body	```declare
	  Vadmin varchar2(1);
	  Vallow varchar2(1);
	begin
	  select admin into Vadmin from app_users where upper(userid)=upper(:APP_USER);
	  if Vadmin = 'N' then
	    select allow_access into Vallow from groups_detail
	      where pageID=:APP_PAGE_ID and itemRole='Create' and groupID=
	      (select groupID from app_users where upper(userid)=upper(:APP_USER));
	    if Vallow='Y' then
	      return true;
	    else
	      return false;
	    end if;
	  else
	    return true;
	  end if;
	exception
	  when NO_DATA_FOUND then return false;
	end;```

Error Message	You're not allowed to create content in database
Validation	Once per page view

2. Create two more schemes (Modify and Delete) using the above code. Replace the string (Create) specified for itemRole with Modify and Delete, respectively.
3. Once again call the Home page. Click on the **ADD_ORDER** button and set its Authorization Scheme attribute to **Create**. Save the change. This button will disappear for all those who are not granted the Create privilege. Repeat this step to apply Create, Modify and Delete authorization schemes to all buttons on all application pages.

Chapter 15
Deploy Oracle APEX Applications

Chapter 15 – Deploy Oracle APEX Applications

15.1 About Application Deployment

APEX application deployment consists of two steps. Export the desired components to a script file, and import the script file into your production environment. Having completed the development phase, you definitely want to run the application in a production environment. For this, you have to decide where and how the application will run. The following section provides you some deployment options to choose from.

No Deployment: The development environment becomes the production environment and nothing is moved to another computer. In this option users are provided with just the URL to access the application.

Application: You will use this option if the target computer is already running a production Oracle database with all underlying objects. You only need to export the application and import it into the target database.

Application and Table Structures: In this deployment option you have to create two scripts, one for your application and another for the database table structures using the Generate DDL utility in SQL Workshop.

Application, Database Objects with Data: In this option you deploy your application along with all database objects and utilize oracle's data pump utility to export data from the development environment to the production environment.

Individual Components: With the development phase going on, you can supplement your deployment plan by exporting only selected components. We will see how this option can be used by exporting our application logo.

For simplicity, we will deploy the application in the same workspace to understand the deployment concept. The same technique is applicable to the production environment.

15.2 Export Application

The section will demonstrate how to export an APEX application that you can import into a new or the same workspace.

1. Sign in to APEX and click the **Application Builder** icon.
2. Click the **Edit** button under **Sales Web Application**.
3. Click on the **Export/Import** icon, as show in Figure 15-1.
4. On the ensuing page, click on the **Export** icon.
5. In Choose Application section, set Application to **Sales Web Application**, File Format to **DOS**, Export Supporting Object Definitions to **No**, and click the **Export** button.
6. Select the **Save File** option and click the **OK** button. A file named **f64699.sql** will be saved in the Download folder under My Documents, or in another folder specified in your browser. Yours might be saved with a different name.

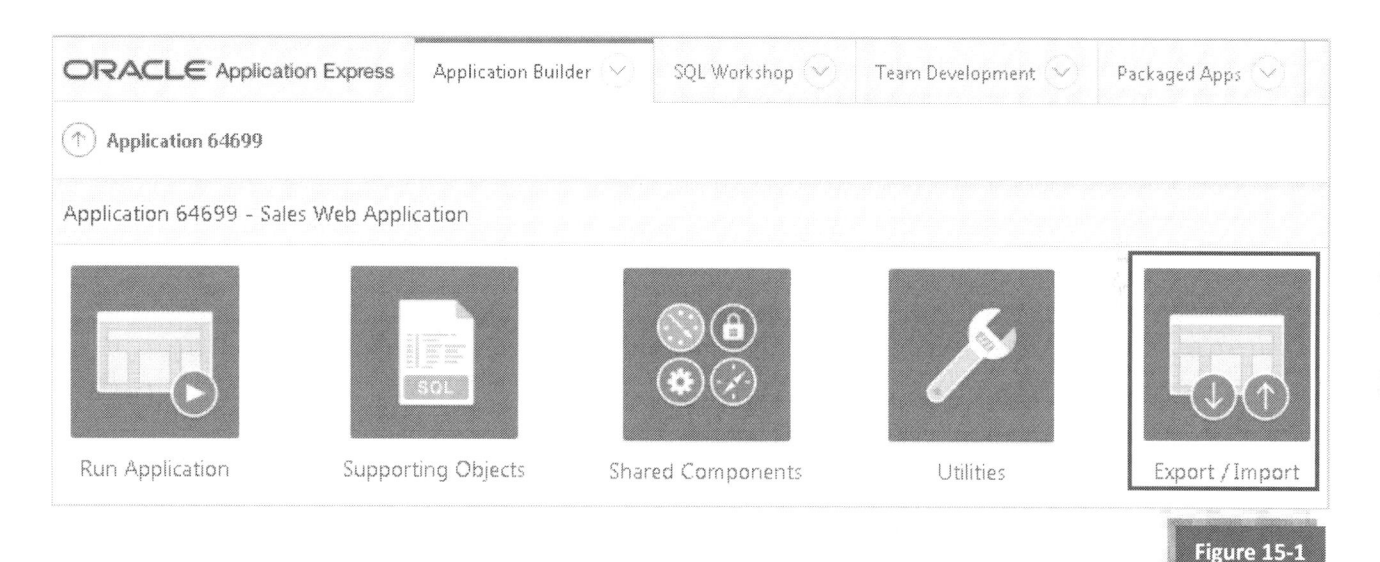

Figure 15-1

File Format - Select how rows in the export file are formatted:
- Choose UNIX to have the resulting file contain rows delimited by line feeds.
- Choose DOS to have the resulting file contain rows delimited by carriage returns and line feeds.

Supporting Object Definitions include all configuration options and scripts and enable an application export to include database object definitions, image definitions, and seed data SQL statements encapsulated in a single file. The No option is selected because you will export and import all application definitions individually.

15.3 Export/Import Data

If you want to also export the data from your test environment into your production environment, then you have the option to utilize Oracle's export and import data pump utilities. Oracle Data Pump technology enables very high-speed movement of data and metadata from one database to another. It includes expdp and impdp utilities that enable the exporting and importing of data and metadata for a complete database or subsets of a database.

15.4 Import Application

In this exercise you will import the exported application (f64699.sql) into the existing workspace you are connected to with a different ID.

1. Go to Application Builder interface and click on the **Import** icon.
2. In the Import interface, click the **Browse** button and select the exported .sql file (f64699). For File Type, select **Database Application, Page or Component Export** and click **Next**.
3. A message, *The export file has been imported successfully* will appear. Click **Next** to move on.
4. Select the default value for Parsing Scheme, Build Status (Run and Build Application), Install As Application (Auto Assign New Application ID), and click the **Install Application** button. After a short while, the application will be installed with a new ID. You can give it a test run.

15.5 Remove Developers Toolbar

The Developers Toolbar is used to access the application source. In this exercise we are going to prevent users from modifying the application by suppressing the toolbar.

1. Call the new application you imported in the previous step.
2. Click on **Shared Components**.
3. Click **Globalization Attributes** link (under Globalization section).
4. Click the **Definition** tab.
5. Scroll down to **Availability section**, set Build Status to **Run Application Only** and click **Apply Changes**.
6. Go to Application Builder interface and see that the new application doesn't have the Edit link. Click the Run button and provide your sign in credentials. Note that the Developer Toolbar has disappeared as well.

That's it. We have successfully deployed our application in the same workspace. You can apply the same procedure to deploy the application to another environment.

Conclusion

Oracle Application Express has come a long way from its simple beginning. With the addition of new features in every release it provides so much possibilities and promises for today and for the days to come. I hope this book has provided you with a solid foundation of Oracle Application Express and set a firm ground to develop robust application systems to fulfill the information requirements of your organization. The sky is the limit, you are limited by your imagination. Be creative, and put the power of APEX to your work. Good luck!

Special Request

From top cover to the last index entry, this book is a one-man effort. Whether you liked this work or not, I'd request you to please drop your valuable comments at:
http://oracleapex5.blogspot.com/2015/05/learn-rapid-web-application-development.html

INDEX

Symbols
\# Column Substitution String 43,47,70
: URL argument separator 40
|| Concatenation operator 40,57
<= (less than or equal to) 84
> (greater than) 84

-moz- Prefix 68,91
-webkit- Prefix 68,91
:APP_SESSION 21,39-40,68,106,114-115,130,132,137,139,141,176,188
&SESSION 21,107,118,150-151,162,177,211

A

Access Privileges 11,210-212
Accessing Mobile Application 32,162
Actions Menu 58,63,71,78,83,86-87,89
ADDROW JavaScript Function 80
Advance Reports 144
Advanced Formatting (mobile page) 166
After Row (attribute) 71
Aggregate Function 7,86-88
Alternative Report 7,83
APEX Collections 7,97,107,115-118,121-123,176,178
APEX URL Syntax *see f?p syntax*
APEX.CONFIRM Function 74
APEX_ESCAPE.JS_LITERAL Function 197
APEX_ESCAPE.HTML 33,90
APEX_UTIL.GET_BLOB_FILE_SRC Function 68,74,91
APEX_UTIL.PREPARE_URL Function 68,118-119,137,141
Application
    create New 23,162
    deployment 214
    export 215
    import 18,216
    in APEX 15
    logo 4
    modify 38,160
    name 4
    packaged 18
    responsive 15
    security 11,210
    segments 11,186
    types 16
Application Builder 15,18,28
    access 23
ApplyMRD Built-in Process 81-82
ApplyMRU Built-in Process 80-81
Attach Report Layout to Report Query 9
Audio Data 66
Authentication Scheme 24
    change scheme 208
Authorization Scheme 11
    create scheme 211-212

B

Backup 14
Badge List 42-43
Bar Chart 8,129,131

Before Rows (attribute) 69
Bind Variable 40,73
    prevent SQL Injection attack 111
Blank Page 16,100,124,129,131,133,154,167,180-182,192
BLOB (Binary Large Object) 66,73
Branch
    built-in 82
    create 99,123,156
    defined 20
Browser 19
Built-in Wizards 2
Button 4
    add to pages 49,189,120,125
    create for mobile app 167,169
    create link 89
    in URL request 22

C

Calculation (add to report) 9
Calendar Report 8,135
    report on mobile 183
Categories LOV 32,71
Central Pane (Page Designer) 20
Change Item Type 61,72,92
Chart Query 44
Chart View 7,85,87
Charts 8,14
    using aggregate functions 87-88
Classic Report 46,48,54,197
Clear Cache 22,43,47-51,71,83,89,99,166-167,169,172,181
Code Editor 19
Column (turn into a link) 42-43,47,83
Column Chart 8,45
Column Toggle Report 171
Comma Delimited Page List (attribute) 31
Commercial Invoice 9,153
Component Gallery 19
Computation (defined) 20
Condition (control appearance of page items) 73-74
Condition (set for buttons) 82
Conditional Formatting 9,144,148
CONFIRM JavaScript Function 81
Control Breaks 7,84
Control Components Display 17
Copy Page 7,94,172,174
COUNT Function 42,68,82,137

INDEX

Create Page 16,21,55,67,78,94,100,166,168,171,202,205
Create Page Item 43,74,95-96,104,125
Create Sub Region 73,75,95-96
CREATE TABLE 186,192,202
Create Links 42-43,47,83
CSS 2-3,6,14-15,19,67-69,160
    defined 100
    editor 16
    override interactive report built-in styles 70
CSS Bar Chart Plug-In 35
Cursor Database Object 110-111
Custom Authentication Scheme 11
Custom Color Scheme 45
Custom Functions 204
Customers Profiling 5,54

D

D3 Line Chart Plug-In 35,133
Dashboard 4
Data
    Display on Mobile Devices 10
    Export/Import 215
    Grouping 9,86-88,146-149,155-156
    Sorting 9,83,85,92,146,155
Data Workshop 18
Database Functions 204
Database Objects 25
Date and Time Format (Set for Application) 24
DBMS_LOB.GETLENGTH Function 68,91
Debug 21,40
Declarative Development 2
Declarative Programming Environment 14
DECODE Function 57,68,91,130,134
Default Primary Report 83
Default (Type) 72,92,95,154,188,193,203,206
Deployment Options 214
Desktop Applications 2,14,16
    create 24
    home page 24
    login page 24
    run 25
    schema 24
    theme 24
    theme style 24
Desktop Navigation Bar (Create entry in) 32
Desktop Navigation Menu 3-4
    add entries 28
    add image 28
    apply security 210
    list 28
Detail View 66,69,71
Developer Toolbar 4,16,58
    remove 216
Development Environment 19
Disable a Page Component 96
DML 5,20,81
DotNet Framework 145
Drag and Drop 45,50
Drag Components 19,45,50

Drill Down 4,8,47,49-50,129,135-136
Dynamic Actions 7,11
    Create 97
    Hide/Show Page Component 94,97-98
    refresh region 198
    to close a page 81
Dynamic Action Tab 19-20
Dynamic LOV 33-34

E

Escape Special Characters (attribute) 90
ESCAPE_SC Function 105-107,109,112
Exclude Default Link Column 58,69
Export Application 215
Export/Import Data 215

F

f?p Syntax 21,39-40,106-107,114, 130,132,137,141,150-151,211
For Each Row (attribute) 70
FOR LOOP Statement 110,112,114
Format Mask (attribute) 42-43,47-48,83,91-92,133
Forms *see Input Form*
Function and Global Variable Declaration (attribute) 62,197

G

Generate DDL 18
GetPK Process 81
Global Page (defined) 16,162-164
Graphical Reports 128
Grid Layout (Page Designer) 19,20
Grid Layout
    to arrange page components 4,5,41,42,44,46,48,59
Groups (users) 11
    create 192
Group By View 7,86-87
Grouping Page Elements 17

H

Hierarchical Presentation of Data 8,11,28,138,186,196
Help (Attribute) 20,39
Help Text 91,96
Hidden (attribute) 43
Hidden Item 6,44,80
Hide Column 43,47-48,58
Highlight Rules 7,84,148
Home Page 4,24,38,162-163
HTML 2,14-15,19,68,70,109,160
    using in PL/SQL 7,108
HTP and HTF Packages 109

I

Icon View 25,66,69,71
Image Handling 6,66,73-74
    remove 74
Import Application 18,216
INITCAP Function 34
Input Form (mobile app) 167,170
Input Form (desktop app) 5,54,61

INDEX

Interactive Report 5-6,54,80
    apply aggregate functions 86-87
    apply Control Break 84
    apply Highlight rules 84
    chart view 85
    customize 6
    filtered 42
    group by view 86
    override default styles 69
    sorting 7,83
Interactive Web Pages 16
Internet 2
Intranet 2
Item (defined) 17 *Also see Create Page Item*

J
Java Runtime Edition 145
JavaScript 2,14-15,19-20,160
jQuery Mobile 3,160

L
Link
    create on a button 89,114-115
    to run report 9,150-151,156
    turn column into a link 42-43,47,83
    text link 4
List 28
    copy from another 165
    create static 30-31
List Entry Current for Condition (attribute) 31
List of Values
    attach to an item 61,72,188
    defined 32
    static and dynamic 33,193
List View 166,168
Logo 36
LPAD Function 82

M
Managed by Database (ROWID) 79,167,202
Mandatory Fields 5,72
Maps 8,136
Master/Detail Form 7,78
MAX Function 68
Messages (Page Designer) 20
Metadata 2
Microsoft Word 145
MIMETYPE (Multipurpose Internet Mail Extension) 66,73
MIS Report 9
Mobile Applications 2,3,10,16
    create 162
    menu 165
    report list 165
    style pages 164
    types 160
Mobile Development 160
Mobile Entry 32

Mobile Input Form 10
Mobile Menu 10
Modal Page 5
Monthly Review (Interactive Report) 83
Monthly Review (PDF Report) 145

N
Native Mobile Applications 160
Navigation 14
    conditional 15
Navigation Bar 4,16
Navigation Menu 16
New or Existing Customer LOV 34,95
NVL Function 68,91

O
Object Browser 18,25
Oracle Application Express
    environment 19
    introduction 14
    sign in form 23
    structure 15
    URL syntax 21,39-40,106-107,114,
    130,132,137,141,150-151,211
Oracle BIPublisher Desktop 145
Oracle BIPublisher 144
Order (Taking) 7
Order Wizard 7,78
Order Wizard List 30

P
Packaged Applications 18
Page
    alias 22
    apply security 211
    copy desktop app page to mobile 172,174,179
    create for mobile app 166
    customization 5
    designer 19
    defined 16
    elements positioning 5
    find 20
    link 5
    lock/unlock 20
    make a copy from another 94
    run 20
    save 20
    style Mobile Pages 10
    styling 6
Page Item
    apply security 212
    make read-only 92
Page Search (Page Designer) 20
pageItemName JavaScript Function 196
Pagination (defined) 47
Pagination Type (attribute) 43
PDF 144-145,147

INDEX

PHP 2
Pie Chart 8,44,131
Pivot Table 9,149

PL/SQL 2,14-15,19-20
    code 104,124-125,195-196,199,207
    defined 104
    incorporate HTML 7
PL/SQL Expression (attribute) 44
PL/SQL Function (returning Error Text) 189,206
PL/SQL Function Body (Returning Boolean) 62,189,207,210-212
Plug-In (Import) 35
Pre-Rendering Process 80
Primary Report 7,71
Process
    add 7
    create 11,14,121-122,195-196,199,207
    defined 20
Process Row of <table> 81
Processing Tab 20
Product Catalog 6,10
    mobile 168
Products With Price LOV 33
Property Editor 14,20
Public Report 7,83,87
Pull-Down Menu 28

Q
Query Builder 18

R
Radio Group Page Item 94,203
Rapid Application Development (RAD) 2,14
Reflow Table 184
Region 4,16
    create 82
    create multiple 39
    defined 17
    delete 82
    hide/show 94
    template 17
Region Display Selector (attribute) 132-133
Rendering Tab 20
Report 14,128
    add chart 149
    advance 9,144
    calendar 135,183
    column toggle 171
    conditional formatting 148
    create template in MS Word 146,155
    formatting 148,156
    graphic 8,128
    grouping 7,9,84,86-88,146-149,155-156
    interactive/classic reports 54
    link 9
    map 136
    matrix 9
    page break 156

    parameterized 9,154
    run 151
    summary calculation 148
    tree 138
    upload template to APEX 150,156
Report Layout 9
Report Query (Create) 9,145,155
Report View 25,66,71,87
Reports (Mobile) 10,180-184
Reports List 30
Request (in URL) 22,40,81,108,115,118-119,121-122,151
Reset Interactive Report (RIR) 40
Reset Password 11,204
RESTful Services 18
RTF 144-145
    upload to APEX 150
Runtime Environment 19

S
Sales by Category Region 45
Sales by Product Region 44
Sales For This Month Region 42
Schema (defined and create) 17
Schema Comparison 18
Search Page Elements 20
Sequence (database object) 5,54,56,67,79
    create 186
Session ID 21
Session State 16
Shared Components (Defined) 28
Shared Components Tab 20
Sign in Form (Oracle APEX) 23
Spreadsheet 14
SQL 2,14,19
SQL Command 18,186
SQL DELETE 81
SQL Injection attack 111
SQL Query 14,18,32,34,42,44,46,57,68,82,90-91,96, 130-133,135,137,146,155,188,193,197
SQL Query (Create Link in) 39-40
SQL UPDATE 81
SQL Workshop 18,25,186
Stacked Bar Chart 8
States LOV 34
Sub-Menu 28
Substitution String 32,36,39,40,43,70,205
SUM Function 42,46,48,68,130-134
SYSDATE Function 44

T
Tabular Form 78-81,90
    add row 80
Taking Orders on Mobile 10,171
Team Development 18
Template (attribute) 61
Text Links 4
ThemeRoller 3-4,15-16
TO_CHAR Function 40,44,48,82,134
TO_DATE Function 42

INDEX

Toolbar (Page Designer) 20
Top Customers Region 46
Top Order by Date Region 39
Top Products Region 48
Transform Column into a Link 42
Tree 8,11
    add region 188,196
    page designer 19-20
    report 138
Tree Query Syntax 140
TRIM Function 114
TRUNC Function 40,82,133

U

Undo/Redo 19-20
UNION Set Operator 139-140
Universal Theme 15
URL Syntax 21
Users 11
    create 202

V

Validation 5,11
    associate to a button 62
    create 61,98-99,189,206-207,
    defined 20
    built-in 81
Value Protected (attribute) 44
Value Required (attribute) 59,61
Video 66
View Chart 85
View Report 85

W

Web Application 2
Web Browser 2,14
Websheet Application 16
Wizards 5,14
    built-in 15
Workspace (defined) 15
Workspace (Get Free) 15,17
Workspace Home Page 17

X

XML Data 9,146
XSS (Cross Site Scripting attack) 33,110

Y

Y or N LOV 34,72

Printed in Great
Britain
by Amazon